UNDERSTANDING DISABILITY POLICY

Also available in the series

Understanding housing policy (Second Edition)
Brian Lund

"An excellent historical and theoretical review of housing policy: thoughtful, well informed, critical and up to date." Chris Paris, Professor of Housing Studies, University of Ulster, Northern Ireland

PB £22.99 (US$34.95) **ISBN** 978 1 84742 631 4 **HB** £65.00 (US$85.00) **ISBN** 978 1 84742 632 1
352 pages April 2011
INSPECTION COPY AVAILABLE

Understanding the environment and social policy
Tony Fitzpatrick

"The inters section of social policy and environmental policy is strategically and morally vital yet haremained a strangely neglected area. No longer. This comprehensive book covers real world challenges, sustainable ethics, a host of applied policy issues, and some bigger questions about the possibility of a green welfare state." Ian Gough, Emeritus Professor, University of Bath

PB £21.99 (US$36.95) **ISBN** 978 1 84742 379 5 **HB** £65.00 (US$85.00) **ISBN** 978 1 84742 380 1
384 pages February 2011
INSPECTION COPY AVAILABLE

Understanding community
Politics, policy and practice
Peter Somerville

"In developing his conception of beloved community, Peter Somerville brings a fresh and radical perspective to communitarian theory and practice. This book will inspire and provoke readers in equal measure." Jonathan Davies, University of Warwick

PB £19.99 (US$34.95) **ISBN** 978 1 84742 392 4 **HB** £65.00 (US$85.00) **ISBN** 978 1 84742 393 1
304 pages February 2011
INSPECTION COPY AVAILABLE

Understanding social citizenship (second edition)
Themes and perspectives for policy and practice
Peter Dwyer

"A second edition of this excellent book is most welcome. Dwyer's understanding of social citizenship is second to none and this new edition provides an updated discussion and assessment of all the practical and theoretical issues that students need to know about this important area of study." Nick Ellison, University of Leeds

PB £19.99 (US$32.95) **ISBN** 978 1 84742 328 3 **HB** £65.00 (US$85.00) **ISBN** 978 1 84742 329 0
280 pages June 2010
INSPECTION COPY AVAILABLE

For a full listing of all titles in the series visit www.policypress.co.uk

www.policypress.co.uk

INSPECTION COPIES AND ORDERS AVAILABLE FROM:
Marston Book Services • PO BOX 269 • Abingdon • Oxon OX14 4YN UK
INSPECTION COPIES
Tel: +44 (0) 1235 465500 • Fax: +44 (0) 1235 465556 • Email: inspections@marston.co.uk
ORDERS
Tel: +44 (0) 1235 465500 • Fax: +44 (0) 1235 465556 • Email: direct.orders@marston.co.uk

UNDERSTANDING DISABILITY POLICY

Alan Roulstone and Simon Prideaux

First published published in Great Britain in 2012 by
The Policy Press
University of Bristol
Fourth Floor, Beacon House
Queen's Road
Bristol BS8 1QU
UK

t: +44 (0)117 331 4054
f: +44 (0)117 331 4093
tpp-info@bristol.ac.uk
www.policypress.co.uk

North American office:
The Policy Press
c/o The University of Chicago Press
1427 East 60th Street
Chicago, IL 60637, USA
t: +1 773 702 7700
f: +1 773-702-9756
sales@press.uchicago.edu
www.press.uchicago.edu

British Library Cataloguing in Publication Data
A catalogue record for this book is available from the British Library.

Library of Congress Cataloging-in-Publication Data
A catalog record for this book has been requested.

ISBN 978 1 84742 738 0 paperback
ISBN 978 1 84742 739 7 hardcover

Cover design by Qube Design Associates, Bristol.
Front cover: photograph kindly supplied by www.alamy.com
Printed and bound in Great Britain by Hobbs, Southampton.
The Policy Press uses environmentally responsible print partners.

Contents

Detailed contents

List of boxes

List of acronyms

AA	Attendance Allowance
ABA	Agricultural Buildings Allowance
ATC	adult training centres
BHPS	British Household Panel Survey
BIP	Benefit Integrity Project
BMA	British Medical Association
BS	British Standards
CIL	Centre for Inclusive/Integrated Living
CLG	Department for Communities and Local Government
CPAG	Child Poverty Action Group
CSCI	Commission for Social Care Inspection
CSIP	Care Services Improvement Partnership
CTC	Child Tax Credit
DCATCH	Disabled Children's Access to Childcare initiative
DCSF	Department for Children, Schools and Families
DDA	Disability Discrimination Act
DEAC	Disability and Employment Advisory Committee
DfES	Department for Education and Skills
DHSS	Department of Health and Social Security
DLA	Disability Living Allowance
DPTA	Disabled Person's Tax Allowance
DPTC	Disabled Person's Tax Credit
DRC	Disability Rights Commission
DSS	Department of Social Security
DWA	Disability Working Allowance
DWP	Department for Work and Pensions
EAZ	Education Action Zone
EDCM	Every Disabled Child Matters
EHRC	Equality and Human Rights Commission
ESA	Employment and Support Allowance
ESN	educationally subnormal
EU	European Union
GDP	gross domestic product
GP	general practitioner
HBAI	Households Below Average Income
HCC	Health Care Commission
HMRC	Her Majesty's Revenue and Customs
IBs	individual budgets
IBA	Industrial Buildings Allowance

ICB	Incapacity Benefit
ICES	Integrated Community Equipment Service
ILF	Independent Living Fund
IPPR	Institute for Public Policy Research
IQ	intelligence quotient
IS	Income Support
IVB	Invalidity Benefit
LEA	local education authority
LSE	London School of Economics and Political Science
MA	Mobility Allowance
NAO	National Audit Office
NDDP	New Deal for disabled people
NEET	not in education, employment or training
NHS	National Health Service
NLBD	National League for the Blind and Disabled
NS-SEC	National Statistics socioeconomic classification
ODI	Office for Disability Issues
ODPM	Office of the Deputy Prime Minister
OECD	Organisation for Economic Co-operation and Development
OPCS	Office of Population Censuses and Surveys
PCP	person-centred planning
PCT	primary care trust
PLM	paid labour market
PMAs	Plant and Machinery Capital Allowances
PMSU	Prime Minister's Strategy Unit
PSA	Public Service Agreement
RAS	Resource Allocation System
RCLTC	Royal Commission on Long-term Care
RNIB	Royal National Institute for the Blind
SDA	Severe Disablement Allowance
SEN	special educational needs
SENCO	special educational needs coordinator
SENDA	Special Educational Needs and Disability Act
SLCN	speech, language and communication needs
ULO	user-led organisation/s
UN	United Nations
UPIAS	Union of Physically Impaired Against Segregation
VAT	value added tax
WFTC	Working Families' Tax Credit
WTC	Working Tax Credit
YDU	Young Disabled Unit

Acknowledgements

We would like to thank Colin Barnes, Saul Becker, Ali Shaw, Laura Vickers, Kath King, David Simmons, Laura Greaves and the production team at The Policy Press for their kind support and keen scrutiny during the gestation of this book. We would also like to thank Dr Robert Drake, formerly of Swansea University, whose previous writings on disability policy were, we believe, the model for all future work and remain under-acknowledged in the wider disability studies and policy literatures.

A note on the terminology

We have used the term 'disabled people' or 'disability' to refer to the social barriers that impinge on someone who has an impairment. Impairment or difficulty is taken to mean the physical, intellectual, sensory impairment that an individual has. We prefer the term 'learning difficulties' to 'disabilities' as the latter conflates impairment and social barriers. We use our preferred terms except where we are referring to statutory terms, for example, the British Department of Health prefer the term 'learning disabilities'. By referring to disabled people we are leaving open to intellectual judgement rather than assuming the causes of disablement. Clearly much of our work here relates to the disabling or enabling effects of social policies.

Introduction

The question of disability policy, or more correctly social policies aimed at disabled people, has always formed a key feature of most modern welfare states. The British welfare state has historically seen disability as being central to many of its overt concerns. Beveridge's identified giant evils including want, idleness and squalor have been particular issues and barriers for people with physical, sensory and intellectual impairments. Breaking the link between engrained poverty and disability remains a key challenge for contemporary social policy. Lack of access to paid work, to humane and robust sources of economic security outside of paid work and lack of choices in daily living have all ensured that wider policy measures have often been 'stillborn' in terms of their wider effectiveness. This book aims to pull together the most up-to-date and engaging materials on the nature and efficacy of 'disability policy' while placing these in a historical policy context. By so doing we have been able to highlight the longer-run policy challenges around supporting disabled people to live their lives to the full and in mainstream society.

A cursory reading of disability policy history or a visit to a government department website might suggest that disabled people in early 21st-century Britain have 'never had it so good'. While major steps forward in policy have characterised the 20th century, there remain many barriers facing disabled people that policies have not managed to erase or for which certain policies, particularly welfare transfers, may actually still be serving as barriers to participation in the mainstream of life. The shift from paternalism to self-direction, from institution to community, is a clear and positive development for some disabled people that will hopefully be difficult or even impossible to reverse. However, paternalism is, to a large extent, entrenched within health and social care and social welfare systems. Policy muddle, professional territorialism, locally managed budgets and increasingly tight local authority settlements from central government have combined to dilute or subvert broader policy aims.

The social model of disability (and its variants) has served as the conceptual glue for much policy change (Barnes, 1991; Oliver and Barnes, 1998; Drake, 1999). The extent to which the model has truly penetrated policy is a moot point (Barnes and Mercer, 2006), while the model itself has come under increasing attack from some commentators (Goodley, 2011). However, it is almost impossible to understand the growth of self-directed support and personalisation ideas without the social model of disability with its focus on choices and rights and its emphasis on giving disabled people the tools to overcome established social barriers. Indeed, the major shift in idealised policy constructions of service user and provider from the National Health Service (NHS) and Community Care Act 1990 onwards seems unlikely to slow down with the shift towards putting disabled people in control of future service formats. The development of the United Nations (UN) Convention on the Rights of Persons with Disabilities (UN, 2006) and two Disability Discrimination Acts in 1995 and 2005 add to the formal legal protections offered to disabled people, which should continue to help substantiate a broader range of supportive policy measures (Lawson, 2008). Evidence points, however, to the barriers to realising the full power of these legislations including cost barriers (Hurstfield et al, 2004), legal processes that favour large organisations (Roulstone and Warren, 2006) and limited educational and national enforcement initiatives. These legislations only add to formal measures and cannot begin to address more substantive inequalities to any great degree. Nevertheless, the newly formed Equality and Human Rights Commission (EHRC) (subsuming all the legacy commissions) did initiate an enquiry into the harassment faced by many disabled people, an action clearly beyond a narrow legal redress and educational framework (EHRC, 2009). Certainly many disabled people welcomed this more expansive vision of policy action.

We do not want to reprise the contribution of the social model here as it is dealt with admirably elsewhere in policy texts. However, throughout this book we benchmark policy achievements against the broad ambitions of the social model and the UK Disabled People's Movement in the quest to achieve greater control of social support. We also bear in mind the longer-run challenges of eradicating poverty and economic exclusion in much of our policy analyses. We devote a chapter to disability policy and economic issues for this reason. This book offers a critical perspective on the extent to which new ideas such as personalisation and self-direction are converging or diverging in official policy rhetoric and use. We present views that question the consumerist and self-directed philosophy as it is used by UK governments. Writers are already referring to a divergence in meaning and language around these terms (Ferguson, 2008; Roulstone and Morgan, 2009), and a failure to alight on these sorts of shifts in meaning attached to key policy terms risks overlooking the limitations of policy. In the same way that community care was initially launched without a firm understanding of community or care (Bornat et al, 1997), self-direction and personalisation run the risk of moving away from the collective imperatives of the Disabled People's Movement that founded the ideas. In so doing it may shift self-direction in a fiercely individualist way, one made more apparent by the looming financial severities of the UK Coalition government's spending cuts.

Disability policy is neither linear, inherently progressive nor equitable, and suffers from the vagaries of time, place and ideological change. Paternalism continues to sit squarely at the centre of the disability welfare system as do employment-related policies for many disabled people. Personalised adult support remains the province of a small minority of disabled people. Most disabled people of working age will never be assessed in the social care system. Policy understandings need to embrace such diversity. Indeed a person may be disabled for one policy sub-system but not for another. Disability policy and the more active measures attaching to conditionality are aimed largely at working-age adults. Arguably disabled children, although receiving much greater attention since the 1980s, are still not afforded the degrees of choice offered to some disabled adults, while older disabled people continue to be construed as health populations or simply deemed 'frail'. In this respect, the UK Disabled People's Movement has not convincingly engaged fully with disabled childhoods and older disabled people. This book aims to redress these issues.

Unlike many areas of social policy, disability policy is too disparate, halting and complex to be susceptible to single models of policy. To that end our attempt to typologise disability policy offers a broad sense of the changing thinking on disability and the typology is not always a neat historical fit with wider policy and ideological systems. While neoliberalism's retreat from 'welfarism', for example, is helpful in allowing us to understand some aspects of disability-related policy since the 1980s, the 1980s also saw the growth of disability welfare and the claimant headcount for a range of disability benefits and transfers. No simple model-based explanation can make sense of these shifts. Similarly the recent shifts towards greater conditionality sit awkwardly alongside personalised social support philosophies. Unless one takes the view that these are all variants of neoliberalism, clearly an absurdity in this context, then we have to acknowledge that we can at best only identify specific policy imperatives set against the longer-run ideological shifts from liberalism via social democratic impulses to neoliberalism. Each remains, in part, evident in specific policies into the 21st century.

What is new is the sense that policy realisations become ever more strained in an era of significantly raised expectations. Whether we view terms like personalisation, choice and control as substantive or rhetorical, the reality is that more disabled people are being exposed to this language in the mainstream, in day centres or even intermediate and residential contexts. The exact playing out of this mismatch between great ambitions and policy fulfilment is hard to gauge. What is likely, however, is that disabled people and their advocates will continue to push for measures which approximate as much as possible to these idealised states of self-determination. Without adequate funding and some sense of equity terms such as choices, rights and entitlements become less meaningful. Disability policy remains something of a misnomer in the sense that policy emanates from a huge array and uses very disparate constructions of disability, desert and entitlement. Health and social care thinking still tends to inhabit different planetary systems, metaphorically speaking. In this sense there is probably no sense that disability policy exists as a separate entity. That said, the pulling together of previous more disparate policies is becoming a feature of certain policy developments as in, for example, individual budgets (IBs), where income streams are pulled together for the first time. Nevertheless, we use the term 'disability policy' in this book as useful shorthand for the range of policies that impinge on the lives of many disabled people.

At the time of writing disabled people have a minister for disabled people without a ministry and an Office for Disability Issues (ODI) whose lineage is as an offshoot of the Department for Work and Pensions (DWP), which was not a department noted for user-led policies. To date, no minister for disabled people has been identified as a disabled person. These may seem trifling considerations alongside issues as challenging as poverty, inaccessible opportunities and social dislocation. However, we hope that in 30 years' time, when someone picks up this by then rather faded tome, they will look back with a wry smile at an age where it was still unquestioned to have non-disabled people as ministers for disabled people. We also hope that disability policy will, by then, be as coherent, equitable and transparent as the term suggests. Disabled people of course deserve this much after so many years of social and economic disadvantage and dislocation.

About the book: structure, signposting and study support

Understanding disability policy is written for a general policy audience and scholars interested in the specificities of disability policy and provision. In addition to the main text are **summary boxes** which draw out the key messages from each chapter. We also provide pertinent **questions** to help lecturers and tutors structure useful questions based squarely on the chapter content. We offer pointers to **further reading** that we think is of particular value for the busy reader.

Early chapters place contemporary disability policy in context. **Chapter One** provides an overview of the general shifts in recorded accounts of disability policy to date by adopting a typology of disability policy with which to grasp the broader policy changes towards disabled people. It should provide a good sense of the ideological and cognitive shifts (for example, attitude change) underpinning policy change. This chapter then explores the shape of disability welfare policy in the latter half of the 20th and early 21st centuries. Alongside laying out specific policy influences, it highlights those longer-run factors that continue to limit coordinated and effective disability policies, for example, the 'activity' and 'inactivity' principles underpinning different aspects of the disability benefits system. The uneasy relationship between social security and social 'care' policy and the increased compartmentalisation of policy by age group at the expense of holistic models of family policy is explored. We also explore the emergent policy ambitions arising out of a social inclusion agenda contextualised by the growth of a mixed economy and a third sector often reliant on 'soft money' to fulfil its key policy objectives. Crucially, the changing construction of the relationship between collective and individual lives is fundamental to this book. Indeed, the mismatch between collective assumptions underpinning user-led organisations (ULOs) alongside the increasingly individualised constructions of choices is perhaps the most pressing issue for the 21st century.

Chapter Two explores the history of paternalist policy ideas that shaped the early welfare state response to disability. It details and critically unpacks those key policy and programme developments that, although now under attack, arguably still underpin much of the current policy environment. Disability policy post-Second World War is contextualised in the wider policy literature. The Beveridgean welfare settlement is discussed because it has had particular implications for many disabled people through its emphasis on paid work and its reliance on the insurance principle. Similarly, Marshall's classic construction of citizenship has left disabled people in an ambiguous position with regard to the substantive benefits of postwar social policy. A detailed appraisal of key developments in education, training, employment and welfare policy is also provided against the backcloth of legislative landmarks and key policy actors who challenged assumed orthodoxies in disability policies.

The chapter begins substantively with the growth of a moral and pragmatic impulse to rehabilitate disabled people, exploring the role of pragmatism and its interplay with policy ideals. An unpacking of the assumptions behind key legislation is undertaken, including appraisals of the Disabled Persons (Employment) Act 1944, National Assistance Act 1948 (Section 48), Chronically Sick and Disabled Persons Act 1970, the Hospital (Closure) Plan, income replacement benefits, the 1988 Fowler reforms, Warnock Report (1978), the Education Act 1981 and the NHS and Community Care Act 1990. Conceptually, the chapter makes clear the paradox of community options rhetoric alongside the continuation of managed choices, marketisation and 'one size fits all' community care policies. Despite much policy change with the 'New Jerusalem' of the British welfare state, the chapter highlights the construction of disabled people's dependence and routes to independence via paid work, something that was very difficult for many disabled people throughout the 20th century. As a consequence, citizenship increasingly eluded disabled people where paid work became the admission fee to an 'advanced welfare state'.

Chapter Three explores more recent developments towards community-based policies. While clearly desirable compared to institutional provision, many disabled people have found the paternalism of institutional regimes pervading community provision. Disabled people have been quick to challenge notions that they are a new burden on the imagined and perhaps idealised mainstream communities. Although some clear advances have been noted and community living has become an expectation for many disabled people, the adequacy and form of social 'care' in a new mixed economy of family, state and private provision has felt distinctly disempowering for many other disabled people. Despite the language of choices, it is argued that the shift towards community care has been combined with paternalist assumptions and imagined notions of community that has lacked the financial and philosophical bases for independence, choices and rights in the community. The continued dominance of a 'cure or care' approach and medically dominated definitions of the 'disability problem' is explored by reference to what has been referred to as the medical or administrative models underpinning disability policy. The ascendancy and pervasiveness of these models has, arguably, perpetuated contradictions in disability policy into the late 20th and early 21st centuries. For people with enduring mental health issues, the early experience of community care was often unsatisfactory and at worst can be summed up as a decanting of former institutionalised residents into highly inappropriate and unsupportive settings, where access to good mental health care and support were at times questionable.

The shift towards community care has spawned a range of cross-cutting debates on the implications of 'care' for those who informally support disabled people (often their closest relatives). We explore the exchanges that have emerged in the wake of the NHS and Community Care Act 1990 that is often dubbed the Ungerson–Morris debate. Clare Ungerson's (1987) emphasis in avoiding an unpaid and individualised 'care' burden falling to unpaid family members toyed with the idea of socialised care which would see paid, collective, planned solutions to the challenge of squaring community provision with the avoidance of an unpaid 'care burden' on (often female) family members. The counter-argument by Jenny Morris (1993) emphasised the risk of such collectivised approaches in possibly leading to greater institutionalisation, which risks defeating the purpose of community care policy. Morris's contribution helps clarify the need to provide community-based solutions that are properly funded, which do not place emphasis on unpaid family members and which offer independence, choices and rights. Morris makes the point that collective solutions need not and should not be based on disempowerment at an individual level.

Chapter Four explores the responses to and position of disabled children since 1997 and the rise of New Labour. The cross-governmental recognition that to eradicate poverty in childhood aids economic and social well-being in later life has permeated strongly into disability policies and programmes for children (PMSU, 2005). *Every Child Matters* (DfES, 2003), the life chances report (PMSU, 2005) and the Bercow Report (DCSF, 2008b) all point to the need to increase opportunities for disabled children and their families. In this chapter we explore key developments in child policy in education, poverty reduction and health services to address whether advances have been made. The shift towards mainstreaming, while strengthened rhetorically, can be seen to have been reversed in some local authorities. Choice has proven to be a double-edged principle in many areas where parents of disabled children have preferred to adhere to 'special school' provision. The educational mismatch between increased credentialism, the sanctity of the national curriculum and the challenge in breaking down the binary between academic and non-academic qualifications all help ensure that some disabled children, especially those with a statement of special educational needs (SEN), achieve less after their school career.

Accordingly, this chapter explores in detail the extent to which post-1997 social policies have placed the lives of disabled children on a stronger footing to achieve greater economic and social security. The impact of these changes are discussed and the question of the funding of disabled children's services is placed alongside other important policy issues such as medical diagnoses and access to services, limited coverage of child wheelchair services and the failure to tackle the crucial issue of disability equality in schools, including the increased mainstreaming of disabled children.

Undoubtedly, the fundamental right to life for disabled children and the right to good healthcare are central to any analysis of disabled children's welfare. At present, the disparate and limited analyses of disabled children are mirrored in the scant attention given to the transition into adulthood. Yet ideas and experiences forged in the crucible of young adulthood and late childhood in general have been officially acknowledged to shape later life ambitions and achievements and are thus deserving of greater attention within disability literature and policy. We know that disabled people's transitions are often fragmented, and the movement from child to adult or adolescent services is a major shock for many disabled people. Given the evidence that early poor experiences of post-school education, training and employment are limited and often inferior to the non-disabled population, we hope that this chapter will go some way to redress that omission (Roulstone and Yates, 2009).

Chapter Five looks at policy changes from 1997 onwards and acknowledges the shift towards much more conditional forms of welfare. A key feature of the post-1997 adult disability welfare policy (regarding social care policy) is the wholesale attempt to redefine the boundaries between 'disabled' and 'able-bodied' in policy terms (Stone, 1984). For many disabled people, the rationing of social support has grown ever more pervasive against a backdrop of greater rhetorical state commitments to choices. Disability welfare policy arguably harks back to a more paternalist age in offering strong discursive criticisms of sick and disabled people who have become dependent on the state. These ideas were far from new in 1997 – the 1980s and the 1990s had witnessed an increased emphasis on getting disabled people to participate in the paid labour market (PLM), and the wider welfare discourses previously reserved for non-disabled people were attached to disabled people for the first time since the Poor Law made attempts to deter sturdy beggars. Thus the chapter looks at the conditions attached to changing disability welfare and asks whether the policies are likely to reduce worklessness and dependency. Although not denying the possible scope for supporting some sick and disabled people into paid work, the chapter points to demand-side issues in some disabled people's worklessness. Worryingly, the emphasis on activating disabled people to be more work-ready has proven of little value to date. Harsher sanctions risk excluding disabled people further.

Chapter Six explores the significant shifts in social care policy away from top-down paternalism to self-directed support and greater personalisation in adult social support. It draws out the key legislative and policy underpinnings of self-directed support while detailing new forms of cash transfers and user-directed policy via direct payments, personal budgets and IBs. A positive view of these changes is that for some disabled people cash transfers and budgetary flexibilities are affording fundamental shifts in the way in which disabled people gain access to and make choices around their support needs. Direct payments are able to afford new ways of supporting choices for disabled people, including direct employment of personal assistants. IBs are challenging previously arbitrarily separate income and service streams by attempting to merge funding and thus provide a more seamless package of support for disabled people. The degree to which power has changed hands from professionals to disabled people is addressed as are issues of equity and the increased means testing of adult social care – uptake of self-directed support is increasing, but not at the rates the UK government had hoped, while many local authorities are restricting social care to those in the highest eligibility categories. The challenges for increased self-direction are explored. The chapter notes the risks of cash-starved authorities shifting much of their administrative burden onto disabled people where insufficient brokerage may result. Cost savings, as opposed to genuine commitment to self-direction, are therefore seen as real risks in some contexts.

Chapter Seven looks at the position of older disabled people, a group often overlooked by much traditional disability policy and by early radical reinterpretations of user-led policy. While much social policy, most notably the life chances report (PMSU, 2005), emphasises the challenge of policy for working-age adults and children, older disabled people are less well accounted for in disability policy. This chapter examines the construction of policy for older disabled people. It argues that beyond working age a great deal of policy emanates from health and safeguarding policies, many (but not all) of which are some distance from an independent living philosophy. Although generational and capacity issues are important here in explaining differences with, say, younger disabled adults, the question of the efficacy of policy for older disabled people needs to be critically engaged with. Greater risks of medical neglect and assumptions that impairment is inevitable in old age are all key policy challenges. There have, however, been significant legislative steps forward in terms of mental capacity, ageing-in-place, and the avoidance of unnecessary institutionalisation and the extension of state-funded, self-directed support schemes (Prideaux et al, 2009) to older disabled people are also issues that are unpicked in this chapter.

Chapter Eight draws together evidence on the overall impact and efficacy of disability policy. It aims to transcend the fragmented nature of disability policy and to draw together indicators of policy effectiveness in aggregate. Links are made to the underlying models and definitions of disability and their links to the performance and value of disability policy. The chapter also raises critical issues as to how policy effectiveness and impact are currently accounted for in official and academic terms. It draws on headline figures on poverty, social inclusion and mainstreaming indicators and, significantly, socioeconomic group profiles of disabled people. The impact of policy by sex, age, ethnicity and sexual orientation is also considered. The question of the redistributive impact of disability policy is clearly important and the complexity of the UK disability policy arena often deters analysts from taking the broader view of policy impact. Alongside macro-level policy impact, we also look at the extent to which specific policies may be furthering exclusion for certain impairment groups. We look at both the redistributive successes of policy where evident and at any of the negative or unplanned consequences of such policy.

Chapter Nine acknowledges the proliferation of evidence that UK disability benefits form part of a complex and at times impenetrable system. The result is a historical build-up of benefits that are based on compensatory, income replacement, extra cost, concessionary and, most recently, motivational principles. This arguably leads to diswelfares and major issues of equity for disabled people who seek welfare support. Indeed there remain a number of 'perverse incentives' in the disability benefits system which makes movement between work and supported lives problematic. The benefits system continues to attribute rates of benefit based on the cause of impairment, often at the expense of careful assessments of actual needs for extra costs, or wider welfare issues such as evidence on relative employability of people with specified impairments. The system thus contends with 21st-century policy issues and with disability constructs drawn from the early and middle period of the 20th century.

Perhaps the key paradox remaining in the UK benefits system hinges on its mix of activity and inactivity principles that it rewards, so much so that those disabled people who are able to do some paid work may have to emphasise their activity to gain in-work benefits or disregards while simultaneously emphasising all that they cannot do in order to secure inactivity benefits such as Disability Living Allowance (DLA) which reward fixed immobility or support needs. This chapter is the first of its kind to explicitly unpack the inner logic of constituent benefits, for example, Incapacity Benefit (ICB) (now Employment and Support Allowance [ESA]) and DLA, while placing these into a wider analysis of how benefits interact in supporting or militating against disabled people's welfare. As a result, the chapter demonstrates how paternalism and a far from personalised welfare system is evident in the early 21st century.

Chapter Ten has altered since the book was first conceived. The book was projected to end with an exploration of the most recent disability policies. The accession of the Conservative-Liberal Coalition to power in June 2010 requires a snapshot of the key proposed policy changes and a prediction as to the impact these policies will have on disabled people. Certainly the rhetoric looks very harsh in general and in some areas of policy in particular. The proposal to cut up to 40 per cent from some departments, for instance, sits alongside a 'cordon sanitaire' of protection for health and overseas development (HM Treasury, 2010). This might suggest that disability, an area increasingly reliant on social care provision, may lose out in major terms. However, the Coalition has mooted an increase in social care funding and a suggested use of some health service monies into adult social care.

That said, the sheer severity of proposed cuts in local authority budgets allocations from central to local government are more than likely to wipe out any small/medium additional investment from healthcare budgets. Major reviews of disability benefits are under way, with all DLAs being reviewed from 2013. ESA, the new mainstay of ICB support, is being tiered to encourage greater work-readiness for most ESA claimants. Critics point to the measures being a consolidation of Thatcherite and Blairite market neoliberalism and a further retraction of the state. In this light, Chapter Ten provides a brief appraisal of the Coalition's plans and attempts to project forward the likely impact on disabled people. At the time of writing, the chapter observes that the future looks very uncertain for many disabled people unable to access paid work and unable to seek the sanctuary of the government's 'supported' group.

We conclude with a brief reflection on recent policy developments in the longer-run scheme of disability policy, asking poignant questions on what has been gained, what is at stake in the next 25 years and where disability policy research and writing might be headed in that time.

one

Contextualising disability welfare policy

This chapter provides a brief introduction to the myriad of factors and issues that have helped shape disability welfare policy in the latter half of the 20th and early 21st centuries. Alongside laying out specific policy influences and positive developments from paternalism to increased control, those longer-run factors that continue to limit coordinated and effective disability policies are highlighted. One important example of this can be seen in the growth of disability provision, whereby benefits are based on the causes of an impairment rather than the extra costs and social barriers faced by disabled people (Barnes, 1991). Drake (1999) provides a guide to the tensions and overlaps in disability policy that are needlessly divisive in terms of the disability welfare category. He devised a four-part typology of historical policy interventions for disabled people. Containment and segregation is synonymous with the English Poor Law and the rise of industrial society and began with institutional attempts to contain and segregate disabled people as perceived threats to non-disabled society. Notions of risk, contagion and moral hazard underlay many of these impulses to contain and segregate. With a growing welfare state in the 20th century and changing sensibilities, industrial and war-related impairment led to concerns to compensate disabled people for the specific losses incurred in social opportunities occasioned by war or industrial injuries. Welfare protection for people with a range of impairments did not happen substantially until the 1940s, with the advent of the British welfare state, and welfare provision, however generous, was based on a firmly paternalist stance that operated on the principle that professionals and the state 'know best'. Only from the 1990s were rights-based assumptions beginning to attach to some disability policy provision. Notions that disabled people deserved the rights afforded in full citizenship were coupled with ideas that disabled people were often experts in their own lives. The challenge to paternalism had begun (see ***Box 1.1*** below):

> **Box 1.1:** Drake's (1999) typology of disability policy approaches
>
> - Containment and segregation
> - Compensation
> - Welfare provision
> - Rights and citizenship

Drake makes clear that, rather than be seen as a linear typology, as we enter the 21st century the forms of intervention are intermingled. However, he notes a general drift away from segregation towards rights-based policies. This approach helps explain the continuance of invidious distinctions in the benefits system based on crude hierarchies of worth among disabled people. In addition to Drake's insights other important and largely unacknowledged tensions in UK disability policy are evident. For example:

- the tension between 'activity' and 'inactivity' principles underpinning different aspects of the disability benefits system, such as the 'activity' assumptions underlying the new 'Employment and Support Allowance' (ESA) as opposed to the inactivity assumptions that underpin the 'Disability Living Allowance' (DLA) system;
- the uneasy relationship between social security and social 'care' policy and the growing separation between deserving and undeserving categories of disability welfare recipients;
- differential rates of benefit and the assumed need for people with what may be the same level of impairment and need, based on the causes of the impairment, for example, injury in battle as opposed to other injuries, accidents and impairments;
- the increased compartmentalisation of policy by age group at the expense of holistic models of family policy.

Crucially, the changing construction of the relationship between collective and individual lives is fundamental to this book. Indeed, the mismatch between collective assumptions underpinning user-led organisations (ULOs) alongside the increasingly individualised governmental constructions of choices is perhaps the most pressing issue for the 21st century (Roulstone and Morgan, 2009). This chapter thus provides outline insights as to how changing policy and political ideologies helped shape the contours of disability policy into the 20th and 21st centuries. Broadly stated, policy in the later modern era has largely followed the contours of policy change, from economic liberalism of the 19th century (Thane,

1982; Fraser, 1984), via social liberalism and Fabianism (Tawney, 1931) through to neoliberalism in the late 20th century (Loney, 1987; Brown and Sparks, 1989; Powell, 2002; Prideaux, 2005). However, the impact of these changing contours on disabled people will be explored in some depth in the following chapters as disabled people have often been prey to a very muddled set of assumptions at any given moment, combining social liberal paternalism through to neoliberal constructions of disabled welfare laggards (Hyde, 2000). Before exploring the more recent history of disability it is important to briefly examine the longer-run factors that have shaped the recent and current shape of disability welfare policies.

Poor Laws, paternalism and the 'relief of disability'

For much of the last 200 years disabled people have served as a 'problem' grouping in policy terms. By definition, to have been disabled for much of this period is to have failed to live up to standards or stereotypes of what are held to be 'normal' measures of success (Finkelstein, 1980), with containment and segregation a key impulse behind disability provision. More than any other social category, disabled people have until recently been defined largely in terms of what they are not able to do – employment, education and being a part of 'normal society'. Only in the last 40 years have disabled people been seen in principle to fit with aspects of mainstream lives across a range of policy issues – education, employment, housing, diverse sexualities and wider civic contributions (Campbell and Oliver, 1996). These policy assumptions have been based on a mixture of ableist constructions of the 'disability problem' and conversely prevalent notions of what constitutes valued and valorised economic and social contributions. In truth, many of the barriers to realising disabled people's contributions have inhered in the very policies aimed to mitigate social disadvantage (Borsay, 2005).

Policies responding to the 'disability problem' have more than any other area of social policy been formed in the absence of disabled people's own voices – or, to use the current expression, to have been 'top-down' developments (Croft and Beresford, 1992). Despite the recent shift towards personalised and tailored packages of support based on consultation principles in social support (DH, 2009a), many areas of disability policy continue to silence or ignore, for example, the views of disabled children (Priestley, 1998) and adults (Roulstone and Barnes, 2005). This is especially true in the areas of welfare, environment, transport and education policies. The recent shift to work-based welfare is particularly significant given the historical connection between poverty and impairment (Disability Alliance, 1975; Townsend, 1979; Barnes, 1991). Recent policy narratives that surround disability and welfare dependency have witnessed some of the most corrosive messages to venture forth from a modern developed economy. The policy landscape then is now a more complex patchwork of assumptions. A shorthand summary of the major changes in policy assumptions over the last 200 years can be summed up in the shift in binary assumptions about disability. Back in 1834, with the passing of the Poor Law Amendment Act, the view many held was that disabled people were not 'made for the mainstream' of economic and social life (Jones, 2000), but should be pitied and supported as legitimate outsiders. The empirical evidence suggested that types of impairment (blindness, deafness etc) left people differentially positioned as regards the mainstream. We need to explore the origins of such thinking a little further.

A forerunner to the principles of the Poor Laws was the Statute of Labourers 1351 which, rooted in feudal bonds, required people to remain on their home manors and to give service to the local landowner (Barker, 1998). Begging and almsgiving were outlawed except for older people and those unable to work. In cementing an early rights and responsibilities discourse, a distinction was established between the 'worthy poor' made up of 'disabled people, dependent children widows, and older people', and the 'unworthy poor', those subjects deemed able to undertake paid work (Borsay, 2005). Early modern assumptions as to the social necessity of supporting the unintentionally needy was mooted in the English Poor Law of 1601. The law introduced the first official recognition of disabled people as deserving of what was then termed 'outdoor relief'. The assumption was that those who could not fend for themselves would receive support from the local Poor Law guardians. Moral concern and fears of social instability underlay the law. The recognition of the unmet needs of sick, infirm and disabled people, although very basic and locally haphazard, did afford basic protection for disabled people to at least survive alongside their non-disabled counterparts. However, notwithstanding the controlling logic of the Poor Law Act 1601, it did provide some rudimentary support for disabled people. Coverage was not even, however, and adequacy of provision were very localised. The Poor Law was wide ranging in its remit and included physical impairment, 'infirmity' and mental frailty. It is important to note that the Poor Law was not designed expressly with the 'vulnerable' in mind, and was equally an instrument of social engineering to ensure that able-bodied people were alerted to the impersonal character of administered relief should they fail to enter a bonded or employment relationship. As Stone very powerfully put it:

> Disabled people are metaphorically "on the move", their handicapping [sic] conditions may be improving or deteriorating

and their ability to move in and out of normal roles may be constantly changing. In poor relief policy the two conditions of vagrancy and disability intersect in the question of how to detect the genuinely needy beggar from the one who feigns disability. (Stone, 1984, p 29)

Stone's quote is helpful as it scotches often simplistic assumptions that disabled people were somehow unambiguously privileged by the Poor Law of 1601 and local relief; the reality according to Stone was one of constant suspicion and distinctions between disabled people, which arguably continues into contemporary disability policy when political expediency requires a narrowing of the disability category to curb costs (Grover and Piggott, 2005). The Poor Law Amendment Act of 1834 that followed over 200 years later was an attempt to remedy what were seen as the perverse incentives of the previous statute in encouraging 'sturdy beggars' and those wilfully outside the realms of employment to desist from their recalcitrant ways. The 1834 Act, according to Barnes, embodied aspirations to uniformity, deterrence and the denial of outdoor relief (Barnes, 1994, p 16). The Poor Law Reform Act 1834 was designed in part to be a key deterrent to worklessness and idleness, and a threat to anyone, disabled or non-disabled, who was able to work but not fully committed to using their labour power in paid employment. The terms and conditions of the new Poor Law were deliberately made inferior to those that could be received from even the lowest-paid jobs of the time (Stone, 1984)

For those disabled people deemed eligible for support, the workhouse or meagre outdoor relief were symbolic of the fate that would ensue for recalcitrant non-disabled workers. In time, disability, Poor Law receipt and begging all became intertwined in the public consciousness. This intermingling of protection and threat has arguably underpinned aspects of the welfare response to impairment throughout the last 200 years.

While the Poor Law had made broad distinctions between 'paupers, children, the sick, insane, defective and the aged/infirm', later decisions in the now crowded context of 19th-century poor relief were made between the deserving and non-deserving, with outdoor relief becoming harder to access for those disabled people who were not as visibly impaired as those who were blind or limbless (Borsay, 2005, p 32). This was arguably the starting point for contemporary distinctions based on legitimacy between the more and less deserving. These decisions were not based on evidence, but simply widely held beliefs that blind and limbless people were inherently more deserving of support.

The factory system and the birth of the abled/disabled binary

The factory system has a key role to play in the story of the development of policy responses to disabled people. The monumental social changes that underpin and are developed in the factory system have served as strong policy narratives around disability and ability. Foucault refers to the development of the notions of abled/disabled emerging for the first time with the factory system (Foucault, 2001). Similarly Stone's comparative study of industrialisation in the UK, USA and Germany (Stone, 1984) noted the increased bifurcation between the 'work-based' and 'needs-based' systems that arose during rapid industrialisation. Even during nascent industrial and agricultural capitalism, disabled people may have had some limited involvement with paid work or petty commodity production (Roulstone, 2002). However, the rise of calculative logic and standardised workplace epitomised in the factory system created a much clearer boundary point between those designed into and inadvertently out of the factory system, as Ryan and Thomas state (see **Box 1.2** below).

> **Box 1.2:** Ryan and Thomas on the impact of industrialisation on disabled people
>
> The speed of factory work, the enforced discipline, the time-keeping and production norms – all these were a highly unfavourable change from the slower, more self determined and flexible methods of work into which many handicapped people had been integrated. (Ryan and Thomas, 1980, p 181)

Alongside the systematic separation of disabled and abled populations, the new asylums of the 18th century also began to take on the characteristics of the factory systems. Somewhat ironically, although now firmly separate, spatially and economically, each system took signals from the other. Foucault and later radical disability writers (Finkelstein, 1980; Ryan and Thomas, 1980) made connections between the discipline and surveillance of the factory systems and of the new large mental asylums. Both were underpinned by an industrial logic that emphasised efficiency, moral hygiene and the diminution of desultory habits that might detract from the new science of industrial efficiency. Although the apotheosis of industrial efficiency was not represented in all factories, this model of standardised production and the notion that time was money did provide a model for housing otherwise refractory populations, both at work and in the burgeoning asylums in the 19th century.

A key aspect of the segregation of disabled people was the increasingly systematised approach to classifying disabled people. With central government taking a fuller legislative role in providing institutional contexts for disabled people, there was an increasing need to differentiate by type of impairment or 'severity' that could be applied locally and as evenly as possible. Hierarchies of concern developed. Early schools for blind or deaf children were in part products of philanthropic concerns as the protection of the most vulnerable (Adams, 1980), while physically disabled children had to wait longer for schools to open their doors as many were simply inaccessible and the rescue imperative more patchy. With the rise of segregated institutions came new professions tasked to deal with these new 'problem populations'. Special educators, almoners, medical officers, Poor Law officials, all had their part to play in the categorisation, assessment and placement of disabled people. Most of these new professionals adopted medical or scientific discourses to underpin their professional projects (Larson, 1977; Langan and Clarke, 1994). The exact set of motivations to segregate were complex, with macro-level concerns as to lack of workableness being overlaid with protective and even eugenic impulses in the case of those deemed 'idiots and imbeciles' (Stone, 1984).

The growth of otherwise protective general trades unions did little to support the plight of those left outside of the employment contract, while craft unions were arguably grounded in intrinsically exclusive social differentials based on skills and qualifying apprenticeships (Pelling, 1971). However, small-scale union-inspired activity was evident in the income-based concerns of the National League for the Blind and Disabled (NLBD) (see Davis, 1998). For many disabled people, however, employment-based social welfare made little sense where they were unable to access employment in the first place. This mirrors the experiences of some women in the first half of the 20th century. The Lloyd George liberal reforms of 1908 and 1911 in the Old Age Pensions Act and National Health Insurance Act afforded some minimal but welcome protection for the small number of disabled people who were able to gain paid employment (Drake, 1999; Borsay, 2005).

It would be wrong, however, to see these developments as the basis of a modern comprehensive welfare state for disabled people. An indication of this was the wholesale continued exclusion of many from the labour market in the early 20th century. A campaign some 10 years after the Lloyd George reforms by the National League for the Blind and Disabled to assist blind people in getting closer to paid work led to the Blind Persons Act 1920 and sheltered employment provision. Perceived differences based on impairments in adulthood created invidious distinctions; the same was also true in educational policy and provision for disabled children. Many of the earliest schools had been attempts to rescue 'the blind and deaf' who were educable. While the Elementary Education Act of 1899 formally recognised epileptic children and those deemed 'defective'. These early developments represent the beginning of the graded and impairment-driven segregations of later special, and often segregated, schooling. Notions of risk and protection were arguably important in explaining the impetus to segregate disabled children. Mainstream schooling, however, remained a challenge for those disabled children who risked lessening the results of schools as, perhaps surprisingly, many schools in the late Victorian era were funded through performance-based payments (Fulcher, 1989).

A key turning point in disability policy came about after the 'Great War' of 1914-18. The scale of lives lost and of severely war-injured prompted a re-evaluation of the needs of disabled people and the rise of rehabilitation medicine and policy. Aside from the medical interventions, the Liberal-led coalition governments, sensing the outrage of war-wounded men not being able to return to a job, developed the King's National Roll Scheme in 1919 (Kowalsky, 2007). The King's Roll was an early form of quota system designed to aid access to paid work. Despite the Lloyd George reforms, the schemes were of limited value for many sick and disabled men who would have ceased paid work or never have had work. Despite the limitations of rehabilitation policy and the sole focus on war injured, the developments that followed the First World War symbolised the changing understanding of and commitment to those injured in the line of duty. Paradoxically, even well after the war had ended, the longer-run hierarchy of support for people impaired in war has led to differentials in benefit levels for disabled people based on the cause of impairment. Wider developments began to have unplanned positive consequences for disabled people. Meanwhile, the Maternity and Child Welfare Act 1918 improved maternal and neonatal care in a way that reduced needless impairment (Hendrick, 2003).

Eugenics, science of difference, segregation and IQ

The 20th century saw the birth of science and science policies emerge in a way that became an additional threat to disabled people's social, economic and cultural lives. Although couched in the language of science, eugenics is firmly within the containment (or elimination) school of thinking. Darwin's *On the origin of species* (1859) provided ideas on long-run natural selection processes that would be abused by what were later dubbed 'Social Darwinists' who suggested that only the fittest would survive in the complex organic social development of the 20th century (Spencer, 1864). This use of the notions of both 'natural selection' and the 'survival of the fittest' were in fact derived from the evolutionist Lamarck and the philosopher Hofstadter. The implications for those who fell way short of a stereotyped image of normality and of 'fit' with society's needs was stark. A new science of categorisation had been born, one which could aid the more careful selection or eradication of those deemed unfit to live. In time, 'fitness' shifted from being a scientific category to a moral judgement. Galton, Darwin's half-cousin, applied a version of his thinking to the new 'science' or more properly ideology of eugenics, one which emphasised the need for genetic purity and social selection to avoid depletion of the strength of the gene pool (Galton, 1883). It is worth noting that eugenics was not simply a genetic science, but a 'science' of social organisation; as Galton noted, eugenics is: '... the study of agencies under social control that may improve or impair the racial qualities of future generations, either physically or mentally' (Galton, 1904).

Institutions in Galton's later work had a key role to play in terms of the long-term development of the eugenic project and later pseudo-scientific constructions of disability. The Mental Deficiency Act 1913 represented a merging of pseudo-scientific Galtonian views with early medical constructions of social risks. Although claiming to separate people who were mentally ill from those with learning difficulties, the Act skated over social niceties in arriving at the four graded categories of: *idiot, imbecile, feeble minded and morally defective*. The Act provided 'legitimacy' for the incarceration of unmarried mothers, people with learning difficulties and those who in other contexts would be deemed 'insane'.

A key weapon in the armoury of the new social categorisers was the development of the notion of IQ (intelligence quotient). The term was popularised by Simon and Binet (quoted in Quigley, 1995) and applied to people deemed idiots, imbeciles, and has been influential throughout the 20th century in terms of providing 'legitimacy' for categorical terms shaping notions of educability, employability and justification for the segregation of disabled people. IQ has of course been used as a system categorising both disabled and non-disabled children alike (Borsay, 2005, p 110), and until late 20th-century scepticism crept in, served to underline what Ryan and Thomas refer to as 'IQ fatalism' (1980).

Beveridge, the postwar context and the New Jerusalem

If the First World War placed war-injured ex-servicemen onto the policy agenda and connected theoretical notions of citizenship to some disabled people, the Second World War witnessed substantive policy developments aimed at supporting disabled people back to work following the war, while war-time labour shortages aided formerly excluded disabled men and women to enter employment (Humphries and Gordon, 1992). At the level of policy this is interesting, providing evidence of the social construction of the disability category to fit with broader changes in economy and society. Both compensatory and welfare impulses underlay changes in policy and programme. The 'New Jerusalem' that the postwar governments ushered in to tackle Beveridge's five 'giant evils' (Glennerster, 2007) (the NHS, Education Act, National Assistance, slum clearances and major housing projects) were mirrored in the field of disability and employment policy with the passing of the Disabled Persons' (Employment) Act 1944 (HM Government, 1944a). The Act, the culmination of the Tomlinson Report (1942), reflected changing attitudes towards disabled people and their economic potential. The report and the Act, originally designed as an annexe to Beveridge's 1942 report on social insurance, took on a life of its own, and can be seen as an early example of effective cross-departmental cooperation.

For the first time, some disabled people were viewed in policy terms as deserving of policy attention to support access to the mainstream of working lives. The Act only went half way, however; Section 2 of the Act noted that some workers were too far from the labour market and would be better suited to sheltered employment. Critics point to this development without questioning the wider paternalist assumptions that lay behind such a forced compromise (Moreton, 1992). What is often not acknowledged was the symbolism of Section 2 employment, its historic attempt to intervene between the values of free market capitalism and paternalist protection, while the labour shortages of the 1940s led to a highly interventionist stance that went beyond voluntarism (Roulstone, 2002). The Tomlinson Report (see ***Box 1.3*** below) made clear that most disabled people should be working in mainstream employment.

Box 1.3: Excerpt from the Tomlinson Report (1943)

In a highly industrialised country such as Britain, the number of separate occupations is so large and their demand on physical activity so varied it is possible to find an occupation within the physical capacity of all save a minority of the disabled. This does not mean that the problem is easy of solution; it means only that disablement need not be a bar to economic employment

Not all disabled people could work, either because employers were unwilling to employ them or because they had impairments (or perceived impairments) that made employment very difficult. Beveridge's 1942 report, *Social insurance and allied services*, acknowledged that for those people unable to build up a contributory record, provision needed to be made.

The National Assistance Act 1948 laid out provisions for disabled people with no insurance history or capacity. Interestingly, despite the evidence that disabled people faced problems accessing paid work, the principle of 'less eligibility' enshrined in the Poor Law continued to underpin the very meagre benefits available and in part helped perpetuate the links between poverty and disability (Harris et al, 1971; Disability Alliance, 1975). In the field of education, developments were also taking place which served to perpetuate the divisive and categorical approach to disability. The Education Act 1944 (HM Government, 1944b), the product of the then Education Minister 'Rab' Butler, is best remembered for ushering in the tri-partite system of education and for its philosophy of education best suited to a child's 'ability, age and aptitude'.

While on paper a promising development for disabled people, the Act did however spawn the parallel and now infamous categories applying solely to disabled people of 'educationally subnormal' (ESN). Notions of mild, moderate and severe subnormality were applied uncritically throughout from the 1940s through to the early 1980s in education and health settings, only being repealed in health policy with the Mental Health Act of 1983 and the Education Act of 1980. It is worth pointing out that children with less significant physical and sensory impairments were entering some mainstream contexts, while many blind, deaf and significantly impaired children were and continue to be educated in the mainstream. As with employment, disabled people were to live in carefully segregated contexts. In many ways the policy imperatives for education were influenced by wider employment policies which often assumed that disabled people were unable to work. In this way, segregated provision was at best a distraction from established curricula, and at worst a form of warehousing. Special schools were at worst brutal and at best highly regimented (Westcott, 1991; Humphries and Gordon, 1992).

Origins of official community-based support

One key finding of much research around poverty was its close association with disability and reliance on disability benefits. Townsend's major study of poverty in the late 1970s established that disabled people were disproportionately represented among the poorest groups in society (Townsend, 1979). Both lack of paid work and poverty level benefits ensured this relationship. The principle of less eligibility enshrined in the Poor Law Reform Act helped underpin poverty level benefit rates. This in part spawned a flurry of policy interest in disability anti-poverty campaigns and programmes and what was later to be called an 'income-based' approach captured the imagination of key policy writers and politicians, for example,

Peter Townsend, Alan Walker and the Labour MP Alf Morris. The Disability Alliance and the Disablement Income Group were formed to pursue what they saw as a better financial settlement for disabled people. Critics pointed to the limited welfarist aims of such early disability lobbying (UPIAS, 1976; Barnes, 1991; Davis, 1998). The National Assistance Act, although allowing benefits to be paid to those who may never have worked or with a fragmentary work record, did not erase the 'evil' of want. Involvement in policy struggle was for some a personal crusade; Alf Morris, for example, had witnessed his father's war injuries and disadvantage following his return from the First World War. His struggle for change was rooted in his outrage at his observations:

> I was the eighth child of a disabled father. He had lost a leg and an eye serving in the First World War, and his lungs were wrecked. He had been a signwriter, but from when I was three-years-old he became unemployable. For the remaining five years of his life, he and his family lived mainly on his meagre war pension. The War Office decreed that his death was not war-related and denied my mother a war widow's pension. That happened when I was seven. It showed that disability entailed deprivation and that disabled people and their families depended on decisions by faraway strangers with no knowledge of their lives and needs. (Alf Morris, *Yorkshire Post*, 2009)

Morris was instrumental in pushing through a key piece of earlier community-based policy in the Chronically Sick and Disabled Persons Act 1970. He met with opposition to the Act and its ambitions, most notably from the Social Services Secretary Richard Crossman and his wider department who felt the Act's provisions would be unwieldy and expensive (*Hansard*, 1969). Morris prevailed and the Act eventually received cross-party support. It captured the social zeitgeist in emphasising disabled people's rights to access public buildings that were otherwise only accessible to non-disabled people, while the orange (now blue) badge scheme afforded disabled people priority on street parking for the first time. The community, mainstream and affirmative nature of these developments was important given the history of paternalist and segregated treatment of disabled people. The Act also made plain the outdated assumption that younger disabled people should be housed with older people. This of course did not signal all disabled people leaving institutions, and the Act was slow to permeate many local authorities. However, the symbolism of disabled people's presence on the 'high street' was important, and arguably part of a general shift towards community that would eventually follow.

Another key development in the 1960s and 1970s was the early questionings of the value and validity of long-stay hospitals for 'the mentally ill' and people with significant learning difficulties (Barnes, 1991, p 22; see also Minister of Health, 1961). A mixture of factors underlay the impetus for change. First, pharmacological improvements allowed greater community options. Changing social sensibilities as to the acceptability of incarcerating sick and disabled people also had its part to play; there is no doubt that financial considerations were also very important.

Beyond paternalism: early struggles for the Disabled People's Movement

The 1970s saw the first awakenings of disabled people rejecting the inevitability of their entering an institution where they were judged to be 'too disabled' to live in the mainstream. If Morris's reforms were advancing the lives of disabled people closer to the mainstream, disabled people themselves had to be at the forefront of more radical challenges of institutionalised lives. Paul Hunt's famous letter to *The Guardian* (Hunt, P, 1972) reflected the growing anger and aspiration to live life in the mainstream and to have choices that non-disabled people took for granted. The Union of Physically Impaired Against Segregation (UPIAS) best represents this tradition, and challenged head on the paternalist heritage that assumed that disabled people did not know how to live their own lives (UPIAS, 1976). The challenge was how to square such new approaches to profoundly traditional policy and delivery models. A key plank of UPIAS's work was to challenge the income-based approach that had to this point been the dominant response to disability poverty. For the first time the document *Fundamental principles of disability* (UPIAS, 1976) floated the idea of disability rights beyond income and statist welfare approaches. This was a challenge for disability income campaigners as their thinking was being questioned while benefits levels remained extraordinarily low (Townsend and Walker, 1981). The nascent Disabled People's Movement was towards 'choices and rights' to control over all aspects of their lives. The mismatch between aspiration and policy reality was very stark. The brute reality for disabled people, whether in institutions or living in mainstream society, was that they continued to have little control over their lives. As Barnes notes:

> It is evident that health and social support systems currently available to disabled people are a product of, and a major contributor to, institutional discrimination. They are organised

around the traditional assumption that disabled people are unable to take charge of their own lives. (Barnes, 1991, p 147)

Mainstreaming and the resilience of segregation

At the same time as radical challenges of disability thinking and policy were happening, developments were afoot in the sphere of 'special education'. The Warnock Report (1978) and the Education Act 1981 (HM Government, 1981) that followed offered new definitions and a new vision for special education. Warnock argued that disabled children should, where possible, be educated in the mainstream alongside their non-disabled peers. The 1981 Act witnessed the introduction of the term 'special educational needs' (SEN) that embraced disabled pupils but also 'gifted and talented' pupils. The underlying philosophy was one of acknowledging a continuum of ability and needs that would reduce the stigma attached to previous labels, for example, ESN. While more children entered the mainstream and previous notions of ineducability were challenged, many disabled children continued to be housed in segregated schools or units in mainstream schools. Warnock did, however, spawn experiments in hybrid approaches where some disabled children spent time in both special and mainstream schools. For some pupils this contrast allowed them to see just how low expectations were in special schools (Roulstone, 1998). Beyond school, those disabled people who were unable to find work continued to be offered very limited day service choices, with most day centres serving as warehouses or repetitive low paid workshop-type environments.

Wholesale shift to community care: the unlikely offspring of neoliberalism?

The impetus to close long-stay hospitals took on a renewed vigour with the evidence to emerge from a number of enquiries over the preceding 20 years into institutional abuse against disabled people, most notably the Ely, Farleigh and Normansfield enquiries (Oswin, 1975). The changing political and policy environment toward neoliberal conservatism and the rejection of the 'nanny state' emphasised 'rolling back the frontiers of the state' (Gamble, 1988, p 223). Together these twin impetuses pushed forward community care reforms in a much more substantial way to that which followed the first wave reforms of the 1960s. Roy Griffiths's report (1988), the White Paper that followed (DH, 1989) and the NHS and Community Care Act 1990 (HM Government, 1990) cemented in the public imagination the view that 'community' was best. After all it was very difficult for anyone to argue against the closure of what were seen as dependency-creating, often harsh and impersonal regimes, and to argue against the value of community. The movement to community-based options fitted well with the Conservative shift to mixed economies of welfare and more localised solutions signalling a weakened central state. Localised market-based or marketised services were seen by neoliberal writers to be inherently more flexible, responsive and tailored to service users' needs (Boyson, 1978). Social work departments shifted roles from service providers to service brokers in the new quasi-market or 'salad bar' approach to 'care' provision (Hoyes et al, 1992). Such approaches, although new, were still based on a 'top-down' welfarist assumption that the most vulnerable in society had to be protected, but now by largely market-driven options.

Changes were not universally well received. The decanting of ex-asylum patients into unwelcoming and unprepared communities and the sense that informal care actually meant greater reliance on family made some commentators question whether the 'community' aspect of community care actually had any meaning (Bornat et al, 1997). A number of critics felt that cost savings were the strong underlying factor in the shift to community care. However, the shift towards consumer primacy based on market principles was seen as the solution to a range of issues in service delivery. The Disabled Persons (Services, Consultation and Representation) Act 1996 (HM Government, 1996a) embodied the logic of consumer sovereignty in placing disabled people at the centre of service consultation and to use an overworked term, 'consultation'. The reality was more complex. There was no evidence that major shifts towards increased consultation or representation were taking place (Drake, 1999, p 71). It is worth noting that the idea of having disabled people's input into local service planning was also evident in the Chronically Sick and Disabled Persons Act 1970 (HM Government, 1970b), and was equally as ineffective in involving disabled people in a meaningful way. Limited social care budgets, resistant professional interests and lack of support for involvement were key factors here, as was the simple refusal to enact certain sections of the 1996 Act. The period 1979-97 was, however, a paradoxical one; it was an era where stringent welfare reforms sat alongside the birth of formal legal rights for disabled people as witnessed in the birth of the Disability Discrimination Act (DDA) 1995 (HM Government, 1995b; see also Gooding, 1995). It might be argued that these developments are not contradictory and that formal equality measures of this type are a preferred policy option to substantive, redistributive, affirmative and civil rights approaches to disability disadvantage. This may be pushing the argument a little too far; however, we do know that the DDA 1995 was constructed as a reluctant legislative sop to those who were pushing strongly for full and enforceable civil rights legislation (Barnes, 1991).

The limits to progress within a neoliberal policy framework are perhaps more easily evinced in a brief assessment of the wider welfare agenda of the Conservative governments of the 1980s and early 1990s. Put simply, the Thatcherite creed, one based on strident anti-dependency perspectives embodied in the work of Charles Murray (Murray, 1996a, 1996b), was that the welfare state had served to foster dependency and a dependency culture among many (Boyson, 1978). Of note, this label began to attach both disabled and non-disabled people alike and may be viewed as the precursor to Tony Blair's later binary formulation of 'work for those who can and support for those who cannot' (Blair, 2002). The supplementary benefits system, one that grew out of the non-contributory principles of national assistance, was placed under severe attack during the 1980s under the Fowler reforms. Specific evidence of fraud was used as a pretext for major cuts in supplementary payments related to disabled people's additional costs. In their place was a single premium which was generally much less generous than the previous system of supplements. Social Fund grants, grants designed for the most needy, were replaced with capped discretionary payments that again equated to cuts for disabled people (Drake, 1999). Perhaps the largest irony of the Conservative government's tenure was their decision to move large numbers of claimants from unemployment to Invalidity Benefit (IVB), arguably to mask their failure to reduce the unemployment of the early 1980s and 1990s. This wholesale shift has stored up perhaps the most significant debate in welfare policy since the Second World War – that of large numbers on IVB, later Incapacity Benefit (ICB) (and now ESA), claimants embodying an electoral and fiscal 'time bomb' for future governments (Roulstone, 2000).

New Deal for disabled people, age-based policies and new dualisms

The accession of New Labour to power in 1997 witnessed perhaps the most diverse and arguably contradictory policies of any postwar party towards disabled people. Some viewed the New Labour project, while hugely ambitious, as a continuity with neoliberal conservatism rather than as a major departure from it (Prideaux, 2005). The carry-over of large numbers of disabled claimants for ICB (ESA since 2009) alongside a growing clamour among a small but vocal group of disabled people towards direct payments based on independent living principles has arguably led to the largest dualisation of disability policy in contemporary policy history. Harsh welfare reform discourses on the undeserving has sat alongside new potentially enabling discourses of personalisation and self-direction best encapsulated in the provision of direct payments for disabled people. By 2010 disabled people represented an increasingly heterogeneous group who, for complex policy reasons, are made up of 'non-legitimate' disability category holders who ought to be working, or 'legitimate' disability category holders who should be supported. To use the words of the former Welfare Reform Secretary Alan Johnson, the challenge of welfare reform is to distinguish between the 'bad backs and genuinely disabled' (Johnson, 2005).

Arguably disabled people as a whole continue to be constructed and narrated by non-disabled policy makers and professionals. However, internal distinctions being made around genuine 'disability' (sic) are now more dramatic, destructive and more easily disseminated. Whether this dualism is a departure from the earlier Poor Law distinctions between deserving and undeserving is a moot point. Certainly the debates have been played out much more publically. However, the offering of direct payments to some disabled people has established that independent living principles and disabled people being placed in the driving seat without undue social care mediation is a very promising development (Barnes and Mercer, 2006).

Interestingly, these same dualised discourses have not been applied to disabled children, perhaps because of greater sympathy towards children more generally, but also partly due to the difficulties some children have accessing support. Indeed the major policy shift towards *Every Child Matters* (DfES, 2003) in the UK has been applied to disabled children. There is evidence that the New Labour government from 1997 had begun to acknowledge disabled childhoods beyond simple categorical approaches based on schooling, safeguarding and so on to make the link between childhood and poverty more generally (PMSU, 2005). The evidence that disabled children faced greater barriers in childhood alerted the government to the need to reduce both those barriers and the wider connection between disabled childhoods and later life poverty (Burchardt, 2003). Disabled children are now more likely to be educated in the mainstream, but the number of special schools has proven resilient to change given the parental opposition to their closure (Rustemier and Vaughan, 2005). Anti-discrimination is in place in the form of the Special Educational Needs and Disability Act (SENDA) 2000 (HM Government, 2000a) and the Code of Practice; however, this does not outlaw continued segregation where this an express wish of parents and/or disabled children. Categories continue to dog progress towards greater similarity between mainstream and segregated provision, while for children with the greatest needs, they may find support elusive without resort to formalised statementing processes. There is evidence that wider access issues, such as poor provision of wheelchairs for younger disabled children, can further reduce their educational and wider living options (CSIP, 2006).

The life chances report of 2005 (PMSU, 2005) laid out a blueprint for better policy responses to disabled people's life chances. It provided a comprehensive picture of the barriers that are evident in disabled people's lives, while recommending a range of programmes and interventions that would ameliorate those barriers in the future (PMSU, 2005). The report is premised on age-based policy approaches. This more explicit approach to age and life stages in UK policy was made more explicit in New Labour policy (Burchardt, 2003). Some critics have pointed to the dangers of such an approach, and its relative under-emphasis on older disabled people.

Self-directed support: choices, self-management or something in between?

As with the first wave of disability-led policy and practice discussed above, some of the most progressive recent disability policy has come from disabled people's own ideas (Barnes and Mercer, 2006). While the significance of direct payments cannot be overestimated, limited take-up has meant that only 5 per cent of eligible people were in receipt of direct payments some 10 years after the Act was passed (Davey et al, 2006). Limited take-up, views that independent living had not taken strong root in adult social care and the growing demographic cost implications of an ageing population have led to redoubled efforts to 'modernise' adult social care and the recent emphasis on the compulsory offering of direct payments for those deemed eligible (DH, 2009b). While not achieving its early ambitions, such self-directed developments did contain rights-based notions that disabled people needed the state to underwrite generous self-directed provision for disabled people meeting eligibility criteria. Of course this shifts the locus of policy decisions to the arena of eligibility, and the Gloucestershire ruling established the severe limits to a rights-based social support system where budgets were not sufficient to respond to the weight of these rights. Indeed rights quickly become contingent in nature, which rather questions the meaning of the term.

Two key policy documents have been built within these contexts – the Green Paper *Independence, wellbeing and choice* (DH, 2005) and the White Paper *Our health, our care, our say* (DH, 2006). These policy documents began to solidify the spirit of earlier changes in adult social care by fostering personalised choices and the requirement for professionals to connect their work while placing disabled people at the centre of the decision-making process on social support (DH, 2006). While these changes are clearly welcomed by many, the exact motivation for their introduction is being hotly debated in an era of stringent planned cuts in public expenditure outlined in the most recent Comprehensive Spending Review. Some examples of cost-driven as opposed to disability-driven changes in self-directed support do beg questions as to the risks of self-direction morphing into self-management and reliance – clearly a return to a Victorian thinking for the majority (Roulstone and Morgan, 2009). Certainly it could be argued that whatever the fiscal position of UK PLC, the self-direction genie has been loosed from the bottle; expectations have been raised. The scope for tensions between policy rhetoric and disabled people's personal expectations has never been so stark, and we shall explore these further in later chapters.

Globalisation and disability policy

The factors shaping the UK economic and legislative dynamics are now of course influenced by some factors well beyond its own shores. UN conventions, European Union (EU) directives, global economic shifts and recessionary impacts all serve to highlight the contingent nature of much disability-related and welfare policy, and not all these developments are negative. While deindustrialisation has profoundly affected many UK regions with major economic relocations, there is no doubt much scope for the emerging economies to invest in the UK in the future and to reverse historical flows of capitalist investment, especially as China, India and other emergent economies are likely to see the development of wage pressures and shifts to greater protective measures for workers. Globalised business, culture and consciousness has afforded the growth of internationalised new social movements, one key one being the global Disabled People's Movement. The terrain of economic and cultural struggle is now equally as globalised as capitalism itself. However that plays out, the influence of wider global and cross-national influences is likely to be important in shaping disability policy into the 21st century.

Conclusion

Policy for disabled people has been seen to shift quite dramatically away from institutional and paternalist thinking towards greater choices and rights-based policy frameworks. However, this process is far from a linear one. The co-existence of, for example, rights-based policy in the form of direct payments and personal budgets, alongside the decidedly paternalist and stigmatised underpinnings of disability welfare policy, presents a complex picture of social policy in the early 21st century. Clearly the blueprint for more disability-led policy has been established, one that acknowledges disabled people as citizen experts. This sits oddly with increasingly harsh rationing as to just who counts as disabled. Increased conditionality and stigma for some benefits make for a very challenging policy climate for those disabled people who fall between the stools of employment and security in recent neoliberal formulations of the binary of 'real' and 'feigned' disability populations. There is a need for a watching brief on the extent to which such binary constructions impact negatively on all disabled people.

Summary

This chapter has provided a historical overview of the development and changes to disability policy. Its aim was to provide a primer with which to explore some of the following issues and themes in more depth:

- the Poor Law shaping of early responses to disability;
- the growth and logic of institutions;
- the impact of industrialisation and industrial logic;
- the rise of the welfare state;
- deinstitutionalisation and community-based policy;
- the birth of disability rights and independent living;
- the increased rationing of services and shifting of the 'disability category'.

Questions

1. According to Drake (1999), what are the key policy traditions that shaped disability provision in British social policy?
2. In what ways were disabled people constructed as 'problem populations' in policy terms during the era of industrialisation in Britain?
3. Did the Poor Law Amendment Act 1834 challenge or reaffirm disabled people as burdens on the progressive state?
4. What is meant by the term 'less eligible' welfare for disabled people?
5. Did the community care reforms of the 1990s end paternalism?
6. What were the key principles of independent living put forward by Hunt. Finkelstein and others?
7. Can neoliberalism and a choices and rights agenda be reconciled?

Further reading

The books by **Drake (1999)** and **Borsay (2005)** are the best overview of the historical developments of disability policy. More contemporary overviews are available in **Barnes (1991)** and **Millar (2003)**. Useful histories are also available in **Ryan and Thomas (1980)** and **Humphries and Gordon (1992)**.

Cure, care and protect: the paternalist policy heritage

Introduction

This chapter primarily concentrates on the period immediately after the Second World War, working its way through to the 1970s. Although Chapter One showed that individuals with impairments have been subject to public hostility for centuries (Barnes and Mercer, 2010), and such hostility was intensified by the onset of industrialisation with its concomitant demand for speed and dexterity from factory workers (Ryan and Thomas, 1980), time and space prevents a longer and more detailed historical exploration of the segregation, marginalisation and exclusion of disabled individuals in the UK. However, any book relating to disability from the 1940s onwards still needs to contextualise the pertinent conflicts, oppressions and concessions surrounding the developments that have driven a succession of political, attitudinal and socioeconomic changes. Suffice to say, such changes have not always been linear or intentional, nor have they been entirely consistent or convincing in terms of application and direction. In part, power struggles, vested interest, pragmatism and acquiescence help to explain the shape of social policies aimed at disabled people. As a consequence of these battles, institutional discrimination, whether it be intended or not, has embodied a culture of oppression against disabled people which:

> ...is embedded in the work of...welfare institutions, and is present if they are systematically ignoring or meeting inadequately the needs of disabled people compared with able-bodied people. It is also present if agencies are regularly interfering in the lives of disabled people as a means of social control, and/or to an extent, not experienced by able-bodied people. It is therefore

> a descriptive concept related to outcome.... It incorporates the extreme forms of prejudice and intolerance ... as well as the more covert and unconscious attitudes which contribute to and maintain indirect and/or passive discriminatory practices within contemporary organisations. (Barnes, 1991, p 3)

In this respect, the domination of medical professionals with their paternalistic approach has played a major part in determining policy during the period this chapter focuses on. Continuing with these themes, ensuing chapters will show how international organisations and trends have also contributed, while resistance and activism from the Disabled People's Movement has attempted to advance the cause of disabled people in recent times. Conversely:

> A great deal of the responsibility for the persistence of institutional discrimination against disabled people rests with the succession of British governments since 1945. While there is a growing consensus throughout the democratic world that disabled people have the same basic human rights as non disabled people, and that it is the responsibility of governments to ensure that they are able to secure a standard of living comparable to that of their fellow citizens, this has not occurred in the United Kingdom. (Barnes, 1991, p 13)

Set against this backdrop, this chapter critically details and unpacks the principal policy and programme developments that, arguably, still underpin many aspects of the contemporary social policy environment despite repeated attacks from many analysts, social commentators and disabled people alike. The chapter thus provides an appraisal of key developments in education, training, employment and welfare policy while placing them within the context of significant legislative landmarks and prominent policy actors who have contributed to the policy atmosphere affecting disabled people.

As a starting point, however, post–Second World War disability policy is situated within the broader scope of policy literature and debate. The Beveridgean welfare settlement, for example, had particular implications for many disabled people, with its emphasis on paid work and the insurance principle. Similarly, Marshall's classic construction of citizenship has left disabled people in an ambiguous position with regard to a substantive amount of subsequent social policy initiatives. The legacies of both Beveridge and Marshall should not be ignored. And both need to be borne in mind when viewing the ensuing disability legislation and the effects on disabled people.

Disability, paternalism and the impact of William Beveridge

During the 1940s, official policy associated with disabled people began to move away from the paternalism best defined as non-disabled professionals 'knowing best' what disabled people want (Charlton, 2000). In other words, 'rehabilitation', 'inclusion' and 'normalisation' embodied in the more pervasive notion of 'care' became subject to the considered opinions of politicians, medical professionals and the non-disabled who knew 'what was best' without any substantial consultation with disabled people over their specific difficulties, obstacles, needs, wants or desires.

A prominent starting point for this changing, paternalistic environment was the work of William Beveridge. His work amply expressed a deep hatred of the means test of bygone years and was significantly influenced by a 'lifetime of experience of insurance' (Glennerster and Evans, 1994, p 58). In 1942, the 'Beveridge Report', or to give its full title, the report on *Social insurance and allied services*, was published to great acclaim, selling an unprecedented 635,000 abridged copies to the public at large. The key aspect of this report, which was adopted in parts by the incoming Labour Party of 1945, related specifically to a scheme of national insurance and national assistance which could proffer a 'cradle to grave' protection if 'any sensible Government would first of all grant family allowances, create a comprehensive health service and maintain full employment' (Fraser, 1984, p 215).

Integral to this 'lifetime' protection was the need to guarantee a basic minimum income which, in the eyes of Beveridge, would further enhance the war-time sense of collective belonging and active citizenship extremes of previous eras despite the continued segregation and containment of some (Drake, 1999). What generally appeared to be a more encompassing approach had great promise. Disabled people were recognised, at last, as an identifiable group in their own right (Oliver and Barnes, 1998), yet social policy from this period onwards leant towards an approach based on notions of 'rehabilitation', 'inclusion' and 'normalisation' (Drake, 1999). 'Rehabilitation' aimed to make disabled people employable, while the avenue of 'inclusion' sought to create a system of benefits that offset the exclusion of disabled people from many aspects of social life. 'Normalisation', on the other hand, had the ambition of establishing specialised welfare services designed to 'adapt disabled individuals to the non-disabled world' (Drake, 1999, p 54).

Taken as a whole, Barnes (1991) attributed this change in emphasis and apparent optimism to the humanitarian influence of the Victorian philanthropists, the general concern felt towards disabled ex-servicemen during and after two world wars, the changing political climate and the prospect of a buoyant economy. Nonetheless, this chapter demonstrates that such an atmospheric change was distinctly paternalistic. Indeed, the Beveridge Report was not immune to such an accusation. Although the report was promoted as a fight against the 'five giants' of 'Want', 'Disease', 'Ignorance', 'Squalor' and 'Idleness', the reality was that 'Want' was the only target. Within this context, the primary focus of Beveridge and his report was not – as one would normally assume – to relieve poverty or inequality, but to restructure the labour market. Ideally, Beveridge wished to promote a universal cum all-embracing sense of security, but that security had to be based on a national contributory insurance scheme in which contributions were set at a 'flat rate' and paid during times of employment. In return, a 'flat rate' of subsistence benefit, that is, an 'adequate' amount for the period in question, would be paid during times of unemployment (Beveridge, 1942).

As touched on earlier, the 'avoidance of mass unemployment' (Beveridge, 1942, p 120) was a crucial ingredient for the success of the planned social security coverage. The long-term dependant on welfare benefits was not a major consideration. Rather, the independent worker, in a regular and well-paid job, was seen as the ideal social welfare client (Harris, 1994). And it was he (and the gendered, non-disabled differentiation which was so prominent in the report) who would be insured against any 'interruption and loss of earning power' (Beveridge, 1942, p 7). Social normality, active citizenship and social inclusion was thus conceived as participation in the paid labour market (PLM) while working contributions into social insurance 'was the indispensable badge of ... [that active form of] citizenship' (Harris, 1994).

Without doubt, it was this emphasis on paid work that was to seriously impact on the lives of disabled individuals during the ensuing years. To compound issues, Beveridge dismissively viewed the long-term unemployment of disabled people as a consequence of a lack of special training schemes (Harris, 1994), and felt that insurance should not carry the 'burden'. Indeed, paragraph 22 of the report was unequivocal in its declaration that:

> The plan adopted since 1930 in regard to prolonged unemployment and sometimes suggested for prolonged disability, that the State should take this burden off insurance, in order to keep the contribution down, is wrong in principle. The insured persons should not feel that income for idleness, however caused, can come from a bottomless purse. The

> Government should not feel that by paying doles it can avoid the major responsibility of seeing that unemployment and disease are reduced to the minimum. The place for direct expenditure and organisation by the State is in maintaining employment of the labour and other productive resources of the country, and in preventing and combating disease, not in patching an incomplete scheme of insurance. (Beveridge, 1942, p 12)

By way of a reinforcing supplement, the desired creation of a National Health Service, Beveridge's famous Assumption B in the report, was an extension of this stance in that such a unified health service would form the ideal mechanism by which comprehensive 're-habilitation services for prevention and cure of disease and restoration of capacity for work' (Beveridge, 1942, p 120) could and should be promulgated.

When viewed 'in the round', it is obvious that the processes of 'rehabilitation' and 'normalisation' were essential for the Beveridge scheme to succeed. Income for idleness could not and should not be funded from a never-ending stream of government revenue. Nonetheless, Beveridge was astute enough to realise that some disabled people were unable to work and therefore were not covered fully by social insurance. As a solution, Beveridge managed to overcome his profound hatred of means testing and proposed that national assistance fill the void. Assistance would be made available to those:

> Persons failing to fulfil contribution conditions either because they have less than the qualifying minimum ... or because they have never become fit for work, or because they are not in full benefit for unemployment, disability or pensions. (Beveridge, 1942, p 141)

Crucially, Beveridge insisted that such assistance 'must be felt to be something less desirable than insurance benefit: otherwise the insured persons get nothing for their contributions' (Beveridge, 1942, p 141). Under these terms, assistance would be subject to proof and examination of needs, invoking memories of the stigma attached to the Poor Law, and would only meet the needs for subsistence. But for Beveridge the determination of subsistence was somewhat elusive. As the report states, 'what is required for reasonable human subsistence is to some extent a matter of judgment; estimates ... change with time' (Beveridge, 1942, p 14), but generally change in an upward direction. Again, Beveridge seriously underestimated the needs and requirements of disabled people.

To be fair, however, this uninformed stance towards the needs, difficulties and barriers facing disabled people was a product of its time. When taken alongside the successful war-time application of Keynesian economics, with its insistence that the government should manage the economy and create work as opposed to letting the laissez-faire market follow its own course, the Beveridge scheme was the focal point for a 'New Jerusalem' where long-term or indeed any form of unemployment would diminish and the government would create and maintain employment. Flat rate benefits arising out of national insurance contributions would only represent a temporary support mechanism for individuals awaiting employment again. Conversely, full employment that Beveridge was to redefine 'as an irreducible minimum of 3 per cent unemployment' (Fraser, 1984, p 217) would, he calculated, allow for an increase in national insurance contributions and thus enable state funding of pensions and benefits as contributions outstripped demand. With the benefit of hindsight, however, 3 per cent unemployment was an impossible and idealistic baseline to work from. And, as the rest of this chapter shows, Beveridge's unrealistic assumptions about unemployment levels, his aforementioned lack of understanding about the obstacles to employment for disabled people and his lack of any realistic focus on the long-term unemployed allowed for the implemented aspects of his report to exclude and marginalise many disabled individuals who were not in a position to participate in the PLM.

Institutional discrimination and implementation of the Beveridge Report

Hindsight, of course, was not available to Beveridge, the existing war-time Coalition government or the incoming Labour Party of 1945. The inclusive, yet paternalistic optimism was still there. As a consequence, the work of Beveridge in tandem with the prevailing environment of political change and concern helped perpetuate a flurry of significant legislation relating directly and indirectly to disabled people during the climax and aftermath of the Second World War (Barnes, 1991). For disabled people, all of this amounted to problems that were overwhelming to say the least. As we shall see in due course, the actual legislation implemented in the spirit of the Beveridge Report (see **Box 2.1**) had the added detrimental effect of perpetuating, intentionally or otherwise, the previously described institutional discrimination of disabled people. In its most tangible form, examples of institutional discrimination:

> ... include the way the education is system is organised, and the operation of the labour market, both of which are influenced by

government and both of which perpetuate the disproportionate economic and social disadvantage experienced by disabled people. (Barnes, 1991, p 3)

Within this context, the first piece of significant legislation concerning disabled people was the Disabled Persons' (Employment) Act of 1944 (HM Government, 1944a). Introduced under the auspices of the war-time Coalition government, this Act followed the recommendations of the Tomlinson Committee Report (see Chapter One for more details) and was noteworthy for its attempt to go beyond a divisive categorical approach with its assumption that many disabled people could work alongside their non-disabled peers. Indeed, the Act was one of the first to acknowledge that the needs of disabled people were not disjointed. It did so through the requirement that health, social and employment professionals work together to help secure employment rights for disabled people or to ensure that all disabled people were provided with a variety of rehabilitation services and vocational training courses (Topliss, 1982; Barnes, 1991; Oliver and Barnes, 1998). Notably, the Act also made provision for a disabled person's employment register, a specialised employment placement service, an employment quota scheme compelling employers to employ disabled workers and a National Advisory Council along with Local Advisory Committees to advise government on the employment needs of disabled people (DoE, 1990; Thornton and Lunt, 1995).

As will become apparent later in this book, the Disabled Persons' (Employment) Act 1944 was a precursor to later Acts which aimed some 35 to 45 years later to connect those aspects of the lives of disabled people which had been fragmented by the industrial system and the growing boundaries that often accompanied the growth of professional spheres of interest (Macdonald, 1995). The Education Act (HM Government, 1944b) that also became law in 1944 was also underpinned by an egalitarian philosophy. In this instance, the intention was that disabled children should be educated alongside their non-disabled peers in primary and secondary education (Tomlinson, 1982). Indeed, the Act was probably best remembered for ushering in the tripartite system of schooling to promote an education best suited to a child's 'ability, age and aptitude' alongside the obligation for 'local education authorities to provide special educational treatment for those thought to need it' (Barnes, 1991, p 21).

In practice, however, both Acts did not live up to their optimistic, egalitarian potential. The implementation of the quota system under the Disabled Persons' (Employment) Act (HM Government, 1944a), for instance, turned out to be more concerned with not upsetting employers rather 'than ensuring that disabled people seeking employment were treated fairly' (Oliver and Barnes, 1998, p 37). Under the Act all employers with 20 or more employees had to employ 3 per cent of their workforce from the disabled person's register. The maximum fine for not complying was £100. The figure was set in 1944 and has never been raised. Since the Act's implementation only 10 employers have been prosecuted, the last of which being in 1975. One of these cases was dismissed, two others received the maximum fine, whereas the total fines for the remaining seven cases amounted to a paltry £434 (House of Commons Employment Committee, 1994). It comes of little surprise that increasing numbers of employers ignored the law. To make matters even worse, no public sector employer in the early 1990s met the quota, while in government departments, which one would reasonably expect to adhere to the laws set in place, only 1.4 per cent of staff were disabled people (Glendinning, 1991).

With the Education Act 1944 (HM Government, 1944b), outcomes fared little better. Despite intentions to the contrary, the Act and its guidance merely served to reassert the divisive, exclusionary approach of old. It did so through the instigation of a quasi-scientific classification of disability that ranged from the 'delicate/diabetic' category to the 'epileptic'. The full range of categories contained within the Act were: delicate/diabetic, children with mild/moderate subnormality, partially sighted, partially deaf, speech impaired, educationally 'subnormal', blind, deaf, children with physical impairments and epileptic children (HM Government, 1944b). In keeping with the spirit of the Act, some children benefited from this categorisation process. Children deemed to fit the 'mild/moderate sub-normality', 'partially sighted', 'partially deaf' or 'speech impaired' categories were allowed, where possible, to be educated in the mainstream.

Nonetheless, this categorisation of disabled people was, in the main, quite disturbing. Specifically, the most disabling feature of the Act and its guidance was the application of the term 'ineducable' to those children with 'severe mental handicaps' (Beveridge, 1999, p 2). These ideas drew on Cyril Burt's application of IQ tests to disability, and resulted in condemning some disabled children to little more than an exclusionary warehousing approach based on segregation (Miller and Gwynne, 1972). As a consequence, children who were categorised as 'educationally subnormal', 'blind', 'deaf', 'physically impaired' or 'epileptic' would ordinarily be educated in the context of a 'special school' and thus removed from the mainstream. To make matters worse, this categorisation process entailed a greater use of professionally trained 'experts' whose decisions were relatively final. The powerlessness of parents to reject the labels attached to their children was clearly evident in the outcomes of the appeals process – there were only four successful appeals registered out of 4,000 parental appeals between 1951 and 1960 (Barnes, 1991).

Box 2.1: Key 1940s legislation relating to disabled people

The **Disabled Persons' (Employment) Act 1944** attempted to secure employment rights for disabled people or ensure that all disabled people were provided with a variety of rehabilitation services and vocational training courses.

The **Education Act 1944** specified that disabled children should be educated alongside their non-disabled peers and obliged local authorities to provide special educational treatment for those thought to need it.

The **National Insurance (Industrial Injuries) Act 1946** enabled the provision and maintenance of equipment and appliances for those injured at work.

The **National Insurance Act 1946** emphasised the importance of work in the PLM. Universal 'flat rate' contributions were expected during times of employment in return for 'flat rate' benefits during unemployment.

The **National Assistance Act 1948** made some provision for meeting the financial needs of disabled people and mandated local authorities to provide residential facilities and services in both the community and institutions.

The **National Health Service Act 1948** provided hospital-based treatment, long-term care for disabled people and helped facilitate local authorities to supply the necessary medical aids for disabled people to live in their own homes.

Source: Adapted from Barnes (1991); Oliver and Barnes (1998); Drake (1999)

After the Second World War, and in the spirit of the Beveridge Report, the key pieces of legislation enacted by the newly formed Labour government were the National Insurance (Industrial Injuries) Act 1946 (HM Government, 1946a), the National Insurance Act 1946 (HM Government, 1946b), the National Assistance Act 1948 (HM Government, 1948b) and the National Health Service Act (HM Government, 1948a) of the same year. The National Insurance (Industrial Injuries) Act was introduced in August 1945 and became law in July of 1946 (HM Government, 1946a). From this point on, compensation for accidents in the workplace became the responsibility of the whole of society, in the guise of the state, rather than employers and private insurers (Fraser, 1984; Page, 2007). With this switch in responsibility for industrial injuries also came the possibility that equipment and appliances could and would be provided and maintained by the state for those injured at work (Barnes, 1991; Oliver and Barnes, 1998).

In the same year, the National Insurance Act (HM Government, 1946b) dutifully enacted Beveridge's belief in a universal, inclusive system of social security deriving from the principle of 'flat rate' contributions when in employment and 'flat rate' benefits when not. The Act also introduced a universal retirement pension for men over 65 and for women over 60. Two years later, the National Assistance Act followed Beveridge's wish that the government should provide a means-tested payment for 'those without a right to national insurance or whose benefits fell below its own minimum standard' (Borsay, 2005, p 161). Through means testing, the Act thus attempted to meet some of the financial needs of disabled people. Furthermore, the Act contained the proviso that local authorities should:

> ... make arrangements for promoting the welfare of persons ... who are blind, deaf or dumb, and other persons who are substantially and permanently handicapped by illness, injury or congenital deformity or such other disabilities as may be prescribed by the Minister. (Section 29, National Assistance Act 1948, cited in Drake, 1999, p 58)

With this proviso, the Act enabled 'local authorities to arrange a variety of services for disabled people, both in the community and institutions' (Oliver and Barnes, 1998, p 37). Arguably, it was this aspect of the Act that acted as a catalyst for the rapid development of social work in the 1950s and 1960s (Drake, 1999). In the immediate years following the war, for example, there was a proliferation of professional medical and psychiatric social workers, childcare officers and probation officers who were the recipients of diverse training schemes and, once the training had been completed, took up different roles in different yet separate service areas (Drake, 1999).

Set within the context of this chapter, the main aim of this professionalisation of welfare services was, of course, to promote the welfare of disabled people. Similarly the National Health Service Act (HM Government, 1948a), which was also enacted in 1948, appeared to supplement this promotion of welfare in that it provided for the acute medical needs of disabled people through hospital-based treatment and long-term care. In addition, the Act also made it possible for local authorities to supply the necessary medical aids for disabled people to live in their own homes (Barnes, 1991). Again, such services would be reliant on professionally trained individuals in their field.

In practice, not all bode well for disabled people. As with the two war-time Coalition Acts cited above, the National Insurance Act (1946b), the National Health Service Act (HM Government, 1948a) and the National

Assistance Act (HM Government, 1948b) had a negative impact. For example, Borsay (2005) points out that there were three major problems arising out of the national insurance and national assistance social security package. The first problem was that benefits made available to disabled people were paid at variable rates according to the cause rather than the effect of an impairment. Consequently, war pensions were more generous than industrial disablement, sickness benefit and retirement pensions.

The second problem arose out of the low level of national insurance and national assistance payments themselves. Mindful of the deprivation many elderly people had suffered during the war years, the Labour government ignored Beveridge's wishes to phase in pensions over 20 years. Naturally, such an undertaking was costly and the government needed to find the revenue from elsewhere. The primary victim of this decision not to phase in pensions was Beveridge's 'principle … [of] adequacy of benefit in amount and time' (1942, p 122). Since 'flat rate' contributions had to be set at a level affordable to the poorest paid worker, the rate of benefits being paid out also had to be low due to the limited amount of revenue accruing from contributions. This meant the government had little to play with, so a 'compromise' was sought through the provision of benefit levels that merely promoted a 'reasonable' and not a total insurance against want (Borsay, 2005). Such a compromise was to have devastating effects for disabled people. Insurance payments would no longer guarantee freedom from poverty and, if claimants had no other source of income, they would have to apply for means-tested national assistance in order to supplement their inadequate insurance benefits. And for those disabled people who did apply, the effect of this 'compromise' was that levels of benefit were far below the standard of living of the time.

The third problem with this social security package was its inability to reach those most in need. Despite Beveridge's belief that the national insurance and national assistance schemes would only create a temporary or diminishing drain on government revenue, and despite a substantial increase of claimants from 1,465,000 in 1948 to 2,840,000 in 1965 (Borsay, 2005, p 163), many 'would-be' disabled claimants took heed of Beveridge's previously recounted belief that national assistance should be less desirable than national insurance. As a result, many disabled people, and especially those who had recollection of the stigmatisation of the Poor Law, often forwent the humiliation and shame attached to means testing. Indeed Borsay (2005) cites the calculations of Atkinson et al, who used Joseph Rowntree's final poverty survey of York, to underline the fact that no more than 51 per cent of those eligible for national assistance actually made a claim (Atkinson et al, 1981). When turned on its head, the inference from this calculation is that disabled people had a high and disproportionate representation within the remaining 49 per cent.

To compound issues, the National Assistance Act (1948b) only empowered local authorities to provide services to enhance the welfare of disabled people. This provision was not a requirement, which meant that wherever provision was provided, it was in the form of institutional provision, leaving disabled people with the choice of either surviving without assistance or having to go into residential care (Oliver and Barnes, 1998). In a similar vein, the National Health Service Act (1948a) provided little beyond acute treatment while long-term care invariably meant living on a geriatric ward whether or not the disabled individual was beyond the age of retirement (Barnes, 1991). In effect, disabled people were being institutionalised inappropriately rather than having their needs met.

One the whole, the discussion of the Acts cited so far (and listed in **Box 2.1**) has demonstrated how the post-world war optimism was misplaced and slightly naive. Acts supposedly designed to promote the well-being of disabled people did not achieve their promise and turned out to be discriminatory when put into practice. Indeed, it was because of these Acts that so many disabled people during this period and after were subject to segregation during their schooling, excluded from the labour market due to a lack of enforcement of the quota system, and economically and socially disadvantaged by the low level of benefits on offer. Such discrimination was not only institutional but it was also patronising. The increase in state-sponsored welfare and the increased professionalisation of the services meant that the newly trained medical professionals and social workers, the so-called 'experts', were increasingly making decisions about what a disabled person's needs were and what support was best for them. Furthermore, this discrimination and patronage contributed to the denial of citizenship rights for disabled people. As this chapter has made clear, the conception of citizenship held by the leading policy protagonists of the time helped to shape policy, yet the vision of what constituted an ideal citizen did not fit the profile of a disabled person: hence the denial of the full benefits of citizenship and the marginalisation/exclusion of disabled individuals from the mainstream.

Citizenship, disability and T.H. Marshall

As this chapter has shown so far, William Beveridge had his own interpretation of active, participatory citizenship that influenced his proposals for social insurance. In turn, Beveridge's position influenced government policy. During the 1950s, however, other influences came into play that would take the concept of citizenship a step further and again the consequences of such deliberations had serious implications for disabled people. The work of T.H. Marshall, for example, was both detrimental and complimentary in terms of social inclusion. In accord with the prevailing logic of the time, Marshall's notion of citizenship focused on the Bevridgean model of the white non-disabled male breadwinner looking after his family while his wife, not partner, stayed at home and brought up the family (Williams, 1989). Within the confines of this logic, citizenship was seen as:

> ... a status bestowed upon those who are full members of a community. All those who possess the status are equal with respect to the rights and duties with which that status is endowed. There is no universal principle that determines what those rights and duties shall be, but societies in which citizenship is a developing institution create an image of an ideal of citizenship against which achievement can be measured and towards which aspiration can be directed. The urge forward along the path thus plotted is an urge towards a fuller measure of equality, an enrichment of the stuff of which the status is made and an increase in the number of those on whom the status is bestowed. (Marshall, [1949] 1992, p 18)

Even though Marshall was 'concerned with protecting individuals from the vicissitudes of capitalism' (Beckett, 2006, p 38), he did not intend to go beyond the moderation of capitalism's worst excesses; nor did he want to remove the social class system. Immediately this raises the question of how and to whom citizenship is bestowed. Clues to the answer, however, come in the way in which Marshall envisaged the historic conferral of civil, political and social rights on recognised citizens (see ***Box 2.2***), his vision of an 'ideal of citizen' and the minimal but telling duties he expected in return. Civil rights, the first conferral in Marshall's deliberations, were about individual liberty, free speech, the right to property ownership and parity before the law (Marshall, [1949] 1992; Dwyer, 2000, 2004a; Beckett, 2006). The second historical bestowment in this account was that of the political. Political rights were about participation in the voting process, the opportunity to stand for election and to exercise political influence that may ensue. Finally, social rights were seen as the embodiment of the civilising process and citizenship itself. Social rights related to welfare protection and the allied notion of social insurance. Marshall viewed these rights as the procurement of an element of economic security necessary for individuals to live a 'civilised' life within the society of that time.

> **Box 2.2: Marshall's historical development of rights: the civil, political and social**
>
> The civil element is composed of the rights necessary for individual freedom – liberty of the person, freedom of speech, thought and faith, the right to own property and to conclude valid contracts, and the right to justice. The last is of a different order from the others, because it is the right to defend and assert all one's rights on terms of equality with others and by due process of law.... By the political element I mean the right to participate in the exercise of political power, as a member of a body invested with political authority or as an elector of the members of such a body.... By the social element I mean the whole range from the right to a modicum of economic welfare and security, to the right to share to the full in the social heritage and to live civilised life according to the standards prevailing in society. (Marshall, [1949] 1992, p 8)

To consolidate his position, Marshall went on to argue that we should all have equal rights and indeed equal responsibilities regardless of the fact that some may be more wealthy and powerful than others. Naively, the duties Marshall attached to the eligibility for continual enjoyment of these social rights again related to the thinking of the time. Indeed, the constructed responsibilities of a citizen were summarised by Marshall as:

> ... the duty to pay taxes and insurance contributions. Since these are compulsory, no act of will is involved. Education and military service are also compulsory. The other duties are vague, and are included in the general obligation to live the life of a good citizen, giving such service as can promote the welfare of the community. (Marshall, [1949] 1992, p 45)

Of paramount importance, however, was the duty to work in the PLM and 'to put one's heart and soul into one's job and work hard' ([1949] 1992, p 46). Without doubt, these statements indicated that Marshall, like Beveridge, based his deliberations on a preconceived profile of an active citizen. The very notion of a civilised being living a civilised life invokes the image of an ideal citizen. And that profile in the eyes of Marshall relied heavily on full male employment (Lister, 1997).

To compound matters, there was an element of inequality built into Marshall's logic despite his tendency to emphasise 'rights' over the above-mentioned 'responsibilities' (Dwyer, 2000, 2004a) and despite his belief in what he termed 'equality of status' (Marshall, [1949] 1992). In this construct, 'equality of status' entailed a separation of economic equality from equal treatment and equal respect. For a number of commentators this separation of economic equality undermines the whole idea that everyone could enjoy equal status. Ultimately, the main problem lay in the historical fact that citizenship presumes equality among citizens and a reciprocal equality in the way in which the state interacts with individuals (Rioux, 2002). In reality, the state guarantee of equal social rights for all citizens has to be more than equal treatment. What is required is an equality of practice or, more poignantly, an equality of outcome (Rioux, 1994) rather than the 'equality of opportunity' that Marshall proposed (Rummery, 2002).

For disabled people, the disparity between equal treatment and equal outcome could not be more obvious. On the one hand, Marshall talks of 'the right to share to the full in the social heritage and to live civilised life according to the standards prevailing in society', whereas on the other he talks of 'a modicum of economic welfare and security' ([1949] 1992, p 8). In plain English, a 'modicum' refers to 'a little; a small quantity; small allowance or share', which would imply that Marshall's 'concept of social rights did not necessarily encompass the right to any particular benefits or services' (Rummery, 2002, p 9). Although Marshall did stipulate that every citizen had the right to register with a doctor, there was no guaranteed right to treatment, services, equipment or appliances. Without these guarantees, disabled people are left outside the realms of full citizenship. Without treatment, support and equipment, many disabled people could not participate fully in the PLM or actively participate in the community. Since participation in these two areas was part of the qualifications for Marshall's conception of citizenship, the inevitable result would be exclusion and disqualification from full citizenship rights.

There were, however, some positive aspects to Marshall's deliberations, and some that benefited disabled people quite substantially. Whether it was by accident or design, the value of Marshall's theory was that it brought the issue of welfare, via its emphasis on social rights, onto the agenda of future debates and contentions. By asserting that welfare rights were part of a tripartite package of civil, political and social rights, Marshall's theory of citizenship acted as a benchmark for the exploration, measurement and recognition of the different dimensions exclusion from the full status of citizenship, the community and society can take (Williams, 1989; Dwyer, 2000, 2004a). And once these varying dimensions of exclusion become apparent, they point the way forward for the making of a more inclusive society.

Moving towards inclusion in the community: the 1950s to 1970

Arguably in the late 1950s, the debates surrounding full citizenship and social rights began to permeate into the policy-making process, especially in relation to disabled people. Realising that disabled people were still not being included in the mainstream institutions of work and education – and that the old exclusionary practices were still being carried out – successive governments made a concerted attempt to reduce the number of people living in segregated institutions by expanding community-based services (Barnes, 1991; Oliver and Barnes, 1998), or 'community care', as it became known in the Report of the Royal Commission on Mental Deficiency of 1954-57 (HM Government, 1957) which considered the problems that arose from outdated mental hospitals and the stigma associated with in-patient treatment.

In a more decisive turn towards community-based services, the government subsequently announced in 1961 that it would halve the number of beds in mental hospitals. By 1962 and 1963 respectively, the Ministry of Health supported this decision with the publication of two papers entitled *National Health Service: A hospital plan for England and Wales* (Ministry of Health, 1962) and *Health and welfare: The development of community care* (Ministry of Health, 1963). Both provided an outline of future plans to increase community-based services and, in the words of the reports, provision would be specifically for mothers and children, 'the elderly', 'the mentally disordered' and 'the physically handicapped' (Jones et al, 1983). Such proposals included an increase in the numbers of general practitioners (GPs), home helps, district nurses, health visitors, sheltered housing schemes and sheltered workshops.

Around this time a number of critical investigations into institutional life and a spate of sensational public expositions by the national press of the cruelty and harsh treatment manifest in institutions for 'the elderly' and 'the mentally ill' undermined public and professional confidence in the health services provided nationally in long-stay hospitals and similar establishments (Goffman, 1961; Townsend, 1967; DHSS, 1969; Morris, 1969; Miller and Gwynne, 1972). In response to this loss of public and professional confidence and the subsequent pressure to reduce the numbers in institutions, the government commissioned the Seebohm Report of 1968. This report looked for a local cum community-based solution by recommending that local authorities must accumulate data on the nature and size of the problems facing disabled people as well as developing and/ or expanding 'services in conjunction with those already provided by the health service and the voluntary sector' (Barnes, 1991; Oliver and Barnes, 1998).

Crucially, these recommendations were subsequently incorporated into the Local Authority Act 1970 (HM Government, 1970a) and the Chronically Sick and Disabled Persons Act 1970 (HM Government, 1970b). The establishment of social services departments in their present form quickly followed and, in conjunction with provision for the other main dependent groups, the new departments were responsible for social services for disabled people. These included the provision of social workers, occupational therapists, residential and day centre facilities, holidays, meals on wheels, respite services and disability aids and adaptations. Section 2 of the Chronically Sick and Disabled Persons Act 1970, in particular, laid out substantive provision that could be made and, more importantly, made it explicit that the home was to be the focal point of delivery (Drake, 1999, p 61).

All in all, the Acts, reports and recommendations discussed above (and summarised in *Box 2.3* below) could be seen as a substantial move towards a more independent life for disabled people. As in previous years, however, not all was as beneficial to disabled people as first presumed. The halving of hospital beds, for example, could be attributed to a pragmatic government wanting to reduce mounting welfare costs. The increase in professional services could be viewed as an increased desire to reassert the paternalist model of 'care' protecting professional judgement and interests in a way that interferes with the lives of disabled people. Indeed this increase in professional service providers 'resulted in the situation where almost every aspect of life for a disabled person had its counterpart in a profession or voluntary organisation' (Barnes, 1991, p 23).

Box 2.3: Key developments relating to disabled people from the 1950s to 1970

The **Report of the Royal Commission on Mental Deficiency of 1954-57** (HM Government, 1957) considered the problems arising from outdated mental hospitals and the stigma associated with in-patient treatment.

In 1961 the government announced its decision to halve the number of beds in mental hospitals.

In 1962, *A hospital plan* was published by the Ministry of Health. This was followed by *Health and welfare: The development of community care* (1963), which was generally referred to as the 'Community Care Blue Book'. Both provided a sketchy outline of plans for community-based services, including proposals for increases in the numbers of GPs, home helps, district nurses, health visitors, sheltered housing schemes and sheltered workshops.

The **Seebohm Report (1968)** was commissioned as a response to a number of critical investigations into institutional life and a spate of sensational public expositions over treatment of in-patients. Among its principal conclusions were recommendations that local authorities should accumulate data relating to the nature and size of the problems associated with disability, and that they should develop and/or expand services in conjunction with those already provided by the health service and the voluntary sector.

The **Local Authority Act 1970** and the **Chronically Sick and Disabled Persons Act 1970** incorporated these recommendations and the establishment of social services departments in their present form quickly followed. These new departments were responsible for the provision of social workers, occupational therapists, residential and day centre facilities, holidays, meals on wheels, respite services and disability aids and adaptations.

Source: Adapted from Barnes (1991); Oliver and Barnes (1998)

To make matters worse, the notion of being 'cared' for in community was not as liberating as one may have initially assumed. For Oliver and Barnes (1998, p 38),

> ... "community" ... within the context of community care suggests life outside an institution within a bounded locality characterized by close social networks between neighbours and friends ... the word "care" means to be looked after and protected. It carries with it definite implications of dependence and is widely used in relation to children and acutely ill or very frail older people.

Conclusion

Under these conditions, what the term 'community care' actually implies is dependence on the community, and when it is applied to disabled people it infers that they are unable to take control of their own lives, which actually goes against the ideal of disabled people living and participating in the community as full citizens. Nevertheless, the trends described in this chapter have revealed a definite move, albeit misconceived and poorly implemented, towards the integration of disabled people into the institutions of community, education and work. These trends, however, can only be seen as the beginning of a more inclusive agenda that was to develop further throughout the rest of the 20th century and the first decade of the 21st. As a consequence, Chapter Three explores these trends further when it examines the rhetoric behind the increased promotion and implementation of community care and compares it to the realities of community care in practice. In particular, the chapter traces the debates, arguments and conflicts that emerged during and after the enactment of the NHS and Community Care Act 1990 (HM Government, 1990). Prominent themes in the chapter thus relate to whether community provision is best implemented through socialised care that involves collective, planned solutions to avoid the unpaid 'care burden' being placed on family members, or whether community care should be properly funded to avoid placing the emphasis on family members and, crucially, to avoid the risk that such collectivisation would lead to greater institutionalisation.

Summary

This chapter has covered disability policy from the end of the Second World War to 1970. It has looked at the different debates, theoretical approaches and conflicts that help explain the differences between disability policy intentions and disability policy in practice. By doing so, the chapter has looked at:

- significant policy legislation;
- institutional discrimination;
- paternalism;
- the influence of the Beveridge Report;
- T.H. Marshall's theory of citizenship and its ambiguity with regards to disabled people;
- the embryonic shift from institutionalisation to 'community care';
- the increased professionalisation of welfare services.

Questions

1. What were the key ideas and assumptions that underpinned the post-Second World War design of disability policies?
2. To what extent were paid work and active citizenship linked in the Beveridge blueprint for the modern welfare state?
3. How might Beveridge's employment-based welfare policies be seen as ableist?

4. What were the key policy interventions to stem from the Tomlinson Report and the Disabled Persons' (Employment) Act 1944?
5. How was national assistance distinct from national insurance in the post-Second World War welfare settlement?

Further reading

The books by **Oliver and Barnes (1998)**, **Drake (1999)** and **Barnes (1991)** give a good overview of all the legislation discussed in this chapter. Chapter Four of **Dwyer's (2004a)** book details T.H. Marshall's theory of citizenship succinctly, while the edited collection by **Hills et al (1994)** provides a deep insight into the thinking of William Beveridge. For those students who want to pursue the earlier history of disability studies and the oppression of disabled people, see **Barton and Oliver's (1997)** edited collection.

three

The rhetoric and reality of community care for disabled people

The changing sensibilities and policy imperatives that led to wholesale deinstitutionalisation and the emphasis on community-based care led to major changes in the way in which policy constructions of disability, need, community and statutory resources were to be interpreted. Although notions of disabled people receiving support in the community date back to pre-history (Richardson, quoted in Grant et al, 2005) and were indeed common before the Industrial Revolution, modern notions of community care were different in assuming:

- that segregation in long-stay hospitals was neither humane nor therapeutic;
- that long-stay contexts were prohibitively expensive and unsustainable;
- that the community is the best place in which social 'care' and support can be offered;
- that a variety of formal and informal support should be made available;
- that the family and wider networks would have a role to play in community care.

Community care was first mooted in official policy terms in the 1950s with the Royal Commission report on Mental Illness and Mental Deficiency (1957) while the Mental Health Act 1959 established the desirability of moving former long-stay mental hospital patients to community settings (Blakemore, 2003, p 205). The Minister of Health's famous 'Watertower Speech' of 1961 added further to the philosophical backlash against institutions which served as little more than forms of incarceration for some disabled 'inmates'. Historically those deemed mentally ill and those with learning difficulties (in the 1950s called 'the mentally deficient') were lumped together with assumptions going back to Galtonian eugenics that both groups represented a moral and social hazard that needed to be contained (Barnes, 1991). Regimes were often harsh and inhumane. County asylums for 'the mentally ill', for example, bore all the hallmarks of what Goffman, the Canadian sociologist, called 'total institutions' which were rigid, managed, staff-centred and institutionalising (Goffman, 1961).

These concerns were reflected in the 1963 Conservative White Paper on community care which, in part, was motivated by a concern over the costs of an ageing population being housed in long-stay hospitals and residential care contexts (Scull, 1984). However, these commitments were not followed up by legislative action with the ascent of a Labour government in 1964. Neither major party of UK politics could or would translate changing approaches towards thinking on institutions into wholesale decarceration until the early 1990s. There were clearly ideological and practical barriers to implementing community care that need to be understood.

Imperatives to deinstitutionalisation

Changing sensibilities in the mid-20th century aimed to challenge those forged in the mid-19th century. The welfare settlement of the Second World War, the increased presence of disabled people in everyday contexts both led to and was part of (slowly) changing attitudes on disability and chronic illness. In 1961, the then Conservative Minister for Health made clear in his famous Watertower Speech the challenge to assumptions that long-stay hospitals were a permanent feature of the social and health care landscape:

> We have to get the idea into our heads that a hospital is a shell, a framework, however complex, to contain certain processes, and when the processes change or are superseded, then the shell must most probably be scrapped and the framework dismantled. (Minister of Health, 1961)

This statement and the *hospital plan* that followed were seen to symbolise the first wave of community care reform with targets to halve the numbers in long-stay mental handicap and psychiatric institutions by 1976 (Ministry of Health, 1962). Although stilted, it could be argued that the second wave of the early 1990s community care reforms would not have taken the form it did without the first wave precursor highlighting the push factor or dependency-creating institutions and the pull factor of mainstreamed benefits of living in the community. Personal testimony of disabled people who had been in long-stay hospitals bears out the concerns of official commentators on the 'perils' of institutions. Many disabled people were sent into institutions against their will and had no idea what to expect of long-stay hospitals and colonies (Atkinson et al, 1997). As one of Atkinson et al's respondents notes:

> My grandfather didn't say where I was going. That's what got to me, he didn't say where. Frightened I were. I felt awful, I wanted to go back out. I felt upset, I couldn't stick it in here. (quoted in Atkinson et al, 1997, p 42)

Not only were day-to-day activities severely curtailed, but also broader social expectations were reversed in long-stay hospitals and colonies. For example, strict sex segregation was implemented to avoid unnecessary contact, as many disabled people were seen as either asexual or a hereditary risk:

> Years ago we daren't talk to the boys. Oh no we had to keep away from them. Girls used to be on one side and boys on the other. If you talked to the boys you could get into real trouble.... I just kept my mouth shut. (quoted in Humphries and Gordon, 1992, p 102)

The Health Services and Public Health Act 1968 (HM Government, 1968) followed the spirit of community care in proposing home help services to avert entry into expensive long-term institutional contexts (Blakemore, 2003, p 205). In reality, it took more than 10 years for the Act's objectives to permeate local authorities whose default approach remained that of supporting disabled people in residential homes and long-stay hospitals (Tinker, 1983). Meanwhile, the Seebohm reforms (Seebohm, 1968) to social care, ones overseen by the then Minister for Personal Social Services Richard Crossman, were clearly premised on conditional principles that they should not distort the underlying belief that families were the key building blocks of social care provision by noting that:

> The primary objective of the Personal Social Services we can best describe as strengthening the capacity of the family to care for its members. (cited in Morris, 1993, p 5)

This gives some clues as to the flawed assumptions that underpin otherwise progressive community-based support principles. It is worth pointing out that there has been a lack of continuity between this first wave of community care and the later policy changes of the 1990s. For example, even in the 1977 White Paper *The way forward* (DHSS, 1977), the pervasive interpretation of community care understood it to include residential homes, staffed community (half-way) houses, sheltered housing and so on. One contemporary concern involved in such a half-baked interpretation of community was that some groups were to experience simply a shift in the context of institutional provision. For example, Young Disabled Units (YDUs) were established to cater for this group in response to the outrage that young disabled people with complex health needs were hitherto being housed in geriatric wards. The response from the Royal College of Physicians (1986) was for YDUs to cater for this age group, without acknowledging that this was simply shifting the institutional context of largely medical care in a way that made independence and choice virtually impossible (Brisenden, 1986). This, then, represented a slow evolution from large-scale institutional provision that often lumped 'dependent population' categories together to more age-specific and localised institutional support. However, these changes were some distance from the fully fledged objectives that would follow in community care. As Barnes observed:

> Throughout the post-1945 period the expansion of health and social services for disabled people has been constructed upon the erroneous belief that disabled people are not competent to make basic decisions about their individual service needs. (Barnes, 1991, p 124)

The 1977 White Paper reflected a more nuanced understanding that by the mid-20th century some long-stay residents were spending part of their time in mainstream community settings and that a binary split between fully integrated and entirely institutionalised were not realities that could be sustained in practice. Indeed some YDUs were allowing home-based living in a way that was inconceivable 10 years before (Benson and Williams, 1979). This was especially true for people with very significant mental health needs. In the early years of community care reform, the overestimate of informal family support coupled with the continued incentives to offer residential places to older and disabled people with high support needs led to a continued rise in residential care throughout the 1980s (Langan and Clarke, 1994). However, the growing costs of most of these forms of institutional care ensured that by the late 1980s the term 'community' was beginning to be used in a more binary sense to mean post-institutional provision for many. Indeed as late as the mid-1980s there were 422,000 disabled people living in long-stay institutions, which prompted the Conservative government to redouble its emphasis on community solutions (Martin et al, 1988). This increased focus on purely community-based solutions was both ideologically more 'pure' but also practically much more problematic as many people decanted from institutions found the transition very difficult to what were, in reality, imagined or idealised communities (Bornat et al, 1997).

During the late 1970s and 1980s, and against the backdrop of national community care developments, the Disabled People's Movement was making small but important progress in fostering greater choices and self-determination based on independent living principles. The development of the Union of Physically Impaired Against Segregation's (UPIAS) *Fundamental principles* document (1976) spawned the first Centre for Integrated Living (CIL) which brought together statutory support with early principles of independent living based on disabled people's own definition of disability and disabled people's seven needs (Borsay, 1986). For the first time notions of disability and the lived policy experience of disabled people were rooted in disabled people's own sense of which services were important and in which format (Campbell and Oliver, 1996). The approach followed the social model of disability (Oliver, 1990; Barnes, 1991) in emphasising the barriers to disabled people's participation and in challenging assumptions that independence equalled doing everything for oneself (Morris, 1993). This was fundamentally challenged so that independence was more closely allied to notions of choice and self-determination. This approach questioned all pre-existing paternalist policy assumptions that disabled people were incapable of engineering and influencing policy and practice in a way that better reflected their needs and aspirations.

These developments arguably altered policy and practice assumptions irreversibly in asserting that disabled people are experts in their own lives and therefore have a key role not simply in determining their own needs but also in acting and thinking collectively for policy change. The exact degree to which these changes represent the birth of a collective disabled identity is hotly contested (Watson, 2002; Shakespeare, 2006). However, most critiques are targeted at social model writers' constructions of shared identities and are perhaps less insightful as they relate to the role of identity reconstructions in helping reshape policy and historic constructions of disabled people as historical categories (Stone, 1984). Such a disability-led approach to policy was clearly very distinct from what might be dubbed the centralised, administered solutions at the core of community care. Nevertheless, this was all to change with a new emphasis on localised 'flexible' community care options. Perhaps the most noteworthy development in 20th-century disability policy is the appropriation by the UK government of some key aspects of disabled people's concern while still falling short of key facets of the Disabled People's Movement's construction of independent living. The following (see *Box 3.1*) have all been common characteristics of a convergence of principles between neoliberal critiques of the historic role of the state and of the Disabled People's Movement's critiques of paternalism (Roulstone and Morgan, 2009).

Box 3.1: Roulstone and Morgan on paternalist policy

1. That remote institutional provision has been an expensive disabling influence on disabled people's lives.
2. That individuals should have greater choice and determination over their lives with less state influence.

Clearly, however, differences remained significant between the two constructions of policy solutions, especially as they related to informal care and the continued role of the family in 'care' networks. The Conservative government's commissioning of the civil servant Sir Roy Griffiths to report on the state and prospects for community care provided a new vision for community care based on projected cost 'efficiencies' and a new philosophy of 'welfare pluralism' (1988, p 71). The report content was consolidated in the 1989 White Paper (DH, 1989) and the NHS and Community Care Act 1990 (HM Government, 1990) itself. A key feature of the second wave of community care reforms embodied in the Act was the shift to neoliberal underpinnings of social and welfare support (see Loney, 1987). Thatcherism and the New Right symbolised a 'rolling back of the frontiers of the state' (Gamble, 1988; Glennerster, 2007), an inherent distrust of 'big' government and a conviction that family dynamics and values had been eroded by the hypertrophied state (George and Wilding, 1985).

The emphasis in both social care and social welfare policy was on self or family reliance and at its most extreme took the form of an advocacy of a dismantling of the nanny state (Murray, 1984). At its more extreme and doctrinaire this political philosophy sounded like a wholesale rejection of the welfare state. In reality, Thatcherism was a more pragmatic project, one that took account of the sentiments that attached to key institutions (for example, the UK NHS) and social policies, particularly as it attached to those seen as the most 'vulnerable in society'. However, there were very harsh elements to the 'New Right' reforms. The Fowler reforms and welfare reform Green Paper (HM Government, 1985) were premised on the view that the benefits system had become too generous while absolute poverty was seen to be almost extinct. As the following passage from the Green Paper of the time suggests:

> Living standards generally have improved substantially and want
> in the sense of absolute deprivation has been largely eliminated.
> (HM Government, 1985, vol 3, para 1.48)

This damaging assumption ensured that supplements to Income Support
(IS) benefits, so important to disabled people's income, were curtailed and
a much more limited single payment system introduced which left disabled
recipients of IS significantly worse off (Glendinning, 1991). The new era
of market liberalism and welfare retraction was a very worrying time for
many disabled people. Social care, at least outside of residential settings
for those who most needed the support of others, proved to be of little
incentive to the market given the limited 'margins' that could be made
from community care (Glennerster, 2007). Overall, Thatcherism, however,
was restricted by its own awareness of the electoral damage wholesale
privatisation might bring, while some of the more thoughtful New Right
acolytes were aware of the limits of the market as a solution to complex
and engrained social problems. In fact an unacknowledged compromise
was evident in the application of market principles to social care services
without resorting to full-blown privatisation.

The approach adopted was to marketise health and social care to
introduce a 'mixed economy' of provision (Loney, 1987; Powell, 2007), what
some have referred to as a 'quasi-market' (Le Grand, 1991) or 'salad bar'
approach that arguably affords the most responsive mix of public, private
and voluntary sector providers. Under the new localised and flexible plans
for community care, social services departments received money formerly
disbursed by the centralised and by now much demonised social security
system, but were no longer empowered to directly provide services. Social
services departments were recast to be purchasers of services from the
mixed economy outlined above. This purchaser–provider split (Bailey
and Davidson, 1999) was the hallmark of neoliberal policy in the 1990s.
Although shifting the locus of policy away from the former Department
of Social Security (DSS), critiques pointed to the growth of a local cadre
of managers who strongly mediated local 'solutions' to care planning and
allocation (Charlesworth et al, 1995). The risks of new barriers being
imposed on an already overstretched social care system (see **Box 3.2**
below) was made very real by a contradictory emphasis on new public
management that emphasised localised solutions with few safeguards that
disabled people could access even the minimum of support received, say,
in a neighbouring borough.

> **Box 3.2:** Limitations of the neoliberal vision for community care
>
> - That it was based on the assumption of a residual state role, that the quasi-market would be the point of last resort, one targeted only at those with the greatest need.
> - That care would largely be provided by the community (Bayley, 1973). This led to an assumption of communities existing that would support, reintegrate and support disabled people as they left institutions.
> - That wider neoliberal assumptions about the family were in tension; this had particular implications for women who were exhorted to be part of the new matrix of formal and informal care while also being encouraged to be part of the paid labour market (PLM) (Levitas, 1986).
> - The continued funding of benefits for residential care and the limited reality of community led to more rather than less residential care in the late 1980s and early 1990s.

The promulgation of new community-based social care alongside residual formal services suggested that any mismatch in the reality of available community and its imagined form would likely lead to funding pressures. This was quickly realised, with the introduction of charging for community care home support shortly after the introduction of community care policies (Baldwin and Lunt, 1996). Recent data on the number of local authorities who now charge and means test for domiciliary support points to a major clawing back of monies from recipients of community support (Wainwright and O'Brien, 2010). Wainwright and O'Brien (2010) note that:

> In 2007-8, local authorities recouped circa 13% of their spending on adult social care services through means-tested charging. With an overall pattern of tightening "eligibility" criteria operated it is now estimated that around 72% of councils only offer homecare services to those with "substantial" or "critical" needs. (2010, pp 3–7)

The imagined community approach (Bornat et al, 1997) was at its most stark during the early years of implementation of community care (1993–99), and led to some dramatic own goals in terms of the rapid shift of people with mental health problems often into hostel accommodation or indeed no accommodation, and a 'cliff-edge' effect in terms of ongoing care. A number of high profile scandals arose which highlighted poor aftercare services in many areas (Coid, 1994). This led to a backlash in some communities and 'nimbyism' regarding the relocation or those decanted from long-stay institutions. A cartoon in *The Guardian* captured the flaws inherent in the assumptions behind second wave community care – it pictures a person in obvious distress having left hospital after many years. He is on the end of a telephone and the speech bubble reads: 'We're sorry, the community isn't in to take your call at the moment'. The zeitgeist was captured in three key questions: would community-based support really cost less? Was there really the level of informal family support required to make community-based options work? And what happened when natural community supports were absent?

In truth these perceptions led to overly pessimistic views of community options for people with physical impairments and many people with learning difficulties. However, the policies were probably too optimistic for those with severe enduring mental health problems whose clinical needs often outweighed their social needs. To add to the challenges of community-based 'care' there was significant inertia and vested interests in the county asylums to community care options. This was the basis of the formulation of a Mental Health Task Force in 1992, one set up by Conservative government 'to help unlock resources from the old, long-stay institutions and to help build up a balanced range of local services, based on best practice'. For a review of the Task Force's remit see Jenkins (1994).

David King, the Mental Health Task Force lead, described his brief to service users:

> To deliver management objectives on flow of capital and revenue for strategic planning....To look at other options/providers/cost structures in mental health apart from traditional health services ones... To get the concept of consumer satisfaction into the mental health arena which is difficult because of the underlying element of compulsory treatment.... To bring in a notion of quality for users.... To inform what is going on – bringing discussion of hospital closure into the public arena, so people understand the issues [as] talk of hospital closures brings strong reactions, and lobbying from MPs. (DH, 2003d)

But just what did 'consumer satisfaction' mean in a context of more restricted public spending and where compulsory treatment remained a key form of statutory response to florid mental symptoms? Arguably the ethos of a more flexible, nuanced community care had so far failed to grasp the real diversity of disabled people and was casting around, looking for old monolithic solutions to a range of very different challenges. It is also noteworthy that unlike notions of independent living and self-determination coming from the Disabled People's Movement (Campbell and Oliver, 1996; Barnes and Mercer, 2006), it was unclear how much overall choice was being afforded to disabled people being moved into the community. King's statement, along with others, at least brought the issues and challenges into the open. There was clearly much work needed, at the time, to get public opinion on side given the high profile afforded to a small but significant number of attacks by former mental hospital residents. The later Audit Commission report of 1994, *Finding a place: A review of mental health services for adults* (Audit Commission, 1994), acknowledged that the government's community care policies were struggling to substantiate the grand vision for community-based services. The disproportionate weight of expectations on carers led to a major backlash, culminating in the Carers National Strategy and the Carers (Recognition) Act 1995 which aimed to place carers' as well as service users' needs centre stage (Roulstone and Hudson, 2007). This emphasis on carers, however, was viewed as inflammatory by key writers and activists. With some disabled service users only just beginning to reap the benefits of the new community care approach, a sudden emphasis towards carers' rights was viewed very dimly by many.

The above makes clear the significant changes that characterised community care reform in the 1990s. What is very clear is an almost total absence of disabled people's voices. Arguably the representational features of the Chronically Sick and Disabled Persons Act of 1970 (HM Government, 1970b) and the Disabled Persons (Services, Consultation and Representation) Act of 1996 (HM Government, 1996a) were now absent from a policy that was underpinned by a notion of market principles and consumer sovereignty. The objective of reducing funding for social care alongside the growth in 'consumer choice' seemed to be directly contradictory. The same mismatch can of course be applied to current attempts to square cuts in public spending with ambitious attempts to offer self-directed support to greater numbers of disabled people (Roulstone and Morgan, 2009). This was a major irony, but one which highlighted the real concerns for policy reform. Clearly key ideological strands of Thatcherism were in tension once substantiated. The New Right emphasis on reducing numbers of lone mothers on benefits, on placing paid work at the centre of its welfare policies, encouraging geographical mobility to follow economic opportunities and assumed family and community continuity all seem to be deeply contradictory and disjointed policies. How could any family live up to the political rhetoric of mobility and stability in the same breath (Levitas, 1986)?

While there seemed to be a least superficial convergence of views on new services for disabled people from the Conservative government and from the Disabled People's Movement based on suspicion of a top–down, centralised, one-size-fits-all approach, in academia another debate was raging between different feminist writers as to the best way forward in squaring the circle on care challenges. For Ungerson (1987) and Finch and Dalley (Finch, 1990; Dalley, 1991), the continued reliance of the state on informal unpaid female labour could only be surmounted by a socialising of social care. In reality this would have amounted to a re-emphasis on institutional solutions for many if unpaid care was withdrawn. Morris, a disabled feminist writer, helped take debates forward by criticising the false binary that sat at the heart of these unpaid carers debates, noting how they characterised women as either 'carers or their dependents' (Morris, 1993) without affording disabled women social rights to be treated as citizens in their own right. This socialised approach to caring for disabled people would simply reaffirm previous policy assumptions that disabled people were not full citizens, but were part of the problem of unpaid care. This was a gross distortion of the reality of disability and of the 'caring relationship', as many carers would not describe their role in this way (Roulstone et al, 2006).

As Morris pointed out, despite the flurry of policy activity around community care, the assumptions that underpinned its working were still those of paternalist assessments of who was in 'need' and to what extent. A top–down policy imperative emerged which converged with some feminist writers around the notion that disabled people were an expensive dependent population. Although quasi-markets were to increasingly hold sway, the resemblance to a fully fledged market was limited. In these terms, just who was the buyer and who was the broker of services is a moot point. In reality social services departments were still in a position to dominate decisions as to who was eligible for 'social goods' and who should rely on family support (Morris, 1993). This is a far cry from the more self-determined notions that underpinned the principles of independent living. However, the issue of who is eligible for service under these two approaches is a very important point and one that is never fully resolved in the literature of the time. Systems of support continued to rely on notions of 'care' rather than support, which leaves many recipients of community care in the traditional mould of 'not being able to do anything for themselves' (McKnight, quoted in Brechin et al, 1980).

The continued under-funding of community-based options beyond family support has meant that institutions remained a feature of the landscape for some disabled people. As the Swedish independent living writer, Adolf Ratzka, has asserted, with the right to community support no one should have to 'live their lives in institutions' (cited in Barnes, 1991, p 129). At the bottom line, we return to the crucial issue of the economics of community care. The political will to fully fund community-based support and the ability to reconcile service users, formal and informal carers, remains a major challenge in the UK, particularly in an ageing population. There remains a severe risk that the promise of independent living, if not fully funded, will simply mean more disabled people are pushed outside of the threshold for community support, or that contribution tapers will be so severe that many disabled people will simply not bother to apply for support. This latter approach is exactly what has happened with the Disabled Facilities Grant. The grant, originally one conceived of as supporting many with more significant environmental access needs to alter their premises, has such a severe taper, or point at which disabled people have to contribute, that many disabled people are simply not bothering to apply or are borrowing at market rates to make access changes (O'Brien, 2003). Later chapters will explore how governments have attempted to square this particular circle, but Hasler sums up the continuing challenges:

> The interests of disabled people, carers and former hospital residents should have been overlapping. All three groups have an interest in state sponsorship of community-based support. Differences in the way each group framed their own needs, however, and in the way care professionals conceptualised these needs meant that a coalescence of aims was rare. (Hasler, quoted in Swain et al, 2004, p 227)

The question of neoliberal approaches to social care policy also needs to be seen in the context of the wider neoliberal project, and, as Chapter Five makes clear later in this book, some disabled people were reassessed as a policy category to be closer to the labour market. The period 1980–95 was arguably a torrid time for some disabled people. The rise in unemployment in the early 1980s led to an increase in the numbers eligible to be moved into the 'disability category'. However, these disabled people were also seen as some distance from core membership of the social care population discussed above, and continued to live in a policy hinterland between the readily employable and 'legitimate' disabled people eligible for packages of social care. Drake (1999) takes a different view, suggesting the White Paper of 1990, entitled *The way ahead: Benefits for disabled people* (DSS, 1990), provided a positive recognition of the additional barriers faced by disabled people and aimed, in a purposive way, to assist more 'workable' (and those perceived to be 'genuinely disabled') disabled people into paid work as this accorded with the broader shifts towards community-based economic security and self-reliance. However, towards the end of the Conservative tenure in the early to mid-1990s a growing spend on community care, residual institutional care and out-of-work benefits, the policy spotlight began to fall on those disabled people who were seen as in any way conceivably close to the labour market. To make matters worse, the failure to move large-scale numbers from benefits to work led to a retrenchment on the part of the DSS against those who were increasingly deemed 'able to work'.

The wider disability benefit system underwent a similar policy assault. Disability Living Allowance (DLA) and Disability Working Allowance (DWA) were introduced in the early 1990s in the wake of the White Paper to help with care, mobility and to support disabled people into paid work (Drake, 1999, p 57). These new benefits were a recognition of the additional barriers disabled people faced in getting about and the lower relative rewards in the workplace. However, with the growing bill for invalidity benefits, community care support, residential care and Disability Living/Working Allowances there was a clear retrenchment by the Conservative government. The newly forged Social Security (Incapacity for Work) Act in 1994 (HM Government, 1994) witnessed the replacement of Invalidity Benefit (IVB) with Incapacity Benefit (ICB). The latter was framed by much stricter eligibility criteria and disabled people were expected to be assessed against much broader appraisals of work–ability, a trend that has continued ever since. In this financially squeezed policy context the Conservative government looked for pretexts to reverse the shift of sick/disabled people from Invalidity/Incapacity Benefit to mainstream out-of-work benefits or ideally paid work. One of the key issues here, one that is often overlooked, is the assumption that the shift to IVB was based on false evidence. The true reality is hard to ascertain, but we now know that many of those moved to IVB/ICB did have impairments often related to work in heavy industry (Nichols and Beynon, 1977), much of which somewhat ironically had been wound up by the wider neoliberal politics of the 1980s.

It is important to recognise that DLA was very well received by those able to establish eligibility for the care and mobility components (formerly called the Mobility Allowance, MA) of the allowance. In terms of Drake's (1999) typology, the benefits were a mixture of welfare and rights thinking as they were seen as going beyond simple compensation, they recognised additional costs faced by disabled people, while being part of the broader shift to personal choice making in community contexts. A decision in the Law Lords in 1997 made clear that DLA as a benefit was intended to go beyond simple personal maintenance, and was a key part in support of a 'normal life'. While the notion of a 'normal' life is contentious, it seems clear that this must equate to rights to mainstream life (including paid work) if it has any meaning at all.

Conclusion

The early to mid-1990s were nothing if not contradictory in messages given out on disability. Despite the retrenchment of certain benefits and the increased shift towards binary distinctions between disabled people and what might politely be seen as those 'seeking disability status', there were significant developments for disabled people with the greatest levels of assessed needs. Alongside DLA, which was designed without a means-test element, the Disability Grants Act 1993 (HM Government, 1993) ushered in the Independent Living Fund (ILF) which provided substantial packages of support and as a sort of early precursor of direct payments was to be paid directly to the disabled person unmediated by professionals once eligibility had been established. Overall, then, the period 1990 to date has consolidated the principle of non-institutional support for many disabled people. The value and efficacy of the key building blocks of community support remained hotly contested, especially in relation to the assumed role of informal care. The reduction in professional mediation of support has been welcomed by many, yet the increased rationing of social support has ensured that those who applied faced increasingly intrusive processes in ascertaining eligibility, while the expansive vision of community options has narrowed to equate to domiciliary support (Kestenbaum, 1993).

The continued dominant role of care managers in community care assessments has arguably shifted power simply from provision to assessment rather than from professional to service uses (Bewley and Glendinning, 1992). The 1980s and early 1990s saw glimpses of later developments – at one extreme, the ILF as a prototype form of direct payments, once supported in principle by commentators across the political spectrum, suggesting that self-determination had been cemented in the imagination of politicians and public alike, and at the other extreme were attempts to stem and overturn the increase in the population entitled to be classed as 'disabled'. The more severe manifestations of these discourses are evident in the policies of New Labour to be outlined in later chapters. The era then provided both progressive and regressive developments (Barnes, 1991; Drake, 1999; Borsay, 2005). Disabled people seen as holding ambiguous social locations, for example, those suddenly deemed 'workable', became prey to long-held notions of dole scroungers (Bagguley and Mann, 1992) being expanded for the first time to disabled people. The community then becomes the crucible for this array of often conflicting messages around an increasingly diverse population of disabled people (Roulstone and Barnes, 2005). The New Labour project ensured that the neoliberal principles of Thatcherism and Majorism were carried over in a way that ensured the contradictions and contrasts of this era were ever more stark.

Summary

- Community care policy is inextricably linked to the desire to close long-stay institutions that had fostered dependency and were expensive.
- Community care had its origins in the 1960s, but was not rolled out fully until the mid-1990s, some 30 years later.
- The early experience of rapid closure of long-stay hospitals created new problems of social dislocation within the 'community'.
- Marketisation is seen by some as helping transcend dependency, while others see markets overlooking those most in need.

Questions

1. How did the early architects of community care view institutionalised living for disabled people?
2. The community care plans of the 1990s are heavily derivative of the plans of the 1960s. Critically discuss.
3. What were the problems of decanting large numbers of disabled people from long-stay institutions? What image of community did policy makers have?
4. Did 'care in the community' transcend paternalism?
5. Has neoliberalism and marketisation been a benefit or barrier to disabled people's community-based choices?

Further reading

There are many books on community care; however, surprisingly few foreground disability in its many forms and then to look only at (the important area of) mental health. However, good overall treatment of the issues is available in **Bornat et al (1997)**, **Blakemore (2003)**, **Hills (1998)**, **Jones (2000)**, and **Langan and Clarke (1994)**. **Oliver and Barnes (1998)** and **Campbell and Oliver (1996)** are explicit evaluations from a disability perspective. **Loney's (1987)** *The state or the market?* remains the best overview of marketisation.

Aiming high enough? Disabled children and mainstreamed lives

This chapter explores the responses to and position of disabled children since 1997 and the rise of New Labour. The treatment of children in the policy process is one that requires careful appraisal given that the impact of policy on disabled children will be mediated by wider policy discourses and treatment of adults, most especially where the latter are under policy scrutiny, for example, if they are out of work or a single parent (Ridge, quoted in Millar, 2003; Lister and Bennett, 2010). Even a cursory glimpse at child policy development since New Labour came to power suggests a major policy commitment to all children, with an attendant and clear commitment to disabled children which arguably knows no parallel in the history of disability policy (Barnes, 1991; Drake, 1999; Borsay, 2005). This commitment helped attempt to overturn a major rise in child poverty during the years of Conservative Party rule between 1979 and 1996 (Lister, 2009). The strength of this commitment was clearly articulated in New Labour's commitment to halving childhood poverty by 2010 and to eradicate child poverty by 2020.

The issue of poverty reduction for disabled children is a significant one and suggests that any analysis of services for disabled children has to be explored alongside the broader socioeconomic position of disabled children and their families. There is evidence that a good economic start early in life can significantly aid socioeconomic status later in life (Burchardt, 2003). This view was largely shared by New Labour and was translated into the language of prevention, establishing opportunity and longer-term inclusion from childhood (PMSU, 2005). There is no reason to believe that disabled children will experience less of a boost than their non-disabled counterparts in these policy discourses. Indeed a disproportionate positive benefit may accrue from early interventions such as Sure Start and now children's centre work with disabled children (DCSF, 2008a) alongside proactive measures such as reasonable adjustments laid out in anti-discrimination legislation. It is worth noting that disabled children have, until recently, been hidden from much policy research. One recent study, for instance, called for research on 'poverty and disability', claiming that research on 'poverty and childhood' had already been well accounted for (LCF, 2010). This false dichotomy is characteristic of a continued paternalism that is attached to some disabled children's lives.

Conversely, evidence suggests that to date disabled children are more likely to live in a context of family poverty. There is a marked class gradient with a much higher prevalence of disabled children in the three lowest social class categories (Pantazis and Gordon, 2000). There is also a greater likelihood of poverty where there is a disabled child in a family, which may in part be due to the extra costs of raising a disabled child and overcoming the additional barriers faced (Burchardt, 2003; Preston, 2006). Wider evidence suggests that disabled children and their families face significantly higher costs related to additional disability-related costs, for example, transport, heating, personal hygiene and specialist dietary needs (Woolley, 2004). Disabled children are also disproportionately more likely to live in lone-parent households (Preston, 2006). Disabled children's families, because of their broader economic position, are more likely to be reliant on means-tested benefits and not able to avail themselves of part-time work given the high opportunity costs associated with extra care and maintenance expenses associated with disabled children (Magadi, 2010). Contrary to traditional assumptions that poverty is inextricably linked to the burden of a disabled child, recent research by Emerson et al (2009) points to the structural limitations of the jobs, education and benefits system that point to a much broader analysis of the problem and call for more mainstream but creative solutions related to social capital and opportunities among the families of disabled children. They noted that:

> While there is no doubt that bringing up a disabled child is associated with some specific stresses – and some specific joys and rewards ... it appears that much of the disadvantage faced by families supporting a disabled child may be attributed to their reduced capabilities and reduced access to social and material resources. As such, improving the life opportunities of disabled children may critically depend on non-"disability-specific" support that enhances the capabilities and access to resources of these families. (Emerson et al, 2009, p 9)

New Labour's cross-governmental recognition that to eradicate poverty in childhood would aid later adult economic and social well-being has underpinned a range of developments in disability policies and programmes for all children since 1997. There has been a plethora of policy changes that aim to positively impact on the lives of disabled children, including *Every Child Matters* (DfES, 2003), *Aiming high for disabled children: Better support for families* (HM Treasury and DCSF, 2007), *Greater expectations: Learners with disabilities* (DCSF, 2006), the Special Educational Needs and Disability Act (SENDA) 2000 (HM Government, 2000a), the life chances report (PMSU, 2005) and the Bercow Report (DCSF, 2008b). In their myriad ways, these policies all support the need to increase opportunities for disabled children and their families if disabled children's longer-term socioeconomic position is to be improved. For the first time, the full range of personal needs has been acknowledged and in a way that radically challenges traditional service delivery models which often treated disabled children's needs in a compartmentalised way or viewed their dependency as inevitable (Priestley, 1998). The many policy developments in this area can be divided into the following useful schema: (1) disabled children's welfare policy; (2) social care and health care support; and (3) educational policy.

Disabled children's welfare policy

In contrast to adult welfare policy, child welfare and child disability benefits systems have remained less prone to stigmatisation and closer to the principles of universalism. The sanctity of Child Benefit, a key universal benefit for all children, remained intact until the recent Coalition review of Child Benefit which, while not questioning its value, an has frozen its value for three years (HM Treasury, 2010; Butler, 2011). The benefit was first introduced in 1946 as the Family Allowance and of all welfare benefits has proven resistant to wholesale reform. One policy writer has described this universal benefit as the 'child's badge of citizenship' (Lister, 1990, p 59). The year 1997 witnessed an uprating of Child Benefit as a recognition of the redistributive impact of the benefit, in line with New Labour's childhood poverty reduction strategy (Ridge, quoted in Millar, 2003). Alongside upratings of child supplements in Income Support (IS) these increases are of importance in beginning to challenge poverty in disabled children's lives (Burchardt, 2003). However, as the Child Poverty Action Group (CPAG) noted in 2006, the benefit in introducing a second tier rate for second and subsequent children has failed to keep pace with rising prices, especially where a second or third child may be disabled. Indeed the advantages of universalism, in focusing on one category, is arguably undermined somewhat by the categorical differentiation of childhoods as deserving of differential levels of support. The continued value of the benefit in reducing the links between poverty and childhood are made clear in the following CPAG statement:

> Child benefit is popular, effective and reaches more children living in poverty than any other benefit or tax credit. That's why we're calling on the chancellor to increase child benefit and ensure that younger children get the same rate as the oldest child. (CPAG, 2006a)

Alongside universal benefits are those benefits that are targeted on poorer children such as free school meals. The continued political support for means-tested free school meals and milk for children under five seems to reflect the belief in the health and social benefits of this provision. That said, the resilience in policy terms may reflect a political expediency of not wanting to repeat the epithet of politicians being 'milk snatchers', an epithet applied to Margaret Thatcher when, as Education Secretary, she decided to scrap free milk for older children. Free school meals are also of significance as an indicator of local deprivation and this is used by schools and local authorities as a proxy for more technical local deprivation indices in some areas. Free milk for under-fives brings together the universal principle with school-based attempts to provide the building blocks of a child's early development. A recent review by the Coalition government of this provision led to a clear statement of the value of the scheme for all children, a decision that has gone against the wider grain of often harsh Coalition policy. One detail that has gone largely unnoticed, however, was the Coalition's decision to reject pleas to extend the remit of free school meals based on evidence that the current provision undershot actual levels of children and families who would benefit (see Hodgson and Blackman-Woods, 2008).

Nevertheless, the evidence of the additional costs for families of disabled children (see **Box 4.1** below) suggests that the above upratings do nothing to compensate for the often substantial extra costs related to impairment and disabling environments. Dobson and Middleton's (1998) study for example, estimated that the essential bare minimum costs for disabled children were three times those for non-disabled children. Recent comparative research entitled *Counting the cost* by the campaigning organisation Contact a Family (2010) established that the extra costs of disabled children and the poverty often attendant on parenting commitments for disabled children mean that there is a link between childhood disability and poverty (see **Box 4.1**).

> **Box 4.1: The link between childhood disability and poverty**
>
> - Almost a quarter of families are going without heating (23%). Up from 16% in 2008.
> - More than half have borrowed money from family or friends (51%) to keep financially afloat or pay for essentials, such as food and heating. Up from 42% in 2008.
> - More than 40% have applied for a charity grant. Up from 25% in 2008.
> - Almost three quarters (73%) are going without days out and leisure time with the family. Up from 55% in 2008. (Contact a Family, 2010)

This suggests that the attempt to detach the enduring bonds between poverty and disabled childhoods has had limited success. There are studies, however, that point to New Labour's impact in reducing child poverty more generally (Hills and Stewart, 2005), but arguably by shifting the benefits from some family formats to others. Even so, one positive development that has emerged for young children was the decision to extend the mobility component of Disability Living Allowance (DLA) to children aged three to four following a hard-won victory from disability groups (children aged 0 to two are assumed to have a universal need to mobility dependency on parents which obviates the 'need' for the benefit). This extension symbolises the recognition that young children may have substantially greater transport (especially adaptation) and wheelchair-related costs than their non-disabled counterparts.

On the negative side, the assumption that a severely disabled one- or two-year-old is, in policy terms, categorised as more generally mobility-dependent is clearly outdated as significant issues relate to behavioural and equipment issues that may legitimately lead to higher transport and care costs currently ruled out by the DLA regulations. DLA is not means tested, it is a passport to other financial support such as Invalid Care Allowance and local concessionary fares and can be used flexibly without statutory prescription as to exactly how it is used. Access to DLA is not uniform, however, even when degree of impairment is held constant. Differences have also been noted across impairment groups, with evidence suggesting DLA is harder to access for children with visual impairments. In fact, children are rarely awarded DLA in the long term as happens more commonly in adulthood (Action for Blind People, 2010). The centralised administration of DLA means it is not part of an integrated support system as originally envisioned by *Every Child Matters*. A recent qualitative study by Preston (2006) found that for the 20 families studied, DLA was very important for the disabled child and their families. Nonetheless, the constant reviews, downgradings and withdrawals of DLA for disabled children could lead to unnecessary stress and hardship for the families of disabled children. The existing evidence that families with disabled children face greater housing challenges and live in poorer and cramped conditions than their non-disabled counterparts adds to the case for a greater recognition of the extra costs and service needs of families with disabled children (Beresford and Oldman, 2002).

Despite the above failings, the withdrawal of the means test for the Disabled Facilities Grant for children was, in the main, a positive step forward. The introduction of a severe taper to the adult Disabled Facilities Grant rules (which required steep hikes in adult contributions with every extra pound attached to adaptations of premises) met with some resistance and, as a consequence, disabled children and their families clearly benefited from the ending of the contributory principle (CLG, 2007; CLG and Welsh Assembly, 2009), a step that has been warmly welcomed by some disabled children's organisations. The decision to cap the grant at £25,000 has, however, been criticised by learning difficulties charities for whom the means test disregard also applies (Mencap, 2008). The financial and economic position of disabled children and their families remains a major concern – the failure to halve child poverty by 2010 for all children is, of course, mirrored in the experiences of disabled children, where evidence suggests poverty is all too closely linked to being disabled. Currently, the scope for building on any positive reforms of the period 1997-2009 is limited given the proposed cuts in public finances by the Coalition government.

Social care and health care support

While substantive improvements to disabled children's health and social care services are arguably still more anticipated than real, there have been major shifts towards greater policy and service coordination in the last 10 years. The challenge for the next 10 years will be that of implementing these ambitions in conditions of predicted severe cuts in departmental budgets that include children's services (HM Treasury, 2010). From the early 2000s, key policy shifts were taking place to attempt to reduce the reported fragmentation of children's services. The Audit Commission report of 2003, *A review of services for disabled children and their families*, a study of 240 families with disabled children, established that some six years after New Labour had acceded to power, children's services were best described as a 'postcode lottery'. Planning of services based on local population profiles of disabled children, an idea first mooted in the Chronically Sick and Disabled Persons Act in 1970 (Barnes, 1991; Drake, 1999), were notable by their absence. Services were often haphazard, disconnected and provider-driven. A recent study of local authorities' population planning and awareness of local disabled children made clear that there was a real deficit of good planning data being gathered by local authorities:

> There is a lack of data at both national and local level on the numbers and characteristics of disabled children and their use of local service provision. Yet, such data is a prerequisite to the planning and delivery of effective services. (Mooney et al, 2008, p 7)

Professional dominance and territorialism have often led to unhelpful demarcations and lack of knowledge sharing (Swain et al, 2004). Hierarchies of credibility are attached to certain professions and this is still the case in child and adult mental health services. Lord Laming's report on the lamentable and catastrophic failure of service profession coordination for 'vulnerable' children proved the final straw in forcing through major policy change in the wake of the Climbié death and the resulting enquiry report (DH, 2003c). The outcome of that report, *Every Child Matters* (DfES, 2003), provided the blueprint for a modernised, responsive, joined-up and family-centred children's service. At its core *Every Child Matters* drew out five important strands of support and development (DfES, 2003) which were seen as a prerequisite of an inclusive and healthy childhood. The five strands proposed that children should:

- be healthy
- achieve economic well-being
- make a positive contribution
- enjoy and achieve
- stay safe.

Clearly some of these, such as economic well-being and positive contribution, require longer-term post-childhood barrier reduction and support for disabled people that makes adult policy issues just as important if childhood enablement is not simply to grind to a halt at the first hurdles of adulthood. They are clear examples of commitment to better children's services, but a critical gaze might suggest their phraseology has all the hallmarks of third way politics (Giddens, 1998), in talking about being healthy and making a positive contribution. Arguably, as with adult welfare policy, conditionality and a rights–responsibilities discourse (Powell, 2002) lies at the heart of the economic and contributory strands of the *Every Child Matters* formulation. Now for disabled children, barriers to education, economic security and inclusion may, as recently suggested (Emerson et al, 2009), be the result of engrained structural factors which, if not erased, and where children fail to thrive in the world of conditional welfare, families run the risk of being blamed for their failure to engage with such 'opportunities'.

As stated earlier, as these are child policies, conditionality is more implicit than explicit in disability policy for children. It remains powerfully implicit in child policy, with the assumption that old centralised redistributive approaches were seen to fail and to have perpetuated family dependency on welfare and social dislocation (Mann and Roseneil, 1994; Levitas, 2005). On the other hand, the question of whether state policy has sufficiently grappled with issues of dependence, independence and inter-dependence and engrained poverty in some disabled childhoods is a moot point (McLaughlin et al, 2008). There is, however, much evidence that policies which aim to make disabled children's transitions to young adulthood smoother are not reaching their targets in the fields of education, health and emotional well-being (Roulstone and Yates, 2009).

What, then, were the key tenets of *Every Child Matters* and their specific implications for disabled children? Key policy and practice challenges in *Every Child Matters* attach to the desirability of knowledge sharing (DfES, 2003), joint commissioning, co-location of social care and education professionals and greater reach-in approaches to working with disabled children in school to avoid unnecessary fragmentation of the child's school day. These messages of seamless working were also reinforced by wider policy developments embodied in *Aiming high for disabled children* (HM Treasury and DCSF, 2007), the *National Service Framework for children* (DH, 2004), *The Early Support Programme* (DfES and DH, 2002) and aspects of the Children Act 2004 (HM Government, 2004), which all emphasised the need to join up planning, provision and review of services. Children and their families were seen as needing to be at the centre of service and local policy influence, with *Aiming high for disabled children* (HM Treasury and DCSF, 2007) requiring children's service providers to listen to the voices of disabled children and their parents and avoid more traditional paternalist assumptions about children's needs.

The exact impact of *Every Child Matters* on disabled children is hard to pin down at this point, and no independent evaluation of the wider initiative has taken place. What we do know is that multi-agency projects to date, many of which predated *Every Child Matters*, have indeed improved the quality and perceived value of services to disabled people (see Townsley et al, 2003). However, we also know that serious cases of failed communication and poor early identification and prevention of undue risk have occurred, issues so central to the Climbié case (DH, 2003c). The most vulnerable children remain 'hard to reach' in practical terms. The strength of professional cultures, budgetary dynamics and professional demarcations are proving exceedingly hard to break down. Recriminations frequently characterise the relationship between central and local government where service integrity and safeguarding have been seen to unravel and trust breaks down further at all levels, with the atmosphere in some London social services departments at the time of the 'Baby Peter' case being described as 'toxic' and thus clearly inimical to positive relations with both disabled and non-disabled children at greatest risk.

As of 2010 the merging of social care and education into children's services in the wake of *Every Child Matters* has, for some disabled children and their families, been less significant than the growing trend towards the further widening of adult and child services in a return to specialist services that existed before the Seebohm reforms backed more generic social work interventions (Seebohm, 1968). This cleaving of adult and child specialisms clearly runs against the grain of the life chances report and transition planning which placed an emphasis on seamless transitions through the life cycle (PMSU, 2005). Such specialisation might be read as greater professional control and even more fractured disabled transitions and can leave some children lacking specialist support, as established in the research commissioned by the National Deaf Children's Society (NDCS, 2010). In terms of the continued risks to the most vulnerable children, many of whom are disabled, Butler (2010) sums up the zeitgeist in some children's services departments and the continued problems:

> The Local Government Association [LGA] said last week that it expects 61,000 children to enter care in 2011–12, an increase of 35% in four years. In March, Cafcass, the children's court service, dealt with a record 832 care applications. The LGA earlier this year put the additional cost of the Baby Peter legacy to its member councils in England at £226m a year. (Butler, 2010)

A more thoroughgoing critique of *Every Child Matters* observed it was/is based around the 'average child' and thus represented an 'ableist' construction of a 'good childhood'. Research by Beresford et al (2007) emphasised the power of a non-disabled model of achievement. In policy terms this represented a hegemonic construction of the 'good citizen' which arguably for some disabled children, particularly those with profound impairments, major health problems and mental health issues, could not live up to, even with support. The study's key findings noted that:

- Disabled children aspired to the same sort of outcomes as non–disabled children. However, what these outcomes meant, the way they were prioritised, and the level of achievement expected, often differed from non–disabled children.
- There is a need to widen definitions of key concepts within the *Every Child Matters* framework to take account of disabled children's views and capabilities. (Beresford et al, 2007)

This latter finding touched on the important point that disabled children are very diverse, and while constructing absolute aims for children is at one level symbolic of a good society, it also has a tendency to foster rather one-dimensional interpretations of child achievement. The question of social policy needing to be sufficiently nuanced in grasping the diversity of impairment and disabling barriers is borne out in a number of areas that have received grossly inadequate attention until recently in central and local policy terms. The report by John Bercow (DCSF, 2008b) on the speech, language and communication needs (SLCN) of children made clear the postcode lottery of services in special and language services. Access to SLCN services in his study were uneven, and unpredictable. Bizarrely speech, language and communication issues often played second fiddle to broader health and social care agendas. These agendas were rooted in traditional assumptions of 'needs' issues relating only to those children with severe and/or complex health or disability needs. In reality, neither medicine social work nor disability studies has focused much attention on the area of speech, language and communication, which is odd given the importance of issues of communication and inclusion of, say, adults with hearing impairments and developments d/Deaf studies and policy. In that sense it is hardly surprising that SLCN issues had not received corresponding policy attention. Bercow noted that:

> Evidence illustrates ... there is insufficient understanding of the centrality of speech, language and communication among policy makers and commissioners nationally and locally, professionals and service providers, and sometimes parents and families themselves. It follows that insufficient priority is attached to addressing SLCN. (DCSF, 2008b, p 7)

In both adding to and reflecting the spirit of *Every Child Matters*, the Bercow Report highlighted the need for early intervention, the need for multi-agency cooperation and for 'whole family' insights which take account of the breadth of family needs and resources. Both school-based special educational needs coordinators (SENCOs) and children's centre workers were seen to have key roles in identifying speech and communication needs as early as possible to help identify the best packages of support. The report actioned greater funding for speech therapists, schools and families to support children with SLCN, and received fulsome cross-party support on publication.

Disabled children and wheelchair services

In a similar vein to the above focus on areas that might be overlooked in policy terms, the issue of wheelchair services, especially for very young children, can easily be overtaken by assumptions that such children, in being dependent on their parents, require less policy and service attention in terms of equipment support. Indeed the Early Years focus in recent policy programmes clearly needs to support even the youngest disabled children to get the best footing in life. A wealth of research points to the shortfalls in wheelchair and equipment provision in the UK. For example, Sharma and Morrison (2007) found that of the 350 families of children requiring wheelchair services, 54 per cent said their local services could not provide the desired equipment and 47 per cent were told that budget restrictions prevented their child's individual needs being met. Similarly, Staincliffe's (2003) study of 145 wheelchair service providers established that a mere 46 per cent provided referrals for under-fives, while few offered indoor power chairs for children under five. A study by the Care Services Improvement Partnership (CSIP), a major social care improvement agency, some three years after *Every Child Matters* had been mooted, found a mismatch between supply and demand in tailored wheelchair services for young children (CSIP, 2006). This was despite official evidence of a shortfall in wheelchair provision for young disabled children in the 20 years leading up to *Every Child Matters* (Audit Commission, 2003). Clearly, the growing rhetoric of child-centred policy and that every child does matter has to be matched in a wide variety of contexts to embrace levels of need, different impairments and the wider configuration of support already available in a locality (EDCM, 2008).

One key resource for parents of children with the highest levels of need is the Family Fund. This little known fund makes grants available to children with high level needs and, as of 2010, was supporting 55,000 families with the additional costs of supporting a disabled child under 18. The fund is means tested and current net income limits are set at £28,000 (Family Fund, 2010). The fund will only pay for items and costs that would not ordinarily be met by a local authority social services department. While a welcome and generous form of support, critics point to the continued low income threshold for exclusion from the benefit where wider family costs need to be met, and ask why the fund should be means tested given the evidence of the actual additional costs incurred alongside normal household expenditure (Harrison and Wooley, 2004; Preston, 2006).

The sense that *Every Child Matters* may not, in itself, live up to the expectations of disabled children and families is evidenced in the development of the consortium Every Disabled Child Matters (EDCM). EDCM was set up five years after the 2003 *Every Child Matters* initiative and is made up of the organisations Contact a Family, Mencap, the Special Educational Consortium and the Council for Disabled Children. Disillusioned by the degree of progress made and the impact of *Every Child Matters*, the consortium has lobbied for additional clauses to strengthen legislation that has derived from *Every Child Matters* to further improve the lives of disabled children. For example, EDCM has lobbied for a greater provision of short breaks by local authorities by adding a clause to the Children and Young Persons Act 2008 (HM Government, 2008). The Act aims to both support 'looked-after' children and to avoid unnecessary movements of disabled and vulnerable children entering statutory care. Short break provision was seen by EDCM members as aiding prevention. In December 2008, *The Children's Plan: Building brighter futures* (DCFS, 2008c) committed an additional £90 million local authority capital funding for short break services from 2008 to 2011, bringing the funding allocation for short breaks to £370 million (DCSF, 2008d), which bolstered EDCM's objectives substantially.

Recent evidence from the EDCM and the Council for Disabled Children (EDCM, 2010) suggests there are still issues that need to be addressed in the implementation of *Every Child Matters* and *Aiming high for disabled children*. This might be expected given their relative newness and the financially straitened times in which they were implemented (Roulstone and Morgan, 2009). However, even before the autumn 2010 review of public spending, research conducted by EDCM established that while services had become more transparent, responsive, preventive and participative, there were still notable variations in the quality and extent of short break services across England and issues of flexible transport, and engagement with family impacts of limited short breaks were still sources of frustration and family breakdown (EDCM, 2010). While *Every Child Matters* proclaims that every child does indeed matter, the wider impact of the report is not being evaluated for disabled children. Only specific components of the policy initiative will be evaluated. For example, there are a number of formal evaluations to assess the outcomes of the various strands of the *Aiming high for disabled children* programme, (Department for Education, 2011). The allocation of 800 million additional money for children's short breaks (funded in part by the ending of the Child Trust Fund) is clearly welcome.

The Disabled Children's Access to Childcare initiative (DCATCH) report is expected to be published later in 2011 (*Hansard*, 2010a). These should all go some way to judging just how enabling these specific programmes are for disabled children and their families.

Two areas with clear potential for disabled children during the last 10 years have been the development of children's centres (formerly Sure Start) and the extension of direct payments to parents/carers of disabled children and to disabled children aged 17-19. Children's centres aim to provide children with a foundation of support via a range of activities and facilities that support both child and parents in the early years of life. The Department for Children, Schools and Families' (DCSF) policy document *Sure Start children's centres: Building brighter futures* (DCSF, 2008a, p 1) made clear the key policy ambitions of children's centres (see **Box 4.2** below) as 'important in the drive to end child poverty, improve life chances for all children and families, close the achievement gap between the most disadvantaged children and the rest, and support parents' (DCSF, 2008a, p 1). Centres were to be set up to achieve the following detailed functions.

Box 4.2: Children's centres and enabled childhoods

- First, early education and childcare which is intended to improve children's emotional, social and intellectual development.
- Second, support for parents in a range of areas including literacy, parenting and targeted interventions for the parents/carers of disabled children.
- Third, child and family health services geared up to local needs but commonly focusing upon immunisations, health reviews and health promotion.
- Finally, support is offered by the Sure Start Children's Centres to parents who need help to find work. (DCSF, 2008a, p 11)

Although aimed at all eligible parents and their children, by being established on principles of inclusion and aiming to include disabled children and those with behavioural and learning challenges, the context clearly holds much potential in providing a good start for disabled children, something campaigning organisations have been focused on and lobbying for during the previous two decades. From the outset children's centre workers have been made aware and, at best, trained to support children with diverse needs and developmental journeys. Here the potential exists for both policy and cultural advances where children grow up in contexts that encourage disabled and non–disabled children to mix and formulate views of each other. This could act to counter segregated schooling and the known problems that emanate from living lives apart.

Sure Start and now children's centres have been tasked from the outset to include disabled children, and to:

> ... enable them to ensure the inclusion of children from disadvantaged and excluded groups such as disabled children and those with special educational needs, children from black and other ethnic minority groups and children from socially excluded families such as those who are homeless or with a parent who is disabled or has mental illness, is abusing drugs or alcohol, in prison or experiencing domestic violence ... activities to facilitate inclusive practice could include providing training, advice and information; giving funding for adaptations, equipment or resources; promoting early intervention and successful school entry planning; supporting multi–agency working and partnership working with parents; adopting the Early Support Programme approaches and tools or providing additional staff or services eg therapy and transport. (DCSF, 2009, p 2)

Precise evaluation evidence for the impact of Sure Start and children's centres on disabled children is currently limited; however, a recent study by the National Audit Office (NAO) revealed there is still some distance to travel in getting the reality to match the rhetoric in supporting children in their early years. The NAO noted that:

> ... less than a third of centres were proactively identifying and taking services out to families with high levels of need in their area, including lone and teenage parents, disabled children's parents and parents from some ethnic minorities in areas with small minority populations. (NAO, 2006)

A further key development which offers disabled children, their parents and carers greater control of their lives is the widening of coverage of direct payments in the UK. The Carers and Disabled Children Act 2000 (HM Government, 2000b) provides for disabled children and their 'carers' to arrange care and services as opposed to direct provision of services from a local authority social services department. Direct payments can be made to parents and 'carers' aged 16 or over, and clearly the payments can be controlled by a disabled person who may employ support work from outside their family rather than, or in addition to, family and established 'carers'. Payments can be spent on a range of support, short breaks, nursery placements (for younger children) and leisure activities. This at least begins to acknowledge the range of needs and preferences that a disabled child may have. It is worth pointing out, however, that the carer, carer breaks mentality does permeate much of the guidance and campaigning activity around direct payments for children. Terms such as 'childcare services' rather than 'independent lives' are pervasive and this runs the risk of confining debates within a 'care' and 'alleviation of burden' approach.

Policy prescription for direct payments for those eligible is strong with mandatory requirements for local authorities to offer the choice of direct payments. Provisions in the Children Act 2004 (HM Government, 2004) ensure that direct payments are not a substitute for good support as the welfare of the child has to be paramount in a decision about offering and providing direct payments. There is some way to go in increasing take-up in this area. In 2004, for instance, 2,400 children were receiving direct payments compared to 29,000 who were receiving traditional services. This has encouraged UK governments to increase their targets for take-up (HM Treasury and DCSF, 2007). The Carers and Disabled Children Act 2000 also empowered local authorities to make direct payments available for 16- and 17-year-olds who can hold the payments in their own right. This development clearly aligns itself with wider impetus to independent living and choice making. Abbott (2003), some three years after the Act's implementation, carried out a study which highlighted the initial excitement and concerns of young people towards direct payments. The provision of support to administer the payments and lack of knowledge of direct payments were two concerns shared by both young disabled people and local authorities as the roll-out took place. This issue of support to and ability to manage direct payments for those individuals aged 16/17 also emerged in the major study by Riddell et al (2006). There needs to be further follow-up research to see how well such issues have been supported.

Educational policy

There is much evidence elsewhere on the educational position and barriers faced by disabled children (Burchardt, 2005; Ainscow and Miles, 2008), and this section aims to simply draw out the links between disability policy and disadvantage. It is important to reflect on how policy constructions of the 'problem' of disabled children and young people's education have been reframed during the period 1997-2009. In outline, what we know is that disabled children and young people are at substantial disadvantage in both compulsory and post-compulsory contexts (Merriman, 2009). The reasons are many. Poorly designed curriculum, historically low expectations, particularly in segregated schooling, illness and treatment requirements and often rather unsophisticated exclusion policies which fail to connect with long-term developmental and educational needs are but four examples. Disabled children are also themselves more likely to complete their formal education with little or no qualifications and to have much lower qualifications than their non-disabled counterparts (Burchardt, 2005). The paradox is that this continued exclusion sits alongside masses of new policy and programme initiatives.

There have been an unprecedented number of education inclusion policies for disabled children since the accession of New Labour in 1997. These are evident in the Green Paper *Excellence for all: Meeting special educational needs* (DfES, 1997) and more recently the Education and Inspections Bill of 2006 (HM Government, 2006; Reiser, 2006). Major impetus has come from key inspection and standards bodies keen to see greater mainstreaming and disabled pupil performance (Audit Commission, 2002; Ofsted, 2004). New Labour were also keen to be associated with reduced school exclusions given the growing evidence on their longer-term educational impact. These have been furthered via anti-truancy projects, Education Action Zones (EAZs), school improvement orders and greater partnership working to reduce disaffection. Despite these efforts, exclusions remain high, while Reiser's work points to a large overlap of school exclusion and disabled pupil populations, noting that '80% of permanent exclusions and 60% of secondary exclusions are pupils with SEN or learning difficulties' (Reiser, 2006, p 46). Pupils with statements of SEN are disproportionately more likely to be excluded from school (National Statistics, 2001a). Disabled children are more likely to be positioned in social class 4 and 5, the social class groups most likely to be excluded in the early to mid-2000s (National Statistics, 2001a). Exclusions reduced only very slightly in the years 2002-07 (National Statistics, 2009a). This is worrying given that the figures were derived from data some five years after New Labour came to office.

Although school exclusions reduced very slightly between 2002-06, with a mathematical drop of 0.04 per cent, the actual figures of children excluded are broadly similar, with 12 pupils permanently excluded per 10,000 in 2002/03 and the same in 2005/06 (National Statistics, 2004, 2007a). It is noteworthy that social class correlates positively with school exclusions. Schools with high exclusion rates also have high rates of eligibility to free school meals (a benchmark socioeconomic indicator). Boys are more likely to be excluded, while boys from Afro-Caribbean families are disproportionately represented in exclusions (National Statistics, 2004).

Notably, pupils with SEN statements are four times more likely to form part of the population of school exclusions (National Statistics, 2004). We know that disabled people (of all ages) are more likely than the general population to be in social classes 4 and 5 (DH, 2001a). The link between class, socioeconomic class and school engagement is significant. In terms of special schools, despite a steady decline in special school placements between 1997-2001, there has been a recent reversal of that trend towards special school or special unit placement, with 33 per cent of local education authorities (LEAs) increasing their placements into segregated provision between 2002-05 (Rustmeier and Vaughan, 2005).

The shift towards mainstreaming, while strengthened rhetorically, can be seen to have been reversed in some local authorities. As the work of the Centre for Studies in Inclusive Education have long illustrated, regardless of some progress in the number of local authorities prompting major mainstreaming initiatives, there had been a shift since 2000 towards a slight growth and retrenchment in the numbers of segregated schools. Despite a decline in disabled children's placement into a special school between the years 1997-2001, a trend reversal took place in the years 2002-05 with a third of LEAs upping their placements into segregated schools during this period (Rustmeier and Vaughan, 2005). New Labour's key policy contradiction here arguably related to its simultaneous belief in greater parental choice alongside major anti-discrimination and anti-exclusion policies. Clearly there are times when central government has to be firm in aligning the new dynamics of an inclusive society with the broader rhetoric of parental choice, especially where the means as well as the will to mainstream are available. This helps explain why the SENDA (HM Government, 2000a) and a myriad of policy guidance on inclusion have been largely ineffective as segregated schooling remains a valued concept in parents' minds.

While parental views are clearly very important, there has arguably been a failure to seriously review the funding patterns for 'special education' in a way that makes mainstream school more attractive culturally, educationally and technically than segregated education. Perhaps the most searching critiques of recent policy contradictions and special education point to the internal tensions between inclusion and a wider educational policy. As radical education writers have made plain, credential inflation, the narrowing of the formal curriculum to measure the three 'Rs' (reading, writing and arithmetic) and the historically exclusive sifting nature of education are all inimical to inclusion in any thoroughgoing sense (Barton and Oliver, 1997). In this way, many disabled children find themselves clustered around the non-academic end of the educational spectrum, with all the negative constructions that exist within the wider educational system.

A reading of vocational and post-school policy over the last 10 years would lead a reasonable observer to conclude that disabled young people had never been as well supported and protected in their search for economic belonging and well-being. Policy has shifted towards mainstreaming and emphasised disabled people's right to live ordinary lives and to realise their expectations (PMSU, 2005). Major policy developments include the *Every Child Matters* framework which promised more joined-up and robust protections of young people's rights and entitlements and included economic well-being as a key policy aim (DfES, 2003). Better transition planning has been a strong feature of a number of recent policy developments in education, social care and health (Disability Rights Task Force, 1999; DH, 2006). There has been a growing and shared acknowledgment that the years 14-19 are critical in the establishment of young people's life chances and opportunities (Nuffield Foundation, 2009). The life chances report (PMSU, 2005) places major emphasis on the needs and expectations of disabled young people and serves as a blueprint for future policy.

If exclusion from the foundational years are significant, the experience of the educational transition to training and paid work are clearly also important. The position of disabled people's education and vocational opportunities and achievements are very worrying despite much policy attention. We know that only 40 per cent of working-age disabled people are low skilled or unskilled (PMSU, 2005). For non-disabled people, the figure is six times higher. Moreover, non-disabled people are six times more likely to make the transition to paid work in any one year, with only 4 per cent (compared to 24 per cent) making this shift annually (Burchardt, 2005). Nearly a third (27 per cent) of disabled young people are not in education, employment or training (NEET); this compared badly with their non-disabled counterparts where 9 per cent are classified as NEET (Dickinson-Lilley, 2010). Worryingly the figure of disabled young people entering NEET status has increased in recent years, with the figure climbing to 15 per cent by 2004 (DRC, 2007). Five per cent of disabled young people were in post-school education (further and higher) in 2003 compared to 10 per cent of their non-disabled comparators (DRC, 2007). Of those disabled young people who did not go on to further or higher education, 30 per cent believe that they were prevented from doing so for reasons to do with disability. There are recorded instances where disabled young people have been refused access to vocational courses where an applicant's impairment was seen, without justification, as unfavourable to working in a given occupation (Roulstone and Yates, 2009).

The Nuffield Foundation review of 14-19 education and training (Nuffield Foundation, 2009) noted that 21 per cent of disabled people aged 16-24 have no qualifications compared to 9 per cent of non-disabled people. At a more advanced level, young disabled people are markedly less likely than their non-disabled peers to have obtained level 3 academic (16.4 compared to 30.7 per cent) or vocational (6.5 compared to 9.9 per cent) qualifications aged 18. Overall, education and employment outcomes of disabled and non-disabled young people diverge quite early on. This is notable at age 18, and even more so by age 26, as both expectations and opportunities seem to diminish. Disabled young adults have, on average, lower qualifications, higher rates of unemployment and longer durations of unemployment, lower pay and lower status employment. Burchardt's (2005) research, entitled *The education and employment of disabled young people*, provides a secondary analysis of the British Cohort Study and Youth Cohort Studies suggesting a dramatic lowering of employment expectations and experiences between the age of 18 and 26. More limited training options, limited access to higher level qualifications and poor access to paid employment all act as forms of attrition in reducing aspiration, expectation and vocational achievement for disabled young people.

Conclusion

Many disabled childhoods remain stubbornly linked to poverty, disadvantage and more limited social horizons, for both disabled children and their families. There is no wholesale evidence of a major reduction in child poverty in line with New Labour's targets set in 2004-05. Indeed, as a recent study by the Institute for Fiscal Studies made clear, the government fell 600,000 short of its 2004-05 target and nowhere near meeting its next 2010-11 target (of half its 1998-2009 level) (cited in Lister, 2009). There are, therefore, a range of policy issues at stake here, while the wider family policy implications that relate to the support and growing conditionality attached to out-of-work and lone-parent benefits need to be accounted for (Dwyer, 2004b). Arguably, disabled children have witnessed a highly valorised and unconditional form of policy support, but one which may be affected or undermined by harsher, more conditional adult and family welfare policy. A good example of this was the recent reaffirmation that Employment and Support Allowance (ESA) and Jobseeker's Allowance recipients would face financial penalties if they did not show evidence of job seeking.

The recent decision by the new Coalition government to freeze Child Benefit for three years has significant implications for disabled children and their families, as does the decision to increase value added tax (VAT) to 20 per cent from January 2010, a tax known to be regressive. Beyond possible contradictions in child and adult policy agendas, the need to ensure greater educational and social opportunities for disabled children is a pressing social priority. Ensuing chapters will begin to explore the policy developments that have taken shape between 1997 and 2011. It is important to understand that the barriers to economic and social participation are more than simply economic, and that they embrace strong cultural assumptions revolving around the twin axes of childhood and disability. Such views are powerful but diverse, some viewing childhood disability as a personal tragedy that creates a double dependency. More recently, a growing understanding of the barriers facing children *and* disabled people may lead some policy commentators to conclude that creative, joined-up policy and legislative enforcement is required to reduce the additional social and educational barriers confronting disabled children. More effective policy is, arguably, not likely to emerge while approaches remain contradictory and legislation unenforced.

Summary

- Childhood disability continues to correlate highly with family poverty.
- Extra costs and additional social barriers each exacerbate poverty.
- The good citizen model fostered by Sure Start and now children's centres do not of themselves help families overcome poverty and social isolation.
- Special segregated education continues to isolate disabled children from the mainstream of social and economic life.
- Barriers in the transition ensures poverty and disability continue to be linked beyond compulsory schooling.

Questions

1. Why does poverty continue to bedevil families with disabled children despite the aim of successive governments to reduce child and disability-related poverty?
2. Do Sure Start-type programmes fully comprehend and deal with engrained social exclusion for families with disabled children?
3. To what extent (if any) do parenting-focused policies bear the hallmarks of third way communitarian principles?
4. The poor are always with us.... Critically discuss with reference to families with disabled children.

Further reading

Lister and Bennett (2010) and **Levitas (2005)** are both very good overviews of family policy. See also **McLaughlin et al (2008)**. More specific references to disabled children are made by **Ridge** and **Burchardt**, both of which are in **Jane Millar**'s **(2003)** excellent collection of essays on contemporary social welfare. The ambitions of the **Audit Commission Report (2003)** and **DCSF**'s *Every Child Matters* **(2003)** are key background reading here.

New Labour and clauses for conditionality: activating disabled citizens

Introduction

Following on from the last chapter that looked at the responses to, and position of, disabled children since the election of New Labour in 1997, this chapter focuses on welfare policy shifts towards self-direction and 'choice making' for disabled adults and the parents of disabled children. In mirroring, at least superficially, the debates in adult social care around self-direction, social policy during the period 1997-2010 has provided fleeting glimpses of the formulation of a rights-based policy agenda for disabled people in the field of work and welfare (Drake, 1999). However, the absence of involvement of disabled people in planning these major policy reforms and the often double-edged and ideologically loaded constructions of self-direction and activation in welfare policy paradoxically leaves some disabled people further from the rhetorical goals of opportunity for all disabled adults and their children. Indeed many features of disability welfare policy sit squarely within the paternalist tradition of social policy. For many, access to welfare has become increasingly conditional and harsh (Hyde, 2000; Burton and Kagan, 2006). Even a cursory glance at the many blogs against social welfare reform makes clear the concerns felt over very forceful policy redefinitions of the boundaries between 'disabled' and 'able-bodied' claimants, 'legitimate' and 'sturdy' claimants. Arguably, the period 1997-2010 has witnessed the most momentous shifts in the disability category (Stone, 1984) and in a way that takes large numbers of disabled people out of the 'deserving category' and back into mainstream and less generous welfare support (DSS, 1998a). The challenge therefore is to give due credence to policy achievements that genuinely provide greater self-determination for disabled people while also fully comprehending the negative or unintended consequences of welfare reform on disabled people.

Despite the change of government in 1997, New Labour continued to pursue a neoliberal ideological platform (Roulstone, 2002; Prideaux, 2001, 2005; Grover and Piggott, 2005, 2007) that personified service users as consumers and committed itself to maintain the spending plans of the previous Conservative government for the first two years in power (Lund, 2002; Walker and Wiseman, 2003). Essentially, this signalled continuity rather than change in social policy. This was particularly evident in the policy areas of social care and welfare during the formative years of New Labour. Even though choice making increased for a small number of disabled people, the context of choice making, and who could 'choose' (Marcuse, 1964; Lukes, 1974), became increasingly constrained by financial restrictions and service retraction (Hills, 1998). This, of course, is not new in disability policy (Walker and Walker, 1991; Drake, 1999), yet the scale of attempts to cut social welfare expenditure during the 1990s and 2000s, alongside the increasingly harsh political focus on so-called social security 'scroungers', has, ironically, led to greater societal, media and political negativity towards disabled people and above all those in receipt of Incapacity Benefit (ICB) (Howard, 2005; Grover and Piggott, 2007).

The increased marketisation of support also created problems, especially in relation to questions of equity and access to a reasonable but minimum supply of welfare provision, the extent of which has meant that some have gained at the expense of others. Even though social care was, and still is, seen as necessary and rightfully due to the most 'deserving' disabled people, the issue of rationing social welfare in the form of disability income and extra needs benefits has been subject to intense scrutiny in the last two to three decades (Hyde, 2000; Roulstone, 2000; Grover and Piggott, 2005; Roulstone and Barnes, 2005). Many of those deemed deserving of support and given access to ICB during the 1980s and early 1990s were now being rebadged as 'fit for work' or as eligible for training and work-related support (Burchardt, 2003). Arguably systems of medical scrutiny and assessment are themselves in some state of disarray and questionable legitimacy as the welfare goalposts move to suit financial expediencies.

New Labour, conditionality and the primacy of paid work

As previous chapters have demonstrated, New Labour's approach towards welfare, employment and disability was not without precedent. The 1980s and the 1990s, in particular, saw an increased emphasis on getting disabled people to participate in the paid labour market (PLM) while discouraging a perceived dependence on welfare benefits (Hyde, 2000; Howard, 2005). This reflected the Reaganite position in the US and its translation of neoliberalism into workfare programmes (Rushefsky, 2002). Debatably, the origins of this new focus on disabled people lay in the controversial 'underclass' ideas of the US political commentator Charles Murray (Murray, 1996a, 1996b; Prideaux 2001, 2005). It was Murray's protestations, initially instigated in the 1980s and accentuated through the proud and persistent support and sponsorship of *The Sunday Times* and the News International Group (Mann and Roseneil, 1994), that allowed Murray, without any sizeable academic following on this side of the Atlantic, to reinforce and vindicate an emergent climate of anti-dependency thought in the UK. By 1987, meetings with representatives from the Prime Minister's Policy Unit, the Department of Health and Social Security (DHSS) and the Treasury Office helped to cement his claims at a higher level. Two years later he addressed the Conservative Prime Minister Margaret Thatcher herself (Dean and Taylor-Gooby, 1992; Mann and Roseneil, 1994). Murray thus began to find a receptive audience and, as a result, was able to successfully promote theories that appealed to growing public and political concerns of the time that the state had become bloated, expensive, overgrown and at worst, had perpetuated rather than tackled dependency (Hall and Jacques, 1983; Gamble, 1988; Brown and Sparks, 1989).

Murray's commentaries, which were permeated with the less controversial thoughts of Lawrence Mead and the authoritarian 'new communitarianism' of Amitai Etzioni before they were incorporated into New Labour's welfare policies (Etzioni, 1998b; Prideaux, 2001, 2005), called for a renewed sense of individual 'responsibility' or 'obligation' (Mead, 1987; Etzioni, 1995, 1997, 1998a, 2000; Deacon, 2002) based on the conviction that there was a growing body of 'irresponsible' welfare recipients who did not want to work, lived a life of crime and significantly contributed to increasing rates of illegitimacy and lone parenthood (Murray, 1984, 1986, 1996a, 1996b; Bagguley and Mann, 1992). This so-called 'underclass', of which commentators and politicians did not originally include disabled people, was commonly believed to represent a significant drain on the public 'purse' and, in part, was seen to contribute to the destabilisation of the economy. Social security spending did grow alarmingly; however, much of this growth was due to an ageing population (see Chapter Nine for more detail). Overall spending in comparable terms rose from £108 billion in 1988 to £145 billion in 1998 (Crawford et al, 2011). Financial pressures over the years and the spiralling costs of welfare soon meant that the focus shifted towards disabled people and, more specifically, towards those in receipt of ICB.

From the outset of the 1997 election to 2010, the belief that an 'underclass' exists heavily influenced New Labour's policy direction. New Labour's self-declared ambition to achieve 'nothing less than a change of culture among benefit claimants' (DSS, 1998a, ch 3.2) bore testament to that. Logically, a powerful catalyst for the cultural change that New Labour desired could have been about achieving full social inclusion and countering the dynamics and multi-dimensional aspects of social exclusion. Inclusion in these terms would entail the involvement of previously excluded individuals or groups in decision making and political processes about making access to employment and material resources easier and about opening the doors to cultural integration so that neighbourhoods would avoid being neglected, marginalised and run down. Policy trends under New Labour did not, however, take such a wide view of social inclusion. Work in the PLM, or at least actively seeking such work, was seen as the only means by which social inclusion could be fully achieved (Levitas, 1998; Prideaux, 2001, 2005). For disabled people, this was also becoming an increasing reality.

Building on the previous focus on disabled people of Conservative governments, yet blending the 'underclass' and authoritarian sentiments of Murray, Mead and Etzioni, New Labour accentuated the trend towards incorporating disabled people into the PLM in a more thorough and comprehensive way (Hyde, 2000). Nevertheless, the irony of greater policy connections being made between disability and the possibility of employment alongside an inclusion of more disabled people into a newly stigmatised dependent population cannot be overlooked. Three days before the general election of 1997, for instance, John Major's government instigated the Benefit Integrity Project (BIP) in the belief that many claims for Disability Living Allowance (DLA) could be fraudulent. The aim of the BIP was basically to check entitlement (Howard, 2005) as part of a broader agenda to tighten eligibility and enforcement regimes for welfare benefits in general (Walker and Wiseman, 2003). Despite the furore that followed the introduction of BIP, and despite its replacement with a periodic review and the Welfare Reform and Pensions Act 1999 (HM Government, 1999a), the basic premises underpinning the project continued to flourish under New Labour (see Chapter Nine for a fuller discussion of the project and the accusation of official manipulation of the extent of disability welfare fraud).

Under the mantra of 'Work for those who can, security for those who cannot' (DSS, 1998a, p 1), and the definitive statement that the newly incumbent government intended to give the marginalised and excluded a 'hand up, not a hand out' (DSS, 1998a, preface), New Labour extended the role of means testing and conditional entitlement to remove the 'perverse incentives' of welfare (Murray, 1984, 1986, 1996a, 1996b) while disavowing the age-old belief 'that people with health conditions and disabilities ...

cannot work' (Secretary of State for Work and Pensions, 2006, p 27, cited in Grover and Piggott, 2007, p 736). Using this philosophy as its baseline, New Labour embarked on its welfare-to-work policies, or 'activation' strategies, as Continental Europe would have it (OECD, 2006), for all categories of the unemployed that, as will become clear, was couched in a rhetoric of 'enablement' in the provision of 'opportunity' but was to have serious impacts on the rights of disabled people. These Smilesian sentiments, that rapid opportunity gains could be had by 'pulling up your bootstraps' (Smiles, 1859), are rejected by major economic studies. Stephen Nickell, an erstwhile member of the Bank of England Monetary Committee, undertook analyses as an academic at the London School of Economics and Political Science (LSE), establishing skills deficits to be at the heart of much worklessness:

> Practical policies discussed include improving education and overall well-being for children in the lower part of the ability range, raising wage floors, New Deal policies, tax credits and benefits for the workless. Overall, I would argue that without reducing the long tail in the skill distribution, there is no practical possibility of policy reducing relative poverty to 1979 levels. (Nickell, 2003, p 28)

Nickell's assertions may be correct; we also know that poor education often holds more significance than disability alone in labour market disadvantage (Burchardt, 2000, 2005). Together, skills, education and training all have key roles to play. However, in contexts of structural worklessness the equation becomes yet bleaker. Beatty, Forthergill (Beatty and Fothergill, 2005) and others have contributed to debates around the economic geographies of worklessness, and in so doing have made clear the key overlapping influence of high levels of ICB claimancy and post-industrial structured worklessness. Clydeside, the Welsh Valleys, ex-mining areas of Northumberland, County Durham and South Yorkshire all hold major challenges for activation policy (Labour Force Survey, 2007), while the low wages that attend most of the available jobs mean that travelling any great distance to work does not pay for those whose families are too far from jobs (Alcock et al, 2003; Beatty and Fothergill, 2005; Fothergill and Wilson, 2007).

   In accord with the sentiments expressed during the Major governments (1990-97), the Welfare Reform and Pensions Act of 1999 (HM Government, 1999a) made it much more difficult for individuals to claim disability-related benefits such as ICB, Severe Disablement Allowance (SDA) and Income Support (IS) on the grounds of incapacity (Grover and Piggott, 2005; Howard, 2005). Would-be claimants of ICB, for example, were subject to added conditions and more rigorous assessments in a response to the growing belief that ICB was either an additional payment for long-term unemployment or an easy way to 'top up' income once in early retirement (Stafford, 2003; Howard, 2005). As a consequence, future claimants of IB were limited to those individuals who had paid national insurance contributions for at least a year during the two years immediately prior to their claim. Moreover, ICB claimants in receipt of personal and occupational pensions were subject to means testing, while eligibility assessment for ICB was no longer focused on incapacity but, instead, on 'assessing an individual's capacity for work, as part of an "All Work Test", now called a "Personal Capability Assessment"' (Hewitt, 2002, p 195).

Finally, prospective ICB claimants were required to attend a compulsory 'work-focused interview' to initiate their claim and subsequently attend obligatory follow-up interviews of up to six in six months under the 'Pathways to Work' schemes set in place. It was also suggested that an ICB claimant had to produce a mandatory action plan setting out the measures they were prepared and/or 'able' to undertake in order to ready themselves for a return to the PLM. Moreover, these 'obligations' placed on the claimant were reinforced with the punitive threat of benefit sanctions should the claimant fail to attend the interviews (Grover and Piggott, 2005).

With this 'hardening' and subsequent enforcement of eligibility criteria, New Labour's primary objective was to take the 'carrot and stick' approach (Hewitt, 2002; Dwyer, 2010) to engage disabled people in the idea of returning to the PLM as quickly as possible (Grover and Piggott, 2005). This reward and punishment approach was the cornerstone of New Labour's welfare-to-work policies in general. In this respect, the aforementioned conditions, obligations and sanctions imposed by New Labour were the punitive stick. Conversely, 'work for those who can' represented the inclusive carrot where the government, under the voluntary New Deal for disabled people (NDDP), or Pathways to Work where NDDP was not available, provided a programme of advice and practical support (see **Box 5.1**). Besides providing information about local job vacancies and supporting disabled people in the first six months of paid employment, the NDDP scheme, which is delivered through a network of job brokers and, to a lesser extent, the Pathways to Work run by Jobcentre Plus, was designed to help disabled people to evaluate their skills and identify available job opportunities, to provide guidance on writing CVs, to provide help in the job application process and the filling in of forms, to help prepare for interviews and to identify and help supply any locally available training needs required (DWP, 2008a).

To overcome the fears of disabled people who felt trapped on benefits because of a potential loss of entitlement if they worked (thus contravening the proviso that ICBs would only be paid if individuals did not work), financial incentives to work in the PLM were extended (Walker and Wiseman, 2003). Notwithstanding the introduction of a National Minimum Wage, from which disabled people are not exempt (Schneider et al, 2001), a one year linking rule was introduced so that disabled people returning to the PLM could re-qualify for ICB at the previous level should they lose employment. Later, this one year linking period was extended to two. In addition, the 16-hour limit for volunteer work was removed while the NDDP was accompanied with tax reforms in the shape of the Disabled Person's Tax Allowance (DPTA) that replaced the Disability Working Allowance (DWA) in 1999. DPTA was specifically introduced to help make work pay (Stafford, 2003), and was supplemented in 2003 with the disability elements of the Child Tax Credit (CTC) and the Working Tax Credit (WTC) (Howard, 2005).

The disability elements of CTC and WTC, in particular, meant that disabled people could claim for additional income while in work. Based on the income received, the 'severely disabled child' element of CTC, for instance, could amount to £1,095 per annum for each child living in a family on the highest rate of the care component for DLA. Moreover, the 'disabled worker' and the 'severe disability' elements of WTC could amount to £2,570 and £1,095 per annum respectively (Disability Alliance, 2010b).

Box 5.1: New Labour's support for disabled people in finding work

Under the auspices of the Disability Discrimination Act (DDA), NDDP and Pathways to Work, New Labour were committed to:

- providing active tailored help (through work-focused interviews and personal advisers) for those who wanted to move into the PLM;
- removing obstacles to the PLM within the benefit system (by removing the one year linking rule so that people returning to the PLM could re-qualify for IB at the previous level should they lose employment and with the removal of the 16-hour limit for volunteer work);
- ensuring work pays through the introduction of the National Minimum Wage (1999) and tax benefits such as the DPTA (1999), CTC (2003) and WTC (2003);
- tackling discrimination and promoting change in the workplace through the Disability Discrimination Act (1995, amended 2005) and through Access to Work (1994) to support disabled employees and employers of disabled people.

Source: Adapted from Howard (2005)

Taken as a whole, it would appear that New Labour had indeed made work look very attractive, financially rewarding and a much more preferable option for those disabled people already closest to the labour market. The tax credits system has been of particular benefit for a number of disabled people motivated to re-enter or remain in the PLM and who can work over 16 hours per week. Moreover, the DDA, which was first introduced by the Conservatives in 1995 and rolled out by New Labour from 1997, made it unlawful for employers to discriminate against disabled people through their recruitment and employment practices and procedures (Gooding, 1995; Grover and Piggott, 2005; Barnes and Mercer, 2010). Further, the DDA required employers not only to make 'reasonable adjustments' to these practices and procedures, but also to their premises and machinery so that employment opportunities and working conditions were made more accessible for disabled employees. Some keynote case outcomes have helped reinforce the value of the DDA of 1995 (Lawson, 2008) even though establishing disability discrimination remained very difficult under the Act (Roulstone, 2003; Hurstfield et al, 2004). A major amendment to the DDA in 2005 instigated by New Labour placed a duty on public bodies to promote disability equality and to embed disability into all its wider corporate planning and awareness (Roulstone and Warren, 2006). In terms of specific workplace support, Access to Work grants, first introduced in 1994 as the successor to the Special Aids to Employment Scheme (Brown, 1984), also helped facilitated job opportunities or retention for some disabled people. Critics of aspects of the operation of the scheme note that it is historically one of the least advertised of all disability support programmes, follow-on support is limited, while portability from employer to employer is difficult (Dewson et al, 2002; Roulstone, quoted in Roulstone and Barnes, 2005). The original aim of Access to Work was to assist disabled employees with any additional costs incurred by their employment. In this context, Access to Work grants could contribute to the purchase of equipment needed to work, help pay for a support worker and/or cover the cost of getting to and from work if a disabled person could not use public transport. On the other hand, employers could also use Access to Work grants to fund the necessary adjustments to their premises and machinery employees may require. Access to Work budgets were increased during the New Labour years to reflect the overall popularity of the scheme (Thornton et al, 2002; Grover and Piggott, 2005).

Paid work, social inclusion and social citizenship

All in all, then, it has become clear that New Labour relied heavily on providing employment opportunities in the PLM for disabled people in fulfilling its vision for activation of the previously excluded. What is more, paid work in the eyes of New Labour and their advocates was viewed as 'the main means of integration' (Levitas, 1996, p 13) into UK 'society'. As such, paid work was explicitly seen as the sole 'route to an adequate income, social networks and personal fulfilment'. Therefore 'attachment to the labour market was the key to breaking the vicious cycle of long-term unemployment and social exclusion' (1996, p 14). Yet social inclusion, as it was originally envisaged in France and Continental Europe, was committed to securing social rights, promoting social citizenship, social solidarity, mutuality and the collectivisation of risk. Therefore 'social bonds, social cohesion, and deeply networked social relations are ... seen as vital to an inclusive, integrated and socially equitable society' (Fergusson, 2002, p 175).

In this guise, social inclusion and the associated concept of social citizenship is couched in terms of available access to the range of resources and conditions that promote a tangible state of social well-being (Ackers and Dwyer, 2002). Clearly this is not confined to participation in the PLM and, as such, helps to highlight the limitations of New Labour's single-stranded approach to inclusion. Frustration had, perhaps, begun to show in 2004 when New Labour altered the terminology from 'claimants' to 'customers', leading one commentator to note that if adopted uncritically the ideological shift to customers might mean, in areas of high structural unemployment, some disabled people would not want to 'buy' that which was not available (Roulstone, quoted in Roulstone and Barnes, 2005). Where social inclusion may be driven through by coercive means the term itself has, arguably, to be reappraised (Burden and Hamm, 2000).

Craig (2004) expands on Ackers and Dwyer's position through the assertion that 'getting by' is completely inadequate, whereas financial remuneration represents only a partial solution to a more general set of problematic circumstances that deny full inclusion into UK society and, in turn, full enjoyment of the rewards of social citizenship. Research (see Cohen et al, 1990; Sadiq-Sangster, 1991; Kempson, 1996; Gordon and Pantazis, 1997; Parker, 2000), argues Craig, has effectively demonstrated how low income and low 'take-up' of benefits has prevented many from obtaining goods and services 'which most in UK society regarded as meeting essential needs' (Craig, 2004, p 99). For disabled people, these problems are acutely manifest. Financial remuneration for work in the PLM remains inadequate despite New Labour's recounted efforts. In this respect, the success of the NDDP has to be called into question. Despite the fact that the employment rate gap between disabled and non-disabled people had decreased from approximately 36 per cent in 2002 to 30 per cent in 2009, disabled people were far less likely to be in employment with employment rates for disabled people being around 47 per cent as opposed to a 77 per cent rate for non-disabled people (ODI, 2010, p 2).

Where disabled people have found work in the PLM as result of NDDP participation, few have benefited from the security of meaningful, well-paid employment (Drake, 1999; Hyde, 2000; Dwyer, 2010). Rather, the quality of work procured tends to be insecure, low paid, manual, relatively unskilled and part time (Barnes, 1991; Barnes et al, 1999) due to the perception that disabled people appear to have fewer marketable skills and qualifications (Hyde, 2000). Moreover, the employment providers working on behalf of disabled people as part of the NDDP have tended to select only those participants who were closest to the PLM in the first place (Stafford, 2005). One explanation why these individuals are closer to the PLM could, of course, relate to the 'capabilities' of the disabled person (possibly underscored by the Personal Capability Assessment, now the Work Capability Assessment) and the costs and requirements of improving the workplace accordingly. It may be that these individuals would have found employment without having entered into the NDDP that, like the other New Deals, only facilitated the supply of labour into the PLM. Certainly early evidence suggested that disabled people, even those desirous of working, were not convinced of the value of the programme, with only 3 per cent of the eligible population availing themselves to NDDP participation (Arthur et al, 1999).

The reasons for many disabled people being restricted to low-paid, insecure employment are numerous. The lack of marketable skills, for instance, can be attributed to the educational choices and opportunities disabled children have access to, while the continued segregation of disabled children has indeed affected the attainment of qualifications. As Barnes and Mercer (2010, p 105) point out, national surveys 'report that over 25 per cent of disabled adults have no qualifications, more than twice the non-disabled rate'. Special schools entered 27 per cent of their pupils for five or more GCSE examinations as opposed to the 92 per cent entry figure for 15-year-olds nationally. Other barriers to secure, well-paid employment stem from employment practices, the (often erroneous) estimate of the costs of altering the work environment, the threat of lost working days because of health deterioration and/or the negative effects that medication can have on a disabled person's working ability (Easterlow and Smith, 2003). In the context of the laissez-faire market and its emphasis on the maximisation of profit, employers often begrudge the loss of working time and the resultant loss of financial gain despite legislation designed to end discrimination and improve employment 'opportunities'. Many of the above perceptions are ill founded, with research pointing to disabled people's higher levels of output often motivated by the fear of being out of work (Zadek and Scott-Parker, 2003).

In truth, disabled people benefited little from the work-first policy efforts of New Labour. In legislative terms, it is significant that the constant use of provisos such as 'reasonable', 'practical' and 'impractical' has dominated the majority of UK regulations. In so doing, these caveats have detrimentally served to dilute the true extent of the requirements laid down by the DDA and its Code of Practice (Prideaux, 2006; Roulstone and Warren, 2006). Numerous permutations have merged together so that businesses are relieved of the obligation to make substantial improvements to their services, machinery and properties. Alterations have been deemed to be ineffective, too costly or too disruptive and, therefore, have not been undertaken. Similarly, modifications have not taken place as they have been seen as unfeasible and an unnecessary addition to the amount already spent on improving access.

With the possible exception of the now defunct Disability Rights Commission (DRC), matters were made worse by the lack of an officially recognised UK regulatory body responsible for overseeing such decisions. Instead, the test for 'reasonableness' was, and still remains, heavily weighted in favour of employers and can usually only be challenged on an individual basis through appeals to the DRC or through the law courts (Prideaux, 2006). More recently, however, the predicament of disabled people has not been helped with the absorption of the DRC into the newly formed Equality and Human Rights Commission (EHRC) and its much broader remit of promoting and monitoring human rights to protect, enforce and promote equality across the seven 'protected' grounds of age, disability, gender, race, religion and belief, sexual orientation and gender reassignment. Inevitably, this broader and wider remit, and the concomitant reduction in commissioners focused solely on disability issues, is bound to impact on disabled people in the fight to overcome disabling barriers.

Effectively, then, New Labour failed to implement a consistent policy agenda that significantly improved work opportunities and accessibility for disabled people. To make matters worse, the availability of financial or other assistance to improve the workplace is severely limited. The aforementioned Access to Work grants, for instance, can indeed be used by employers to modify the working environment. Even so, this is not a source of funding that will cover all of the costs for improvements. Rather, the employer generally has to share the costs and the precise level is determined as follows:

- employers of 1–9 employees are not required to share costs;
- employers of 10–49 employees are required to pay the first £300 and 20 per cent of costs up to £10,000;

- employers of 50-249 employees are required to pay the first £500 and 20 per cent of costs up to £10,000;
- large employers of 250 employees or more are required to pay the first £1,000 and 20 per cent of costs up to £10,000.
  (Directgov, 2010)

Other sources of funding come in the form of favourable tax incentives rather than full financial assistance (Prideaux, 2006). For example, the Inland Revenue argues that the cost of building or installing a permanent ramp to facilitate access would not normally be allowable for tax relief (HMRC, 2005). However, relief would only be forthcoming for the expenditure at the rate of 4 per cent a year under the Industrial Buildings Allowance (IBA) or the Agricultural Buildings Allowance (ABA) if the work was to be carried out on an industrial or agricultural building.

A similar situation has also arisen when it comes to adjustment of toilets and washing facilities. The costs of making building alterations to widen doorways to facilitate wheelchair access, for instance, have not been allowable for tax purposes if the building being altered is a commercial building, such as a shop or office. But in the case of an industrial or agricultural building, the alteration costs would have qualified for IBA or ABA capital allowances at 4 per cent a year. That said, the costs of minor adjustments, such as changing doors on cubicles from opening inwards to opening outwards, have been wholly deductible for tax purposes. In addition, the cost of any new sanitary ware has qualified for Plant and Machinery Capital Allowances (PMAs), and the costs of altering the premises, which are 'incidental' to the installation of that sanitary ware, have also qualified for allowances at the plant and machinery rate of 40 per cent of the up-front cost of the items in the year when the expenditure is incurred. Likewise, the costs of permanent signs in toilets and elsewhere, the replacement of handrails and the installation of new, or the replacement of old, lifts would also qualify for PMAs (HMRC, 2005, p 23).

No matter which way you look at it, however, full reimbursement for premises and machinery adaptation is not forthcoming. Only a percentage is made available and set against this background, favourable tax incentives have not provided enough motivation for some employers to make alterations; nor has the 'light touch' approach to regulatory control epitomised by the debate about what is 'reasonable'. Yet no analysis of the impact of policy on disabled people would be complete without a more in-depth discussion of the inherent tensions, contradictions and dynamics of capitalism embodied in the laissez-faire principles so beloved by all governments of whatever hue from 1979 onwards.

A careful analysis of policy discourses would suggest that disabled people fluctuate between being cast as 'victims and villains' at any given historical moment (Brown, 1984). The exact determination as to whether disabled people are one or the other of these very disparate and contradictory discourses depends on the wider intersection of the health of the UK economy coupled with the political ideologies that compete to frame these problems. At times disabled people are referred to as the 'missing million', as wasted lives, the forgotten (Stanley and Regan, 2003; DWP, 2007a, 2010a), clearly ideas that point the finger at broader economics shifts, for example, deindustrialisation. At other times disabled people and those deemed marginal to the disability category are demonised as the authors of their own exclusion (Johnson, 2005). The question as to whether harsh stories about disabled 'scroungers' and 'malingerers' can set the scene for greater employment of people with impairments and health conditions is a moot one, however.

Disability and a return to laissez-faire policies?

In the discussions presented so far, this chapter has demonstrated that New Labour, like the Major government before 1997, largely encouraged disabled people to take existing employment opportunities. In so doing, New Labour embarked on a path that embraced a mixture of laissez-faire economics, cherry-picking employment schemes and victim blaming in a way which previous Labour governments would find unrecognisable. Arguably, the approach failed to significantly improve the lives of disabled people. Critics pointed to the 'supply-side fundamentalism' (Peck and Theodore, 2000) that underpinned New Labour's view of economic dependency, a view that focused 'on improving access to "existing" employment opportunities rather than addressing the nature of available employment' (Hyde, 2000, p 338). To echo Craig's (2004) words cited earlier, 'getting by' on low wages is not enough for disabled people to promote their own social well-being. By way of further elaboration, Grover and Piggott (2005) and Russell (2002) contend that disabled people are now adding to the swelling ranks of a 'reserve army of labour'.

The shift towards market solutions and a growing distrust in the big state has led the UK government to seek contracting organisations from the private and voluntary sectors for employment support work. These organisations were added to the list of service providers to increase competition and, theoretically, to provide greater choice and improve the quality of provision at the best possible price. Notably, the 2007 consultation on the review of specialist employment support for disabled people (DWP, 2007b) managed to emphasise the importance of Public Service

Agreements (PSAs) alongside a discussion of the possibility of an enhanced role for private and not-for-profit contractors (2007b, p 16). If we take PSAs along with the public sector duty requirement, much of this shifting of delivery of substantive service provision to the private and third sectors goes against the grain of greater public accountability for the government's performance on disability issues. Atos, the major multinational delivering on IB/ESA and DLA medicals for the DWP, have come under unprecedented attack from disabled people, disabled people's organisations and even the Atos employees union, PCS (Public and Commercial Services), over the rigour and objectivity of their operations. Rumours abound as to whether Atos are given targets for benefit reductions, while PCS has publicly stated its members' concerns over the role of bonuses in the payment structures that Atos use (PCS, 2010). Even the British Medical Association have raised their disquiet as to the operations of the fees structures adopted by Atos:

> The Professional Fees Committee has had concerns about the fees paid to sessional doctors undertaking work for the DWP for over thirteen years. During this period, the contractors responsible for delivering medical services to the DWP have consistently refused to enter into fee negotiations with the BMA, despite intense pressure from the Committee and senior representatives from the Association. The concerns of the Committee have also been raised at ministerial level. (BMA, undated)

The risk of 'perverse incentives' in a contracted out system, one very evident in the early days of community care reforms (Griffiths, 1988) and already mired in controversy over issues of fairness and human rights issues, is very real. These risks are not simply that of harsh and inhumane targets to delist numbers of disabled people from ICB/ESA and DLA but equally there is evidence of over-generous allocations to DLA applicants in the run-up to contract renewal, where fear of appeals leads to over-awarding. The case of Dr Gail Young is a case in point. The following report appeared across the print media:

> Dr Young's allegations centre on claims that she was victimised for attempting to highlight practices in which applicants were classified as having higher levels of disability than was the case. The doctor, who was a Sessional Doctor Performance manager at Atos, claimed she attempted to raise concerns about the practices by carrying out studies into applicants with high medical assessment scores, which signified high disability levels.

She claimed the company carried out this practice to ensure that complaints against doctors or reworks (mistakes in applications) were kept to a minimum. Dr Young claimed statistics on complaints and reworks would have been monitored by the Department for Work and Pensions at the same time as Atos was attempting to secure a £500 million seven-year contract, which it subsequently obtained. (*Birmingham Post*, 2008)

Internal government differences obtain over the fine print detail of benefit reform. The following is an excerpt from the House of Commons Select Committee on Work and Pensions' review of Pathways to Work and ICB reforms:

We welcome the Government's laudable aim of reducing the incapacity benefits caseload by one million. However, it will be very challenging to do this by 2016. Success depends very much upon the effort and resources that are invested by the Government, particularly over the next few years.... We are disappointed that the Green Paper did not contain any detail on how the new Personal Capability Assessment will assess those with fluctuating conditions. This is a difficult area on which DWP should consult extensively with stakeholders, including employers, to ensure that those with fluctuating conditions receive the right assessment and do not continue to be excluded from the labour market.... We are not, however, content with the process that we understand the Department has now begun. Disability organisations as well as medical experts must play a key role in advising the Department on the content and delivery of the PCA. (House of Commons Select Committee on Work and Pensions, 2006)

Crucially, private contractors are already responsible for the assessment of eligibility for these services and there is real disquiet over the role of the private sector in assessing just who is disabled. It is quite conceivable that assessment, eligibility and service delivery begin to be operated by the same companies searching for economies of scale. The temptation to cut corners and cherry-pick based on biased interventions that create the best market return rather than, for example, acts that challenge the most engrained workless positions furthest from the labour market, are very real. If the private and not-for-profit sectors are to play an increasing part in everything from initial assessment of disability, work capability, employment placement and benefits entitlement, one has to ask where the countervailing checks and balances to ensure humane, equitable, accessible and consistent service interventions are taking place (DWP, 2007b). Indeed, the private sector is not known for its central attachment to social values over increased margins. This is a key explanation as to why there are too few contractors from the private sector entering, for instance, the residential care market, since margins are so low. Markets fail when it comes to providing for those with little or no marketable income and wealth. This is clear if one views any of the 'sink estates' across Britain. Grover and Piggott (2005) assert that a potential employer seeking employees generally looks for the best person available at the cheapest possible price in order to maintain a competitive edge in the laissez-faire market. The evidence is more nuanced, in the sense that a small number of disabled people are in relatively secure and high status jobs (Roulstone and Barnes, 2005; Shah, 2005; Berthoud, 2006). However, we know that disabled people are more likely to be outside of paid work (Labour Force Survey, 2008) and when in work, to be concentrated disproportionately in lower paid work (Burchardt, 2000, 2005; Berthoud, 2006).

In this sense, we can sustain the view that disabled people are generally disadvantaged in the labour market, while those with limited education capital, poor health and erratic employment records may be viewed as a reserve of labour. Cheaper labour allows for competitive pricing of goods and services or greater profit margins, whichever is appropriate within the existing market conditions, especially where companies are competing on price. Either way, cheaper labour is essential. Beyond the confines of employers and employees, Grover and Piggott (2005) also argue that the state has the duty of ensuring that there is a greater supply of labour competing for employment. It is this pool of labour that gives potential employers a greater choice. Moreover, when the supply of potential labour begins to outnumber the availability of employment opportunities, downward pressure is placed on wage levels as employers have greater choice and control over the costs of labour. When the labour markets tighten, however, the supply of a ready and competitive 'reserve army of labour' for employers to choose from diminishes. At this point, the state, in accordance with the demands of capital, has to 'consider disabled people as workers if it is to maintain profitability through paying the cheapest possible wages' (Grover and Piggott, 2005, p 711). And it was this consideration that New Labour opted for with its welfare-to-work and NDDP strategies (see **Box 5.2** for a further insight into New Labour's position).

Box 5.2: New Labour, welfare-to-work and the market

... the Government is targeting groups of people who are at risk of becoming detached from the labour market. Long periods of dependence on benefits are deeply damaging for individuals.... They are also *costly in economic terms....* If more people can be helped back into the labour market, we can increase the numbers who are in a position to *compete for the job opportunities that exist.* That means that the economy can grow more rapidly *without running into skills shortages and wage inflation.* In other words, the welfare to work programme ... [of which the NDDP is an integral part] can help raise the sustainable level of employment. (HM Treasury, 1998, para 4.17, cited and adapted from Grover and Piggott, 2005 [emphases added])

This quote underlines the 'reserve army of labour' thesis and New Labour's conscious or sub-conscious adoption of it. Over time, the ramifications of this approach were threefold. The NDDP was part of a concerted welfare-to-work strategy intended to reduce the economic cost of benefits and alleviate the problem of perceived fraudulent claims for ICB in particular.

This approach, said its supporters, brought disabled people closer to the labour market and they would be fully equipped (through the NDDP, its job brokers and 'back to work training schemes') to compete for existing, as opposed to new, state-funded jobs. Third, New Labour concluded that welfare-to-work (which NDDP was part of) would maintain the necessary skills requirement demanded by employers yet, crucially, the availability of this skills 'pool' would prevent a rise in wage costs. As the 'reserve army of labour' thesis indicates, wage costs would not simply be prevented from rising but would, over time, decrease in real terms, and this has particularly devastating consequences for disabled people.

Reassuringly there has been no evidence of wage suppression due to government-sponsored schemes. In part, the National Minimum Wage has seen to that (Schneider et al, 2001). However, most government employment support schemes have not been that effective either. Stafford et al's (2007) long-term evaluation of the NDDP established that 39 per cent of participants (57,000) has progressed into paid work. This seems heartening, yet the scheme is voluntary – the evidence suggests that those volunteering are already closer to the labour market and tend to be younger, fitter candidates with musculo-skeletal impairments. This contrasts greatly with the very low take-up of NDDP and job brokerage by people with mental health problems, those with complex needs, older disabled people and those furthest from the labour market (Stafford et al, 2007).

The extent to which these employments are sustained in nature and long term requires further evidence. As Chapters Eight and Nine make clear, the limited efficacy of a range of employment support programmes is borne out in the continued stock of ICB claimants some 10 years after NDDP was first rolled out. The major study by Grewal et al (2002) emphasised the importance of greater policy and legislative efforts required to fight disability discrimination and disadvantage (see also Williams et al, 2008). The NAO's review of Pathways to Work (NAO, 2010) also made it patently clear that despite the commitment of much funding in the attempt to reduce ICB claimancy, the programme had been woefully limited in placing large numbers of sick and disabled people into paid work. Pathways to Work, a compulsory ICB-related programme for all new claimants (voluntary for existing claimants) had by, 2009, cost £538 million, while the DWP could not assert with any certainty just how many individuals had left ICB due to the programme intervention by 2010. As the NAO pointed out:

> The Department is not able to say precisely what proportion of the 125,000 reduction in incapacity benefits claimants recorded between February 2005 and August 2009 is directly attributable to Pathways. We would expect it to be small, given the relatively recent expansion of Pathways, the Department's estimate of the overall contribution of Pathways to 2015, and our understanding of the impact of Pathways. (NAO, 2010, p 22)

As with the New Deals prior to Pathways to Work, the exact attribution of factors as to why someone leaves benefits and enters paid employment is difficult to disentangle. It seems reasonable to say that beyond pilot programmes, where arguably artificially high levels of per capita funding are pumped into employment support schemes, NDDP and the broader Pathways to Work programme have had limited long-term significance in narrowing the employment gap between disabled and non-disabled people. What the NAO did establish in their audit of Pathways to Work was the relative 'effectiveness' of the compulsory strand of the programme and conversely the limited impact of the voluntary 'Condition Management' and 'Return to Work Credit' are much less effective (NAO, 2010, p 24). The conclusion NAO drew was that the Pathways effect was less attributable to active intervention, as those who moved into paid work would, they argued, have entered anyway due to the negative impact an obligatory interview and early medical assessment may have had on them. This is rather worrying as it seems to offer a technical appraisal with little concern as to whether the assessment and interview are coercive. Nonetheless, the lack of clear impact of any one programme is interesting. While many pilots have proved effective as they provide the intensive labour market support disabled people require to return to or enter paid work (Corden and Thornton, 2002), the broader economic dynamics of the labour market and employment system have arguably been left untouched by the above schemes. Indeed, increased coercion may be seen as the main factor in increasing orientations to paid work, whether or not opportunities actually exist. As stated earlier, New Labour has made disabled people compete against other disabled people and non-disabled individuals for employment in the PLM. This is particularly disturbing in that:

> When competition, individualism, dog-eat-dog capitalism are unchallenged dominant values, cooperation, interdependence and social justice suffer.... Identity groups are competing for "our" piece of a reduced pie, when what we need to do is demand transformation that delivers a bigger pie – one that is big enough for all of us. (Russell, 1998, p 231)

Accordingly, disabled people have at best been left fighting for poorly paid jobs or at worst fighting to prove they are eligible or still eligible for benefits that are subject to constant review and attack. Naturally, of course, the principles of laissez-faire capitalism are not confined to the competition over employment and the conflict between profit and the cost of labour. This is only one side of the coin. The other side relates to consumer choice and the availability/accessibility of that choice. Theoretically, the 'free market' avoids discrimination. It only responds to the needs and wants of the consumer. It avoids arbitrary decision making from so-called experts and professionals. In the words of Sir Keith Joseph, one of the UK's early champions of the 'free market':

> ... the blind, unplanned, uncoordinated wisdom of the market ... is overwhelmingly superior to the well researched, rational, systematic, well meaning, cooperative, science based, forward looking, respectable plans of government. (Joseph, 1976, cited in Lawton, 1992, p 6)

Although this advocacy of the virtues of the market was declared in 1976, the sentiments and stern belief contained within it has persisted to a large extent under the auspices of Conservative and New Labour governments alike and, arguably, will be continued under the embryonic Coalition government elected to power in 2010. Based on notions of choice (read market choice), the conviction that market competition would promote greater efficiency and, as a direct consequence, provide 'value for money' (or the interchangeable term of 'best value'), New Labour continued with the market philosophy, especially in relation to the provision of welfare services. Within this scenario, disabled people were gradually being viewed as consumers of welfare services. The extent to which a welfare consumer model can be applied without inherent contradictions surfacing is a moot point. There are political voices expressing disquiet, but at the time of writing neoliberalism is reaching its apotheosis.

Conclusion

This chapter has explored the growing impact and shape of conditionality in the disability welfare system. Whereas disabled people have, since the Second World War, at least been afforded positive attributes as welfare recipients, despite much continuity between Thatcherism and Blairite policies more generally, the view connecting disability with non-legitimate welfare subjects has changed since 1997 with the accession of the New Labour government. Views on the justification of these major policy shifts depend on one's standpoint – the architects of the ICB/ESA and DLA reforms point to the growth in numbers of disabled people despite there being no general decline in ill health for the wider population. Critics of the reforms highlight the manner in which disabled people were legitimately awarded ICB and DLA benefits, even though they acknowledge that goalposts may have been moved during the Thatcher years to reduce the unemployment count by shifting claimants onto ICBs. This is clearly not the fault of claimants, according to this view. Similarly the clumsy and at times oppressive detail of some aspects of ICB and DLA reduction led some to conclude that subsequent governments are using increasingly inhumane methods to reverse the growth of these benefits.

There is evidence that shifting contract delivery for welfare reform to the private sector may further distort the relationship between official eligibility and objective measures of impairment. Disabled people remain outside of these assessment decisions at both a personal and organisational level. The policy shift to public sector duties, PSAs and equality impact assessments sit badly with the ideological shift to the private sector at all costs. These shifts arguably stereotype the weaknesses of the public sector and overhype the benefits of the private sector. The dynamics of capitalism cannot be ignored on the one hand, while the 'private sector' is valorised on the other. Disability welfare policy bears superficial similarities to the choices and rights and personalisation agenda into which some employment support (for example, Access to Work) sits.

Nonetheless, even a cursory glance at the detail and assumptions of welfare reform creates an image of a major mismatch between the choices offered in the social care system and those in the social welfare system. Disabled people have very little input into even momentous policy shifts in social welfare. The latter is going some way to demonising disabled and sick people and placing them in a position where attitudes run the risk of reverting back to extreme prejudice, in some instances.

Summary

- There is evidence of a clear tendency in UK disability policy to shift the 'disability category' to fit with broader fiscal priorities.
- Disabled people wholly reliant on the welfare system are significantly more likely (regarding adult social care) to experience conditionality and stigma attaching to disability welfare.
- Work-first agendas characterise much of the post-1997 disability policy terrain; there is, however, an absence of symmetry in the rights/ responsibilities binary reaffirmed by New Labour.
- Marketisation has been a key plank of much disability support since 1997.

Questions

1. Why was it felt necessary to instigate more 'searching' welfare regimes and tighten eligibility to disability welfare benefits?
2. What are the likely effects of increased conditionality on disability welfare policy?
3. Who gains from a harsher work-first agenda?
4. Did New Labour welfare policies represent a change to or continuity of neoliberal ideology?

Further reading

A good overview of the Thatcherite changes to disability policy are contained in **Drake (1999)**. New Labour welfare and disability reforms are well covered in **Grover and Piggott's** many articles; see also **Roulstone (2000)**, **Prideaux (2005)**, and on wider New Labour reforms, see any of **Powell**'s edited collections and **Levitas (1998)** on New Labour ideology. If you are interested in Murray's formulations of the underclass and policy writers' responses, see **Murray (1996)**.

six

Supporting disabled adults: new paradigms or new paternalism?

This chapter explores policy developments for those disabled people who generally sat more squarely within the remit of 'deserving' of 'social care' support from local statutory services throughout the period of the New Labour government (1997-2009). It is worth noting, however, that for the first time since the post–1944 welfare settlement, some disabled people formerly supported by social care may, due to changes in eligibility, now be entirely reliant on more stigmatised social welfare for the first time.

Even so, since the late 1990s there has been significant, some would say momentous, developments around service philosophies (DH, 1998), relationships and experiences for some disabled people (Prideaux et al, 2009). The development of the Disability Discrimination Act (DDA) in 1995 also added to the sense that disabled people were to be treated as fully fledged citizens in this new dawn of legal and social entitlements (Gooding, 1995). It is also painfully clear that some of these very important gains have been at the expense of a tightening of the criteria for just who qualifies for social 'care' support (Clements, 2008). It is also worth pointing out that although this chapter is largely about social care rather than social welfare, disabled people in receipt of social care services will also often be reliant on forms of social welfare embodied in, for example, the Disability Living Allowance (DLA) which has, over the last 10 years, been a crucial source of added welfare conditionality and critical public scrutiny (Roulstone, 2000). Also important is a critical reflection on the broader implications of what are increasingly dubbed self-directed approaches to adult social care. Self-direction does, at some levels, parallel forms of activation in social welfare policy around incapacity and worklessness (Ladyman, 2004), the key difference being that activation and self-direction within the welfare arena are inherently urgent, conditional and stigmatised.

Moreover, in the social care arena, there is a more gradual sense that greater self-direction might occur over the longer term and be supported by advocacy and brokerage services. These differences are reflected in the fact that social care reforms have been built on wholesale consultations and recently policy co-production of policy change (DH, 2005; SCIE, 2009), whereas the arena of social welfare has been largely hermetic and departmentally driven with little or co-production elements (Roulstone and Barnes, 2005). This chapter looks at the key policy shifts and ambitions around modernised social care, while also looking briefly at other key areas of policy that support or hinder independent lives in the built environment, for example, community safety and transport.

Modernised adult social care: personalisation and self-directed support

Self-directed support and personalisation as a new means of public service delivery, despite being a new policy, is not actually a new idea. Arguably, the underlying principles of community care are to support greater personal community-based choice and to protect a policy that has been in place for almost 20 years. However, what is different about the current thrust towards personalisation (see ***Box 6.1***) is the determination to embrace so many of the tenets of independent living that have been at the heart of the disability movement campaigns for so long. The following captures the English Department of Health's construction of personalisation.

Box 6.1: Personalisation: a Department of Health perspective

To make this happen the sector needs a shared vision. The direction is clear: to make personalisation, including a strategic shift towards early intervention and prevention, the cornerstone of public services. In social care, this means every person across the spectrum of need, having choice and control over the shape of his or her support, in the most appropriate setting. For some, exercising choice and control will require a significant level of assistance either through professionals or through independent advocates. (DH, 2008a)

Likewise, self-direction in British disability policy did not begin with direct payments, but is best epitomised in that form. The closure of long-stay institutions was, of course, an important precursor in symbolising the end of the least self-directed forms of 'care'. The shift to person-centred practice and planning embodied in *Valuing People* (DH, 2001c) provided a key impetus towards disabled people having greater self-determination in their lives. *Valuing People* was about a philosophical change in social and professional attitudes towards people with learning disabilities, while also keen to encourage joined-up practices in assessing, planning, delivering and monitoring support towards greater choices and independence (Burton and Kagan, 2006).

Valuing People first applied the key principles of personalisation in the form of person-centred planning (PCP). For the first time, it placed disabled people's needs at the centre of policy and practice attention (DH, 2001c). The potency of choice, control over one's daily life and carefully personalised solutions and options was a new development. Clearly this could not happen without the active input of disabled people, which was facilitated in part by the development of Learning Disability Partnership Boards, where area-based planning of services and joined-up professional thinking was seen to connect with the voices of people with learning disabilities. It is noteworthy that such developments were impairment-specific and reflected the perceived urgency of providing greater choice for disabled people who have traditionally faced the greatest barriers to independent lives (Grant and Ramcharan, quoted in Grant et al, 2005, p 617). Equally important was a shift towards recognising that outcomes of this personalised choice making were the key measure of policy change (Netten et al, 2009); after all, why make major structural changes if disabled people would not feel any tangible changes in their lives? This is significant as the risk of a gap forming between policy rhetoric and reality is very real, especially where the choice horizons of disabled people outstrip available professional visions for independent lives (see Roulstone and Morgan, 2009).

The need to involve all disabled people, including those with complex physical needs, is very important, with recent evidence that this 'group' has not benefited as fully to date from PCP (Black, 2000). At a strategic management level, the statutory requirement for health and social care authorities to plan through a Joint Strategic Needs Assessment has also not been that effective for disabled people with complex needs that substantially straddle primary care trust (PCT) and local authority social services (CSCI and Health Care Commission, 2009). The Commission for Social Care Inspection (CSCI) and Health Care Commission (HCC) report noted that:

> Councils and trusts also had underdeveloped strategies for commissioning services for this group, while only a minority of service users had a person-centred plan, and in many of these cases the plans were poor. (cited in *Community Care*, 19 March 2009)

At the time of writing, PCTs are being phased out, and discussion in the new Coalition government hinges on a range of healthcare professions in both primary and hospital care taking a fuller role in commissioning services.

Direct payments, on the other hand, were conceived of by the outgoing Conservative administration and enshrined in the Community Care (Direct Payments) Act of 1996 (HM Government, 1996b) that was rolled out by the New Labour government in 1997 (Pearson, 2004). Direct payments were, in part, the government's response to pressure from wider disabled people's organisations, their push for greater self-determination and control over their support, social and environmental needs (Barnes and Mercer, 2006). It is important to note that unlike *Valuing People*, direct payments were seen from the outset as a pan-impairment development. Direct payments, as the name suggests, were to be payments that, once needs were assessed, would be made directly to a disabled person with no uninvited professional direction as to how the payment or should be spent. So, what were previously seen purely in terms of care packages assessed and provided by social service professionals were now only cash transfers that fundamentally altered the role of social services staff in the provision of funded support (Hasler et al, 1999). Direct payments are means tested and provided in lieu of directly commissioned services, and designed to give disabled people and their families the means to buy in support and thus have greater control over their lives (Glendinning et al, 2000; Woodin, 2006). There is also evidence that some cash for care schemes proved less costly than their directly provided equivalent (O'Neal and Lewis, 2001; Leadbeater et al, 2008). There are, however, a few studies that contest this claim, where direct payments were introduced in a haphazard or unsupported manner (Audit Commission, 2006).

The major benefits of direct payments was seen to be the freedom afforded to disabled people to use the money in the best way they saw fit in meeting their support needs, the ability to connect their own solutions and to take control of their lives in a way that best suited their needs and wider life choices (Pearson, 2004). Cash for care or self-directed solutions to disabled people's support are also recognised in many country contexts across the globe (Ungerson and Yeandle, 2007). Direct payments also squared well with government emphasis over the previous 15 years with respect to less dependency on professional decision making and a more direct relationship between disabled people and the newly pluralised markets in care/support (Ladyman, 2004). April 2001 saw direct payments being extended to 'carers', parents of disabled children and to younger (aged 16-17) service users. Availability was also extended to people with short-term needs, like those recovering from an operation, and to

Children Act services to help disabled parents with their disabled children's support requirements (HM Government, 2000b). Young people were seen to benefit most greatly compared to older disabled people (Glasby and Littlechild, 2002; Woodin, 2006; DH, 2007). Direct payments were also seen to offer social citizenship because of their transcendence over the paternalist assumption that receiving services confirmed a disabled person to be below the presumed norms of social contributions and engagement that earn people citizenship status, as per Marshall's class formulation. As Rummery rightly pointed out:

> This enhanced sense of control over the quality, timing and delivery of a service mean that direct payments users have found that they are more able on the one hand to enjoy the benefits of citizenship by sharing "in the full social heritage and to live the civilised life according to the standards prevailing in society", as Marshall would recognise, and on the other hand to carry out their citizenship duties and participate in society in a way which enabled them to "live the life of a good citizen, giving such service as can promote the welfare of the community". Direct payments enable disabled people to enjoy the rights of citizenship while fulfilling their duties. (Rummery, 2006, p 643)

This is helpful, and in valuing and valorising the contributions of disabled people outside of the productivist domain of paid work this affords the recognition of a valued role in the private and familial sphere. This does not, of course, confront the barriers to citizenship in the public domain of work and community any further, but it does question where the boundaries for measuring citizenship should lie. A key shift in the move to direct payments, one so far not widely acknowledged (Cree, 2010), is that disabled people who use direct payments to employ personal assistants are essentially challenging the assumed binary between welfare/work in much policy thinking. Historically those claiming substantial social care support were assumed not to be working. Not only are some disabled people using direct payments to facilitate their own paid work, but some are acting as employers. The latter is about as far away from the image of welfare recipients as it is possible to be. However, this insight has not permeated government quarters, as the following quotation attests:

> In policy terms, it is remarkable that despite notions of "independent living" underpinning state funded, self operated support, the "independence" of disabled people is not freed from the wider policy discourses of welfare dependency.

> In this respect, it is noteworthy that direct payments and individual budgets continue to emanate primarily from the UK Government's Department of Health rather than the Department for Work and Pensions and/or the Department for Business, Enterprise and Regulatory Reform (BERR). (Prideaux et al, 2009, pp 558-9)

This placement of direct payments within the aegis of the Department of Health fails to understand the changing 'social relations of care' at the heart of direct payments, and:

> In explicitly acknowledging the true economic costs and benefits of self operated support systems use ... [the] aim is to challenge the traditional, "welfarist" assumptions that characterise disabled people using these schemes as "benefit claimants". The other challenge is to place the analytical framework of user controlled services into a more appropriate theoretical, economic and policy context. Indeed a new language of "social entrepreneurs" or "active citizens" should be applied to those disabled people who employ PAs. (Prideaux et al, 2009, p 563)

One disappointing aspect of the early application of direct payments was the low take-up of these payments, with predictive factors hinging on often unacknowledged policy mediating factors such as the political profile of the local authority, the presence or absence of a local Centre for Inclusive/ Integrated Living (CIL) and fears over job losses that might ensue if direct payments were introduced (Riddell et al, 2006). Recent surveys of direct payments also point to the preponderance of certain forms of impairment groups benefiting most fully from the shift to direct payments:

> Direct payments were found to be provided most commonly to people with a physical disability or sensory impairment, compared to other groups, and least commonly to people with a mental health problem, but there was considerable variation across local authorities, underlining how some local authorities have risen to the challenge of implementing user-centred care through direct payments while others lag behind ... 15.5% of the budgets of English authorities for people with a physical disability was spent on direct payments, compared to 1.1% for people with a learning disability, 0.8% for older people and 0.4% for people with a mental health problem. (Davey et al, 2006, p 1)

In this respect, a key development that has aided the roll-out of direct payments has been the continued growth of CILs. While the first of these was formed in the 1980s, the recent action by the cross-governmental Office for Disability Issues (ODI) to foster user-led organisations (ULOs) (DH, 2008b) has helped encourage further developments that could support disabled people to manage their direct payments. Detracting from the value and virtue of these changes are the reported major struggles of CILs and now ULOs as to how they manage their own finances with the current cutbacks in statutory funding to local support centres (NCIL, 2008). There is a very real challenge in policy terms to sustain the development of self-directed support approaches while averting a crisis of funding that would place a more comprehensive implementation of self-directed support in jeopardy. Previous shifts to rationing social care in charges for domiciliary support (DH, 2002; Ahmed, 2008) and for adult Disabled Facilities Grant (Care & Repair, 2007) do not augur well for a growth in funded self-directed support, particularly given the recent proposed severe cuts in public spending where health spending was protected, but social care was not (HM Treasury, 2010).

Recognition of the lower than anticipated uptake of direct payments and the legislative reform of social care delivery models going back to the NHS and Community Care Act 1990 (HM Government, 1990) provided impetus to further shifts towards self-directed support. The *Modernising social services* White Paper of 1998 (DH, 1998) was an early statement of New Labour's intent to place disabled people at the centre of decision making in adult social care, and to go beyond the paternalist assumption that receiving social care support equalled social dependency and helplessness. Independence was a recurrent term that featured in the White Paper and chimed with third way constructions of rights and responsibilities (Giddens, 1998; Powell, 2002). Two further policy documents were compiled within these contexts during the lifetime of the New Labour governments. The first was the 2005 Green Paper entitled *Independence, wellbeing and choice* (DH, 2005), while the second, published the following year, was the 2006 White Paper *Our health, our care, our say* (DH, 2006). Both policy documents began to solidify the spirit of earlier changes in adult social care by fostering personalised choices and the requirement for professionals to connect their work while placing disabled people at the centre of the decision-making process. *Independence, wellbeing and choice* highlighted the benefits of wider take-up of direct payments and the need to look further at joined-up commissioning and provision of support. Again this exhortation stems from earlier precursors in the NHS and Community Care Act 1990, Section 31 of the Health Act 1999 (HM Government, 1999b) through to *Valuing People*, and was captured neatly in the following quote:

> A strong strategic and leadership role for local government, working in partnership with other agencies, particularly the NHS, to ensure a wide development of new and exciting models of service delivery and harnessing technology to deliver the right outcomes for adult social care. (DH, 2005, p 14)

Independence, wellbeing and choice (DH, 2005), alongside *Our health, our care, our say* (DH, 2006), made clear that it was about more than simply 'care' and that policy makers had framed the document to best foster an expansive way of thinking about independence to include disabled people's 'health, quality of life, economic well-being, support for disabled people in making a positive contribution, to exercise choice and control, to be free from discrimination and harassment and to have personal dignity' (DH, 2005, p 10). The document continued the thread of health and social care policy since 1990 in emphasising the mixed economy of support and the need to coordinate provision based on existing services:

> Not all of the costs of offering wider and more flexible packages fall within social services department budgets. We want to encourage a more flexible approach to putting together packages using the wider resources of the community. A package could include a mixture of more traditional social care items, use of universal services already provided by the local authority, and a contribution from the local voluntary and community sector. (DH, 2005, p 39)

These were clearly well intended and linked to the long voiced concern that disabled people's services were seen in isolation (Davis, 1998); and the assumption that unused community resource could be tapped into. Rather like the NHS and Community Care Act some 16 years before, there was a real risk that community resources were 'imagined' rather than real and substantive (Bornat et al, 1997). There were also challenges for local statutory organisations where they worked increasingly with the voluntary sector in facilitating services. *Independence, wellbeing and choice* and *Our health, our care, our say* (DH, 2005, 2006) also made great play of the role of preventative strategies among agencies. The emphasis on prevention perhaps sat oddly in a policy document that was primarily concerned with independence in its fullest sense. However, the 2005 paper aimed to embrace the circumstances of a very diverse population of disabled people. Specifically it aimed to avoid unnecessary hospitalisation for some older disabled people as a result of, for example, falls or dementia-related crises. As the Department of Health stipulated:

> Social care services can also help to prevent inappropriate use of specialist healthcare. For example, too many older people are admitted to hospital, often as an emergency, when this could be avoided if the right community services were in place. (DH, 2005, p 46)

Similarly, the White Paper commented that:

> Prevention begins by building good health and a healthy lifestyle from the beginning of an individual's life. We are strengthening the provision of antenatal, postnatal and health and early years services, including through our proposals for the new NHS "Life Check". (DH, 2006, p 46)

Clearly we need to remain alert to the potential for disempowering assumptions being made in otherwise progressive documents where it is perhaps misapplied, as many disabled people who might have benefited from the independence and choice facets of the White Paper may have felt that words like 'prevention' and 'well-being' were inappropriate or that they resonated with past medical constructions of disability. The *Putting people first* document seemed to follow in this medically-led vein, despite claiming to be first and foremost about 'putting people first' (DH, 2007). It is worth reflecting that disabled people are often heard to say they want choice and independence and that it could one day be within their control. The same has not been said about well-being, arguably because it is the result of complex social processes that are, in part at least, beyond the control of the individual. Indeed even a cursory glance at the use of the term 'preventive' in official documents has the word 'contextualised' most commonly alongside illness narratives and secondary healthcare. It might be argued that the White Paper was trying to achieve a too differentiated set of ideas and over-reached itself. A more critical interpretation is one that is borne out by the wording of the White Paper itself. Hospitalisation is linked to a lack of independence while independence and well-being are integrally linked (DH, 2005, p 39). This seems to misunderstand the relationship between disability, impairment and illness (Roulstone and Warren, 2006) as hospitalisation can be due to neglect, sudden illness, poor services and so on, and a more self-directed social care framework has to accommodate these nuances to avoid victim blaming.

In practical terms the advent of *Independence, wellbeing and choice* (DH, 2005) required professionals working in health and social care, work, training and education to identify a range of proactive approaches from preventive strategies through to multi-disciplinary protocols for supporting people with more complex needs. For example, they needed to think in terms of options for short-term respite, intermediate care and lifetime homes which were pitched at differentiated assessed levels of need. At senior levels, the Green Paper required the use of Local Area Agreements and joint commissioning and budgetary protocols that both offered joint working while placing disabled people as close to the centre of decision making as possible.

Fair Access to Care Services and *Putting people first*: rhetoric and reality

A policy analysis of reforms in adult social care might suggest that by 2005 everything was falling into place and new visions for adult social care being realised. In fact the reality with such policies in the 1990s and 2000s was one of grander ambitions set alongside increasingly limited funding. This dilemma had characterised disability policy for many decades and helped limit the effectiveness of policy, most notably the Chronically Sick and Disabled Persons Act 1970 (HM Government, 1970b) and the Education Act 1981 (HM Government, 1981), where funding limits arguably undermined key features of planned policy change. Disillusion among some disabled people and their families was perhaps inevitable. Alas the same is also proving true of adult social care. There is a risk of an increasingly Orwellian one-dimensional language of self-direction over time to increasingly equate to self-management and reliance in the face of severe funding shortages and critical discourses on the cost of disabled people's services (Ferguson, 2008; Roulstone and Morgan, 2009). It is imperative that uncritical use of terms such as choice, control and self-direction are not applied where large numbers of previously eligible disabled people find they are suddenly not part of a population who are eligible to make any choices, however meagre.

The *Fair Access to Care Services* guidance issued by the Department of Health in 2002 (DH, 2002) laid out the need for local authorities to be fair in their assessment and allocation of support for disabled people. The guidance followed the logic of the earlier White Paper *Modernising social services* (DH, 1998) in drawing on Section 47 of the NHS and Community Care Act 1990 that provided substantive access to social care provision. The guidance was underpinned by fiscal optimism, the projection of increased annual funding from 2003 of 6 per cent (that is, an above-inflation settlement). It laid out the need to assess and provide consistently and openly, while acknowledging the likely diversity of certain local conditions (population density, economic profile). In this respect, it noted that:

On a related point, it is not the intention of the Department of Health that individuals with similar needs receive similar services up and down the country. This is because, although all councils should use the same eligibility framework to set their local criteria, the different budgetary decisions of individual councils will mean that some councils will be able to provide services to proportionately more adults seeking help than others. (DH, 2002, p 3)

It is clear that since the publication of the *Fair Access to Care Services* guidance, the above optimism was misplaced. Official recognition was made that severe forms of prioritisation of those in the two highest bands of assessed need (substantial and critical) had taken place since 2002 but there was an admission that some disabled people had been reassigned to lower categories of need. The figures for the number of older people receiving social care support was illustrative of this, with a 26,000 decline in the absolute numbers of over-75s receiving care between March 2003 and March 2006 (Clements, 2008; CSCI, 2008). This shifting of the disability category is a feature of the history of disability policy, especially at times of fiscal crises (Stone, 1984; Roulstone and Barnes, 2005). What was new was that this was being done under the banner of fair access, a linguistic paradox in social care terms. The evidence came to light in a rather embarrassing report for the UK government which revealed:

There is evidence that in recent years, financial pressures have influenced local authorities to shift their focus towards those groups with the highest needs.... Many councils have raised the level of their eligibility threshold, leading to concerns that some people who ought to be receiving support are now being ruled as ineligible. This is despite evidence indicating that limiting access through raising eligibility criteria has only a modest and short-term effect on expenditure. (CSCI, 2008, p 15)

The issue of prioritisation of support was also a key feature of the recent guidance *Putting people first: A whole system approach to eligibility for social care* (DH, 2010a). Interestingly the guidance (see **Box 6.2**) emphasises yet further the way to square scarce resources with disabled people's growing ambitions of choices and rights.

> **Box 6.2: *Putting people first*: intelligent service use or passing the buck?**
>
> - Fullest use of universal services.
> - The use of the wider community in preventing the need for social care.
> - Signposting of benefits and community support.
> - Promoting access to employment.

The following summed up the vision distilled from the *Putting people first* document. A critic might easily argue that the document could have been retitled: *Putting savings first: Externalising the risks of adult social care*. Indeed:

> Before setting eligibility criteria for social care, councils should consider their strategy for investing in a more universal approach, which prevents or delays the need for more specialist social care interventions. Low cost interventions may also have considerable impact on day-to-day quality of life. This could include signposting people to information relating to benefits they may be entitled to or community support groups. Councils should also consider the potential of low-level services in helping carers, of any age, to have a life outside of caring. All of these interventions can support people to maintain their independence and wellbeing and reduce or delay the need for more targeted social care interventions ... [other low/no cost options include] luncheon clubs or befriending; healthy living advice and support; employment advice and support, physical recreation and leisure pursuits; community safety; housing support and transport. Only a minority of these universal services will be funded through social care and many will be reliant on a community-base.... (DH, 2007, p 13)

A more positive interpretation, however, would note that alongside the above policy imperatives mandated in *Putting people first* (DH, 2007), the initiative also laid a duty on local authorities to 'significantly increase' the number of recipients of direct payments and personal budgets. Certainly, personal budgets – that is, budgets that have at least some element of direct payment – were seen as the baseline from which local authorities should build and signal an end to previous models of support. The initiative claimed the first co-produced policy on adult social care and made great play of the need to jointly organise assessments in a way that supported seamless services across health and social care.

Changing day services

Another key challenge in putting disabled people first was the need to review the nature and function of day services for disabled adults. Day services had traditionally been seen as a dependency-creating form of adult social care. Barnes' (1990) study of day centres pointed to the benign but passive character of these centres by situating them within 'warehousing' or 'horticultural' contexts in which disabled people rarely developed or moved on. The reform of day services goes back to the 1971 White Paper *Better services for the mentally handicapped* (DHSS, 1971). It was stressed that although numerous centres were avowedly vocational or rehabilitative, the reality for many was that day centres and also adult training centres (ATCs) were not helping the majority of disabled people to progress. In reality, day centre attendees were broadly seen as those unable to enter mainstream or sheltered employment (usually operating within minimum productivity assumptions of 30 per cent 'normal' outputs). As Powell (1996) neatly summarised, the White Paper made little difference to the lives of attendees as the true reasons for day attendance were complex, and employment seemed the respectable but largely unconvincing rationale for such centres. Without doubt:

> ... part of the heritage of the 1971 Better Services White Paper included day centres falling short of the known aspirations of adults with learning difficulties and tending to operate a narrow range of programmes on a part-time basis, leaving many with too much unstructured time.... (Powell and Flynn, quoted in Grant et al, 2005, p 402)

Day centre literatures have often concentrated on working-age people with learning disabilities. Nonetheless, it is important to note that people with physical and sensory impairment have also featured as large day centre populations, some sharing space with older (disabled and non-disabled) people. The common denominator seems to be that these groups are out of the run of mainstream life, while the personalisation and choice agendas are beginning to challenge the nature and rationale of day services that seem to sit awkwardly in an era of mainstreaming. One local authority recently announced the closure of its day centres as part of its modernisation programme and shift to personalisation (Dunning, 2010). A review of day activities for people with learning disabilities by the Social Care Institute for Excellence (SCIE) (2006) (see **Box 6.3**), entitled *'Having a good day?'*, established the following as characteristic of good days:

> ## Box 6.3: Changing days? SCIE tenets of good day services
>
> - Doing things that have a purpose.
> - Being in ordinary places.
> - Doing things that others would be doing.
> - Doing things that are right for you.
> - Receiving support that meets your needs.
> - Being in touch with local people, meeting people.
> - Developing friendships. (SCIE, 2006, p 2)

The findings of this review were mixed; there were good examples of community-based projects and support which afforded voluntary work, paid employment and recreation. The best projects were generally recipients of short-term 'soft'-funding. Services for people with the highest needs were scarce, which may have reminded local authorities that often there were no 'markets' for people with higher needs, which was a sobering idea that counselled against rapid day centre closure and the assumption that communities would provide. There were, however, greater reappraisals of how disabled people spent their days and used disability benefits for more flexible travel use. The extent to which disabled people could avail themselves of community activities (for example, the number of days per week) and any shift of responsibilities back onto families was unclear from this review.

Recent reflections from critical adult social care researchers points up the challenge of meaningful choice by asking: just what are communities? Can choices continue to include day service provision in day centres, community centres or resource centres where disabled people so choose? In other words, disabled people need to make choices and under conditions of their own choosing, rather than a fixed range of 'choices' being made available (Marcuse, 1964). Choices also need to be supported throughout the process of decision making, given how new concepts and options might feel. Choices have to be presented accurately and in good faith. The dilemma at the heart of choice is that disabled people's choices may not accord with more critical conceptions of 'mainstreamed' community lives. Indeed research by Roulstone and Morgan (2009) begged questions around individualism and collectivism in day services. While fully committed to the choices and rights agenda, their research, in what might be described as a 'critical realist' framework, established that many disabled people using current day centre services saw those as their communities. It could rightly be argued that people can only 'know what they know' based on their social horizons at that point.

Crossing provider boundaries

The shift towards joint provisioning has also been evident in key health policy documents. The Darzi Report, a major review of health policy in the New Labour era, argued forcefully for much greater joined-up working across health and social care functions (DH, 2008c). Alongside more seamless working, the report also referred to the value of greater reliance on self-assessment among service users. This was an exciting shift but one that was not without policy challenges, given the potentially conflicting personal and official constructions of needs, wants and rights in an assessment context (DH, 2007, p 1). Certainly there is much anecdotal evidence that self-assessments are currently 'moderated' by professionals, while the question of how we can square often very different personal constructions of need with social equity, for example, as laid out in *Fair Access to Care Services*, is a moot point. We need to ensure that such moderation is motivated entirely by equity concerns as opposed to developing cultures of constraint which limit assessed support as custom and practice. The latter would clearly conflict with personalised support principles. Both of these issues are central to progressive assessment regimes, otherwise care access is subject to levels of power, knowledge and articulacy of service users and professionals.

Individual budgets

Perhaps the most far-reaching policy experiment to date has been the shift in piloting of individual budgets (IBs). Such developments acknowledge that disabled people's needs are not, as far as they are concerned, separate in the way that service providers and care managers might traditionally have assumed. Notably IBs are not sanctioned by new legislation but are a policy reinterpretation of duties laid on local authorities under the NHS Community Care Act 1990 and Chronically Sick and Disabled Persons Act 1970. The IB pilots were given policy momentum by overt support in the 2005 Prime Minister's Strategy Unit report on the life chances of disabled people (PMSU, 2005). Relatedly, it is not unusual for disabled people with complex needs to have a plethora of different assessments for a variety of resources from a range of separate professionals (Finkelstein quoted in Swain et al, 2004). Assessment, then, has been needlessly repetitive and time consuming, while service provision has often been fragmented. IBs reflect the personalisation agenda in placing disabled people at the heart of the service delivery process, while a focus on outcomes as opposed to inputs should hopefully lead to more responsive services in the longer term (DH,

2009a). The period 2005-07 witnessed the piloting of IBs in 13 social service contexts across England. For the first time attempts were made to integrate the activities of health, social care and work-related assessments, cash transactions and wider service delivery. In this respect, an IB pilot report recommended that:

- The pilot projects should test opportunities for integrating resources from several different funding streams into a single IB.
- The multiple assessment processes and eligibility criteria should be simplified and integrated or aligned, although adult social care should be the gateway to an IB.
- Merged and simplified assessment and eligibility approaches. However social care organisations remained the proposed gateway for accessing IBs during the pilot phase.
- Support should be available to help individuals plan how to use their IBs. Additionally, brokerage support should provide individuals with information on the costs and availability of different service options. (Glendinning et al, 2008)

In addition to social care budgets, IBs can include social care needs where adaptations to premises are required, something that is currently separately funded in the Disabled Facilities Grant and Integrated Community Equipment Service (ICES), and also day service options from *Supporting People* and the Independent Living Fund (ILF). Most daringly, IBs allow in principle the assessment for work-based support that has its incarnation as the Access to Work scheme. The latter is provided with an employer's approval and with a proportionate contribution made by employers after a disabled person has been in work for at least six weeks. Not only are we talking here of different funding streams, but also of very different application methods. At the level of central government, the symbolic transcendence of formerly very much separate funding is evident across the Department of Health (ICES), Department for Work and Pensions (DWP) (Access to Work, ILF) and the Department for Communities and Local Government (CLG) (*Supporting People* and Disabled Facilities Grant). From the outset, the ILF was designed to support disabled people (18,000 in 2010) via cash transfers that could be spent on a wide array of social goods including leisure services. In this sense the ILF has always been more expansive in its remit than traditional social care transfers, including direct payments. What the above points to is the significant diversity of approaches to the use of each traditional funding stream. The challenges have been very real from the outset. The pilots, however, established some success in being able to draw previously disparate funding streams together for the benefit of a few disabled people, while outcomes were seen to be better, according to self-reports from disabled people (Glendinning et al, 2008). That said, there remain a number of challenges. As the following quote from the pilots report made clear:

> Early experiences with aligning funding streams prompted a number of concerns. These included how to disaggregate social care resources from jointly-funded services (such as ICES), the exclusion of NHS continuing care systems from IBs, and aligning Access to Work eligibility criteria with those for adult social care. Major changes in care co-ordinators (front-line staff, often known as care managers in some sites) activities and processes were anticipated, as were needs for new accountability and risk-management processes. (Glendinning et al, 2008)

There are other concerns attached to IBs. The deliberate aim of targeting certain individuals that might be more favourable to IB use can be seen to distort the pilot and perhaps overestimate the potential for take-up. As the quote above suggested, budgetary alignment is a continued challenge; indeed health budgets and professional cultures have proven difficult to penetrate at times (see **Box 6.4**). There are also concerns that IB expansion might encroach on the numbers deemed eligible for support; this has led to some suspicion among some disabled people. There are voices which suggest IBs may not be as widely disseminated and available as once envisaged (Samuel, 2009). Nevertheless, it could be predicted that the principle of merged budgets is likely to be a feature in future social care roll-outs, whether or not they are working in practice.

Box 6.4: The challenge of merged budgeting

- The combination of needs and means-tested systems in the English context that make for an overly complex approach.
- The impairment-specific challenges – the internationally greater take-up rates have been registered for younger people with physical impairments, while very few people with mental health problems have been trialled for IBs.
- Older people piloted on IB had a reverse benefit effect with less good outcomes than the control group comparator.
- Unit costs seem high in the current English context; beliefs that roll-out costs would be lower per capita remain unevidenced.

> • Very different pilot interpretations of the Resource Allocation System (RAS), the process by which resources are judged based on assessed needs. Some care coordinators view the RAS process as an outline checklist, others as a prescriptive and purely mathematical approach to assessment and resource quantification.

In policy terms, the complexity of pooled budgets, gateways, resource allocations and differential reliance and allowance for self-assessment in certain localities give some clues as to the complexity and challenge of implementing IBs. The extent to which professionals are more rather than less central to such processes is a moot point, as is the scope for personal preferences distorting the wider population needs of disabled people. We have to wait to see how the roll-out operates and the likely impact of severe budgetary constraints on the numbers of disabled people receiving support. It is noteworthy that some disabled people felt they had lost out because of IB-related developments, while there was no evidence in the IBSEN (Individual Budgets Evaluation Network) report of people feeling they had gained financially from the IB pilot (Glendinning et al, 2008). Clearly policy analyses has to go beyond just evaluating beneficiaries of IBs and indeed direct payments to understand the impact of specific policies on the health of social care systems in the round. Furthermore, we also need to be aware that the evaluation of IBs was largely completed by academics who are in preferred provider relations with many of the funding departments that support IBs and self-directed support more generally. Perhaps the key issue here is to use IBs to reflect back on the self-direction project. It thus stands or falls on whether it is adequately and equitably funded or not. If it is, in part, a 'Trojan horse' for widespread social care retractions, the authors would then have to align with the following early warning on IBs and self-direction in being aware of:

> ... the dangers [with IBs] of just passing on to disabled people the requirement and responsibility to be the restrictors of their own ambitions. (Beresford and Jones, 2008)

The following from the former minister responsible for social care adds to some commentators' concerns:

> ... by "person-centred" I mean we have to move away from mass produced services. Services that too often created a culture of dependency and move towards a future that seeks to develop the potential that is in every single individual. (Ladyman, 2004)

On the specific question of the Disabled Facilities Grant, a major feature of the attempts to merge budgets has been the mainstay of environmental improvements to allow disabled people to grow older in their own homes, a key plank of disability and ageing policy in the UK (Sixsmith and Sixsmith, 2008). It is worth noting that this reliance on retro-fitting inaccessible premises is partly exacerbated by neoliberal changes in housing policy and one person's self-direction can be deleterious to another's. Explicitly, the 'Right to Buy' policy ushered in during the Conservative government's tenure in the 1980s severely depleted the number of mobility and wheelchair-accessible homes available for disabled people (Rowe, quoted in Barnes, 1991).

The refusal of successive governments to ensure growing percentages of new housing to meet mobility and wheelchair standards complicates matters further. This has led to a position where the majority of homes are inaccessible to wheelchair users and those with significant mobility impairments (Imrie, 2003; Burns, 2004). To date pledges have been more evident than enforcement – for example, the unfulfilled mandate to increase the numbers in social and private housing that meet mobility and wheelchair access standards (CLG, 2008). There have, however, been some successes in ensuring greater provision of lifetime home features that will benefit disabled people with mild to moderate needs in the future (Sopp and Wood, 2001). Even so, the New Labour government's pledge to ensure all new built social housing would meet lifetime home standards remained in doubt at the end of their tenure in office (FLHN, 2010). The rather uneasy relationship between self-directed selves and the sovereignty of markets is notable in the context that we would need less self-directed struggle if the market was to design disabled people into building plans and encourage the growth in the number of lifetime homes. On this issue, Imrie commented that:

> If one accepts that housing quality is maximised by responding to individual needs, then the social and economic relations of the building industry need to be modified or changed. (Imrie, 2006, p 371)

Similarly, and somewhat ironically, the decision to place the Disabled Facilities Grant in the IB pilots sat oddly with an increasingly severe contributory taper that was attached to all adult applicants for the grant. This summed up many of the challenges of modernisation, that progressive philosophies do not always themselves dovetail with specific policy changes that relate to particular benefits and services. The shift towards activated citizens in social welfare and to a lesser extent in social care is arguably not matched by the activation and scrutiny of markets. This seems to be a dangerous, some might say deliberate idiosyncracy in neoliberal social policy. Meanwhile, the assumption that disabled people can and will always 'activate', that we can minimise and prevent social care needs this way, can arguably be seen to store up policy and fiscal issues for the future.

Conclusion

There have been many welcome developments in adult social care. The challenges that remain include taking on the 'care' system itself and paternalism. In concrete terms direct payments are now well established and working well for some disabled people. Although personal budgets and IBs are less proven at the time of writing, the underlying philosophy of choice is not likely to diminish in future adult social support policy. IBs are especially exciting in trying to break down funding and, by implication, professional barriers. There is limited but promising evidence that some barriers are reducing; however, professional and budgetary territorialism remains a major challenge. This is made more difficult by the inherent unresponsiveness of constituent-funded schemes such as the Disabled Facilities Grant and Access to Work that have been seen to require increased contributory elements for disabled adults and employers respectively. Personal budget take-up has been very disappointing. Meanwhile direct payments are struggling to make a mark beyond working-age physically disabled constituencies and, therefore, take-up is much less for people with mental health problems and learning difficulties. Housing, transport and employment barriers remain missing pieces in the jigsaw of independence for disabled adults. Increasingly, it seems probable that severe rationing will continue, with the Local Government Association (2009) arguing that only those in the 'substantial and critical need' category will be likely to receive funding from many local authorities in the future.

Summary

- Policy innovations such as direct payments have been very welcome for those disabled people taking up their use.
- Direct payments do not attract the stigma that attaches to welfare transfers although they are means tested.
- In policy terms a range of innovative choices now exist around direct payments, personal budgets and to a lesser extent IBs.
- Coverage and take-up of self-directed support has been limited and has benefited certain groups rather than others.
- A narrowing of eligibility criteria has been clear of late, which is likely to narrow the recipient profile yet further.
- Wider barriers such as poor housing options, limited access to paid work and public transport limit the degree of independent living experienced by some disabled people.

Questions

1. Can self-directed support and broader equity issues be squared in adult social care?
2. Why has take-up for self-directed support been so patchy?
3. Will the narrowing of eligibility criteria undermine the prospects for disabled people in terms of self-direction and choice making?
4. Can independent living be achieved with direct payments alone?

Further reading

On self-direction and personalisation see **Barnes and Mercer (2006)** and **Ramcharan and Grant** in **Grant et al (2005)**. On conceptualising self-directed support see **Prideaux et al (2009)** and **Roulstone and Morgan (2009)**. **Riddell et al (2006)** and **Pearson (2004)** are also very good policy and practice appraisals of direct payments. On individual budgets see **Glendinning et al (2008)**.

seven

Older disabled people: choices and rights in old age?

Introduction

While much social policy, most notably the life chances report (PMSU, 2005), emphasises the challenge of policy for working-age adults and children, older disabled people are less well accounted for in disability policy. This chapter explores the construction and impact of policy for older disabled people. It is argued that beyond working age a great deal of policy emanates from health and safeguarding policies where many, but not all, are some distance from the philosophy of independent living. Although generational and capacity issues are important in explaining differences with younger disabled adults, the question of the efficacy of policy for older disabled people needs to be critically engaged with. Greater risks of medical neglect and assumptions that impairment is inevitable in old age are all key policy challenges. Nonetheless, as *Box 7.1* below makes clear, there have been significant legislative and policy developments in the fields of 'care', housing, unnecessary institutionalisation and state funding for older disabled people that need to be acknowledged.

Box 7.1: Policy developments with implications for older disabled people

- The Royal Commission on Long-term 'Care' (Sutherland Report, 1999).
- Developments in intermediate and continuing 'care'.
- *Putting people first* (DH, 2007).
- Direct payments and individual budgets (IBs).
- *Fair Access to Care Services*.
- Age-in-place and telecare developments.

Despite the fact that the occurrence of impairment is inextricably intertwined with the ageing process and the majority of disabled people in the UK are likely to be older people (Priestley, 2002), there is a tendency for policy makers not to view older people with impairments in the same light as younger disabled people. Statistically, 34 per cent of those individuals aged 50-64 in the UK are deemed disabled (DRC, 2000, p 13), whereas the figure for those over 80 rises to 70 per cent (Martin et al, 1988; Craig and Greenslade, 1998). According to the ODI, estimates covering disability prevalence over the period 2008-09 indicate there were over 10 million disabled people in Britain, of whom 5.1 million were over the state pension age (ODI, 2010). Yet in spite of this disproportionate imbalance, UK disability policies have 'consistently focused on the concerns and needs of younger disabled people' (Priestley, 2002, p 362). In part, this myopic focus can be attributed to the government emphasis on 'active citizenship' and their attempts to encourage or cajole disabled individuals to participate in the paid labour market (PLM). Work-based welfare can be seen to have ignored the needs of those who have left or never been able to access the PLM (Roulstone and Barnes, 2005). In this sense, younger disabled people are seen by government to be less problematic in terms of finding suitable employment. Indeed, their close proximity to the PLM has thus led to the policy distinction between older and younger disabled people whereby older disabled people are associated with 'perceived dependency and devalued human capital' (Priestley, 2002, p 363).

In part also, the myopia in UK disability policy is a product of the lack of coordination between the campaigns of the Disabled People's Movement and campaigning groups representing older people. Despite a considerable overlap in their claims to entitlement, where the Disabled People's Movement has campaigned for a more 'enabling society', 'accessible housing' and claimed for the 'additional costs of impairment', and where the representations of older people have embraced the vision of a 'society for all ages' which includes 'housing for life' and 'cold weather payments' (Priestley and Rabiee, 2002), neither group has viewed the other as fully representative of the interests of older disabled people. Traditional charities and pressure groups have tended to be better funded (Drake, 1999) and more concerned with specific single-issue concerns and embraced the notion of 'social care' as central to their concerns. Disabled people's organisations have been concerned with choices and rights to control one's life. Despite the development of an independent living strategy (ODI, 2009) and the policy imperative to have a user-led organisation (ULO) in each locality, most disability organisations are struggling severely with financial solvency. However, broader historic and cultural factors have also limited the reach of disability-led organisations to older people. The exact reasons for this dichotomous development requires further research and policy reflection.

On the one hand, it is evident that the experiences of older disabled people have been under-represented by current disability studies literature (Boyle, 2008), whereas on the other, the impairments of older disabled people have been 'socially constructed as intrinsic to the ageing process' (Boyle, 2008, p 301). As a consequence, older disabled people have not automatically viewed themselves as disabled people. On the contrary, the self-identities of this group have concentrated on age or traditional models of caring which, in turn, has led to collective representations that have made pension rights a dominant theme as opposed to independent living (Boyle, 2008; see also National Pensioners Commission, 2005). Yet despite this apparent lack of focus on older people's independent living, older disabled people are, nonetheless, highly concerned about the funding of adult social 'care'. This distinction between independence for younger disabled people and social care for older disabled people requires much greater policy attention in the future. The recent extension of direct payments to older people represents the first real step to challenge this dichotomous view (Prideaux et al, 2009). For older disabled people, such 'care' or support has traditionally embraced a range of options and is more likely to include provision for residential and home 'care' support, both of which were investigated by the Royal Commission on Long-term Care in 1999 (RCLTC, 1999).

The Royal Commission on Long-term 'Care'

The Royal Commission on Long-term Care report entitled *With respect to old age* (also known as the Sutherland Report) was established to look, among other things, at the best options for funding and providing long-term 'care' in an ageing population. The Commission argued that elderly people were being pushed into institutional 'care' far too early due to the lack of alternative support in their own homes (see also Barlow and Venables, 2004). The eventual report also looked at the funding of 'care' for all disabled adults in both domestic and residential contexts and it was recommended that free adult social care in England and Wales should be provided in order to end the anomaly where health 'care' was provided free in nursing homes but social 'care' remained mean tested. Crucially, however, the report reflected the growing support for the ideals of independent living as health and social 'care' policy increasingly strove to enable older disabled individuals to live in the circumstances of their own choosing.

As this chapter makes clear later, achieving this choice of where to live and receive the necessary support has been supplemented by further government initiatives to empower older disabled people. Besides a growing concern over intermediate and continuing 'care', successive governments have championed the cause of state-funded self-directed support schemes to pay for personal assistance (Prideaux et al, 2009), promoted the idea of 'choice' and 'control' and facilitated new approaches to the design, construction and/or adaption of homes. Arguably, all represented a more rounded and complete package designed to improve the lives of individuals who are disabled and past retirement.

Intermediate 'care' and support

Intermediate care is that support provided between home and hospital (or other residential setting) (DH, 2001d). In principle the term relates most fully to independent living principles where it supports disabled people to make the move from hospital or residential care to home-based living (Melis et al, 2004). In practice intermediate care can support the shift from home to residential provision, although this goes against the grain of the recent policy emphasis on 'ageing-in-place' and home-based support (CLG, 2008). A crucial issue here is that of discharge processes and the smooth transition from a residential or hospital setting to home. Despite the partial effectiveness of the Department of Health's discharge from hospital practice guidance (DH, 2003a) in promoting working relations between health and social care services, there remain significant barriers to more joined-up and seamless approaches to connecting older people's lives between home and hospital. This is significant as although disability policy discussion often fights shy of connecting disability and declining health, there is clear evidence that declining health is a characteristic of disabled and non-disabled adults alike (Martin et al, 1988; DH, 2009c).

The area of discharge planning for older disabled and frailer older people is one which requires further policy attention to avoid early discharge and the potential for otherwise unnecessary prolonging of acute health problems and possible readmission to hospital. Intermediate and continuing care are important in helping bridge this gap. There is much evidence on the barriers to greater joint working. Such barriers can be poor communication between health and social care professionals and service users and 'carers' having to deal with sometimes challenging healthcare procedures at home. There are numerous reasons for premature discharge. Hospital overcrowding, perceptions of 'bed blocking' and notions that older disabled people are never likely to recover acute health bouts and a blurring of chronic and acute health status have all prompted premature discharge. Badly planned hospital discharge can be disempowering for service users and their 'carers', while in clinical terms there is an increased risk of readmission (Bauer et al, 2009). Such practice clearly runs contrary to the spirit of *Independence, wellbeing and choice* and the older people's *Prevention package* (DH, 2005, 2010b) and their emphasis on preventive approaches.

An over-delayed discharge can also militate against older disabled people's rights where health and social care professionals deem a person too ill to return home despite evidence to the contrary. Such a delay can often be a distraction from the real causes including poor health and social care coordination (Chadwick and Russell, 1989). The negotiation of discharge or continued hospitalisation has to be dealt with on the balance of all available evidence and take account of home and family circumstances. In some health and local authorities, the *Putting people first* (DH, 2007) and *The case for change* (DH, 2008d) agendas take in both supported and appropriate discharge and the identification of preventable hospitalisation. This makes sense as both are about personalised solutions and also aim to ensure reduced risks of hospitalisation. Intermediate care is intended to be free and is mandated under the Community Care (Delayed Discharges etc) Act 2003 and aims to reduce future health and social care costs by supporting intermediate support (DH, 2003a). The recent publication of a revised and updated statement on intermediate care makes clear that health and social care authorities have not always understood the principle or been prepared to let their paramount definition yield to others, as exemplified in different models of care in residential and independent home settings (Martin and Sturdy, 2010). The severe constraints on future home-based support may continue to limit effectiveness and symmetry of health and social care services where health retains its broad funding base in the face of severe cuts to social care budgets. The potential cost savings of reducing needless long-stay hospital or residential home use and of supporting home-based approaches has in turn to be underpinned by a transfer of funds from health to social support in the longer term. The recent finding that 22 per cent of English local authorities were charging illegally for reablement, a key facet of intermediate support, suggests a continued misunderstanding as to how independence can best be fostered and funded for those who need it most in the 21st century (Pitt, 2010).

Putting people first

In keeping with the ideals of independent living, the foreword penned by Patricia Hewitt in the White Paper *Our health, our care, our say* declared that under the future auspices of the New Labour government:

- People will be helped in their goal to remain healthy and independent.
- People will have real choices and greater access in both health and social care.
- Far more services will be delivered – safely and effectively – in the community or at home.
- Services will be integrated, built round the needs of individuals and not service providers, promoting independence and choice.
- Long-standing inequalities in access and care will be tackled. (Hewitt, quoted in DH, 2006, p 4)

Accordingly, the government set itself four main objectives within the White Paper. The first was to provide better prevention services in the area of health and social care services. It would do so through early intervention as a result of closer working ties between GP practices, PCTs and local government, 'to ensure that there is early support for prevention' (DH, 2006, p 7). Second, the government declared that it needed to improve access to community services and increase its efforts to tackle inequalities. Third, the government was committed to providing more support for people with long-term needs by assisting and supporting individuals to manage their condition for themselves. With the fourth objective, the government proposed to give people a louder voice and greater say. Patients would be guaranteed a more simplified system of registration onto a local GP practice list to help them choose a relevant practice and available services. To ensure that people were provided with real choices, the government also proposed to 'increase the take-up of direct payments by introducing new legislation to extend their availability to currently excluded groups and will pilot the introduction of individual budgets' (DH, 2006, p 7).

Direct payments, independent living and individual budgets

As noted earlier in Chapter Six, direct payments were first implemented in 1997 with the passing of the Community Care (Direct Payments) Act. This enabled local authorities to make discretionary cash payments to those disabled people under the age of 65 assessed as in need of community 'care' services (Leece and Leece, 2006). Indeed, the experience of direct payments has been a major contributory factor in the decision to pilot IBs during the period 2005-07. In accordance with the ideals of independent living (promoted by numerous In Control projects developed with and on behalf of people with learning difficulties during this period), the aim of IBs was to extend the choice and control aspects of self-directed support to a much broader range of service users (Rabiee et al, 2009). Significantly for this chapter, such an expansion included older disabled people over retirement age. To achieve greater choice and control, IBs were thus designed to:

- Combine a variety of resources from different funding schemes
- Coordinate assessments from these funding streams
- Encourage recipients to plan their personal support package
- Be flexible in their deployment. (Rabiee et al, 2009)

In particular, IBs attempt to give the user more flexibility in the use of their funding by pooling the resources from council-provided social care services (which include direct payments), Access to Work, the Independent Living Fund (ILF), *Supporting People* funding, the Disabled Facilities Grant and Integrated Community Equipment Services (ICES) (Glendinning et al, 2008; Boxall et al, 2009). To coordinate the assessment procedures, IBs are also premised on self-assessment (where possible) and, crucially, incorporate a transparent Resource Allocation System (RAS) whereby each recipient is fully informed of their financial allocation and from which resources it has been composed. Older people have, however, been less likely than younger disabled people to avail themselves or to get access to individual or personal budgets. Issues around an adequate social care infrastructure and availability of affordable and well-trained support and advocacy staff are also of clear significance given the current association between low pay and social care work (CSCI and HCC, 2009; Baxter et al, 2011).

As a consequence of this transparency, the recipient, on the award of an IB, is in a position to decide on the level of control they wish to take over their allocation, plan (through advocates, brokers or others if necessary) how they will use their budget to get help best suited for them and, subsequently, able to purchase the required support from either social services, the private sector, community groups, family and/or friends (Boxall et al, 2009; Rabiee et al, 2009; Duffy, 2010). Indeed, the amount of control that a recipient can decide to take ranges, by degree, to receiving and managing a direct payment at one end of the scale to full local authority control at the other, thus enhancing the flexibility of such schemes even further.

Whether the older disabled person is a recipient of direct payments or is the holder of an IB, the most attractive element of such schemes is that they promote a discourse of emancipation which emphasises choice, control or independence for disabled people and older people alike. True to the ideals of independent living, individuals are in a position to determine their own support needs in a manner that is relatively independent of the state and local authority 'care' systems. By contrast, the framework set out by the New Labour government in the *Fair Access to Care Services* (DH, 2003b) went against individual choice and control in that it was designed to help local authorities decide who should and, more crucially, who should not, receive adult community care services from social services departments.

Are we witnessing *Fair Access to Care Services?*

Fair Access to Care Services aimed to provide a blueprint for fairer access to care services and support. By systematising a national approach to threshold eligibility and developing a graduated typology of need (ranging from low, to moderate, to substantial and to critical), the decision as to who would rightly receive support in a given local authority would be fairer. The guidance did not aim to prescribe just who should receive care, while budgetary, population and customary differences ensured that the guidance was used flexibly. For example, some authorities set the threshold at only those assessed to be in moderate need and above, while in others it was restricted to those assessed as having substantial and critical needs. The Commission for Social Care Inspection (CSCI) study established that in 2007/08, 72 per cent of local authorities were no longer funding low or moderate assessed needs. People who did not meet established thresholds with savings above a set level (currently £23,000) have had to find the cost of social 'care' themselves. This 'cliff-edge' effect was acknowledged in the Green Paper *Shaping the future of care together* (DH, 2009b). For important adaptations to homes under the Disabled Facilities Grant, disabled people have to contribute on the basis of a sliding scale which, although less steep than for personal 'care', does make some work prohibitively expensive for disabled people who live just above Income Support (IS) or Jobseeker's Allowance benefits levels. This has led to what can best be described as a lottery of provision, where service eligibility and response to older disabled people's needs depends on where they live as much as the level of their personal needs. To reiterate, this sits awkwardly with the personalisation agenda discussed above and in previous chapters, and it is hardly surprising that the take-up of direct payments and personal budgets by older disabled people has remained low. The government is currently reviewing these guidelines and the wide interpretations of its domiciliary 'care'.

Age-in-place and telecare

As this book has made clear throughout, the development and thinking of the UK Disabled People's Movement since the 1980s has, in the main, helped ensure that community-based independence was part of the rights agenda for disabled people. More recently this agenda has been expanded to incorporate older people. While government policy has increasingly converged with the idea of community-based solutions, and while the exact motivation for embracing community options is debatable (see Roulstone and Morgan, 2009), a key plank of the independence agenda is the role of assistive technology in helping disabled people gain greater control over their social environment. The recent emphasis on ageing in one's home, or 'age-in-place' to use official terminology, increases the emphasis on home and community support (Means, 2007).

Naturally the drive towards home and community support was underpinned by the need for appropriate housing or housing adaptations. In terms of new homes for older disabled people, three approaches to design and construction predominate. On one level there is the concept of 'universal design' which 'aims to create products, processes and environments that are usable by people with the widest possible range of abilities' (Barlow and Venables, 2004, p 797). On another, there is the proposition of 'lifetime homes' where emphasis is placed on design features that allow for a degree of flexibility across the life cycle of both the occupant and the dwelling itself. Put simply, 'lifetime homes' are premised on foresight and anticipation in that they are designed to accommodate the need to adapt through, for example, the inclusion of additional space for future installations such as stair lifts or elevators as, when, or if, the need arises. Finally, there is the notion of 'open building'. Here again, the focus is on future adaptation to meet changing needs. This time, however, design and construction is less concerned with social housing but with retail and office space.

In this respect, Part M of the UK Building Regulations is seen by some as an important 'stepping stone' to the achievement of accessibility. It requires builders to construct new dwellings to minimum standards of accessibility for wheelchair users (Imrie, 2004), and it was the emergence of this regulation that signalled a much broader shift in socio-political values, advocating policies 'to enhance sustainable and socially inclusive neighbourhoods and patterns of living' (Imrie, 2003, p 391). Indeed, New Labour actively encouraged builders to incorporate flexible design in their new constructions so that usable dwellings were created to cater for changes in bodily capacities and capabilities over a lifetime. In theory, this would help avoid the need for expensive adaptation or the need to move home.

Where adaptation is still necessary, however, it is also important to note that the aforementioned Disabled Facilities Grant represents a key resource for disabled people ageing in their own home. That said, it is still conceivable that a person may need to move to a more accessible house. The provision of 'wheelchair standard' housing is significant here. The lesser category of mobility standard is more likely to be achieved through a retro-fit (after a house is built and lived in) approach, using, say, the Disabled Facilities Grant.

Wheelchair standard housing may be required where retro-fitting would be difficult or prohibitively expensive. Local authority plans have to follow the broad British Standards (BS) guidelines set out in the aforementioned Part M of the Building Regulations (ODPM, 2000). Professionals do not need to be experts on the details of these regulations. Rather, an understanding of the importance of accessible housing and being able to aid a disabled person's decision as to whether to retro-fit a current house or to initiate a joint professional application for a wheelchair-accessible house is important here. Social workers, occupational therapists and sometimes community nurses may need to start the process of looking at accessible housing options. Whichever approach is taken, the direction of travel in policy terms is towards 'age-in-place' in the community and that is likely to hold true for many disabled and frail older people.

For people with profound and complex impairments, such as late-stage dementia or where sustained health 'care' is required, options are likely to include residential 'care', nursing 'care' or a specialist health unit. Notably, intermediate 'care' options are becoming increasingly important in treating the health needs of older disabled people in community units designed to avert needless entry into long-stay residential or hospital settings. These units also aim to reduce bed blocking or too rapid discharges of older disabled people and act as a half-way option between hospital and home environments (British Geriatrics Society, 2008). One key factor in age-in-place approaches is the perceived importance of new assistive technologies in supporting older disabled people's housing needs. There has been a tendency of late for academic and practice writers to equate enabling technology (Roulstone, 1998) with telecare (remotely operated health and safety monitors or alarms). This is only one small part of the required picture. Indeed 'technologies of independence' is perhaps a better way to understand the assistive technologies that can facilitate older disabled people to stay in their home environments. A good working definition of these assistive technologies is offered by the Royal Commission on Long-term Care which states that telecare is 'an umbrella term for any device or system that allows an individual to perform a task they would otherwise be unable to do, or increase the ease and safety with which the task can be performed' (RCLTC, 1999, p 1). Future possibilities include the provision of passive sensors to build a more comprehensive picture of the activities of older disabled people in their homes. Notwithstanding the cost benefits of telecare and assistive technologies (in that it is less labour intensive), such applications of technology have the advantage of delivering a more person-oriented form of 'care'. Moreover, widespread deployment of these schemes has the potential to reduce the need for relocation to institutional care or, for that matter, enable older disabled people to leave institutions.

Telecare could also 'unblock' hospital beds, providing health service gains. More specifically, however, the perceived advantage of telecare alone meant that the previous New Labour government set itself the ambitious but commendable target of providing telephone-based 'care' to all homes that needed it by December 2010 (Barlow and Venables, 2004).

Ambitious holism, realism or ineffectual rhetoric?

Taken as a whole, it could be argued that the policy direction and debates entered into by New Labour did indeed impact positively on the lives of older disabled people. Certainly it is possible to argue that New Labour adopted a holistic approach that advanced the opportunity for older disabled people to achieve the ideal of independent living. Nevertheless, this is not to say that in practice the ultimate objectives embodied within the independent living philosophy were realised, nor is it a suggestion that each element of New Labour's approach avoided distortion as a result of conflicting ideals/ambitions, pragmatic acquiescence and unintended consequences. It cannot be said that reform was uniform across the UK either. Older people are still much less likely to avail themselves of self-directed support options.

The cost implications of some of the recommendations of the Sutherland Report meant, for example, that social 'care', in the main, is still means tested in England for domiciliary, residential and nursing home personal 'care' unless the extent or specialist nature of nursing 'care' makes nursing/personal 'care' inseparable, or where health 'care' is the clear primary purpose of the 'care' package. By contrast, Scotland has broken with the continued links between means testing and the more stigmatised elements of the English Poor Law of 1842 to create a system where free personal 'care' is currently available for older disabled people, although 'hotel' costs have to be met by individuals entering 'care' settings (Scottish Parliament, 2008).

To compound issues, the requirement on disabled or sick older people in England to sell their own homes where means testing establishes their 'ability to pay' (Hirsch, 2006) remains a policy prerequisite. This has, of course, provoked heated political debates over fairness and equity. Of major concern is the fact that once a house is sold, the option of moving back into the community is often lost (Hirsch, 2006), thus 'institutionalising' the affected individual and denying them choice, control and the right to independent living. There is also evidence of health authorities attempting to close facilities or refuse free 'care' where personal and health 'care' are inextricably linked. Again, individuals are being denied choice, which has implications for older disabled people achieving the goals encapsulated within the philosophy of independent living. The above evidence on the unlawful charging for intermediate care suggests that there remains confusion as to support that falls between home and hospital, between health and social care. Budgetary boundaries and territorialism remain very real issues affecting the lives of some disabled people.

On a more positive note there is little doubt that IBs, like direct payments, have plenty of potential for the good. Because of the (quasi)-market system on which personalised budgets are premised, disabled people and, in particular for this chapter, older disabled people over 65 years of age, can secure both choice and control over their lives through the services that they purchase from a range of service providers. There are, however, a number of tensions, problems and potential conflicts that have to be considered when evaluating the full effectiveness of such schemes (Boxall et al, 2009; Duffy, 2010). On a practical front, there have been problems in merging the various funding sources since each has maintained different eligibility criteria and regulations. Moreover, the original idea that individual brokers would help users plan and utilise their budgets has not been encouraged by councils in practice (Boxall et al, 2009). The recent survey of personal budget take-up has established that targets for take-up were significantly undershot (NHS Information Centre, 2010). In addition, the market principles that underpin these personalised budgets are also problematic.

By way of an illustration of this point it is interesting to look at the social justice discourse of the Disabled People's Movement and contrast it with the market-oriented approach of government when introducing direct payment reforms. Indeed some writers are begging the question as to whether the British government and the UK Disabled People's Movement are talking the same language around self-directed support (Ferguson, 2008; Roulstone and Morgan, 2009). Here issues of individualism and collectivism are very important. Older people may be less likely to attach to the more overtly individualist constructions of self-direction and management underpinning modernised adult social care. As a consequence, it is dangerous to assume that there is a lack of conflict and that all parties interested or promoting the personalisation of funds have a shared common purpose. On the contrary, many commentators and practitioners alike simply object to approaches that transform 'care' into more business or market-based relationships.

It is also worth noting that the design and construction approaches embodied in Part M of the Building Regulations, lifetime homes, universal design and open building philosophies are not without their limitations. According to Imrie (2003, 2004), Part M, for example, only relates to a focus on making a dwelling 'visitable'. This is an entirely subjective term and is therefore entirely open to individual interpretation. 'Visitable' in the eyes of a builder, for instance, may have an entirely different meaning to that of a disabled person (for other debates on the subjective terms used in relation to access and adaptation of the built environment, see Prideaux and Roulstone, 2009; Roulstone and Prideaux, 2009). Either way, the term 'visitable' definitely does not imply 'liveable'. Moreover, as with design and adaptive approaches, there is the very real danger of corporeal reductionism whereby complex disabilities are accommodated within a narrow range of physical and technical solutions rather than considering the vast range of needs and adaptations separate individuals may require (Barlow and Venables, 2004). At present, space and accessibility appear to be the major but not wholehearted concerns of builders and architects who do not fully understand the concept of 'visitability'. As a consequence, there is little consideration, and in some quarters resentment, of what constitutes universal provision (Heywood, 2004). Granted wheelchair users tend to be the major recipients of such an approach, but it must also be remembered that bodily impairment is neither fixed nor static, and so housing quality cannot be understood or defined separately from an understanding of the experiences, interactions and meanings disabled people attach to life in their own homes.

Reliance on telecare is also problematic. Government aspirations for widespread deployment were seriously limited by the technical problems surrounding the use of such complex systems. Furthermore, there was, and still is, the considerable danger that the deployment of this technology could provide the wrong model of care as a consequence of a misunderstanding of the social context in which the technology is placed (Barlow and Venables, 2004). The lack of standardisation of these systems does not help the cause either, although it is envisaged that this will be overcome as the market for such assistance increases. More importantly, however, is the concern over ethical and legal considerations. There are very real fears that the implementation of advanced telecare systems which monitor the activities of older disabled people could remove choice and control from the user due to the effective 'substitution of technology for more personal forms of care and support' (Barlow and Venables, 2004, p 803).

Conclusion

To reiterate an earlier observation, there is little doubt that the policies introduced by New Labour enhanced opportunities for disabled people. Despite the above-mentioned contradictions, tensions and conflicts, disability policy under New Labour had been moving in a more positive direction until the onset of the economic decline instigated by the global financial crisis. Indeed, the policy direction of New Labour began to harden during the final years of Gordon Brown's government. Recent developments from the Conservative-Liberal Coalition provide some concern that although engaged fully with the notion of independence, their wider fiscal severity may limit adult social care to an ever smaller group of older disabled people. This is set against the projected rise in adult social care demand of 1.7 million people by 2031 (HM Government, 2009). There is a very real risk here of a return to crisis intervention and pillar-to-post welfarism for many of those who have to navigate the difficult waters between health and social care funders. The recent announcement of a wholesale review of DLA also adds to concerns as reduced headcount is now an explicit feature of the reviews. After an initial decision to withdraw of DLA from those in residential care a recent impact assessment (DWP, 2011b) has concluded that the availability of DLA for this group will continue until the Personal Independence Payment (PiP) successor to DLA is fully operationalised. A benevolent view is that this aims to ensure no duplication of funding from adults social care and welfare (DLA) sources. A less sanguine view is that DLA targeted reductions will see pressure to reduce the headcount of recipients in residential contexts.

Summary

- Older disabled people are beginning to be recognised in wider disability policy.
- Direct payments extensions and *Putting people first* are examples of positive developments.
- Disabled older people have received less substantively supported social policy in an era of work-first welfare. The UK Disabled People's Movement has arguably not won older disabled people's attentions, while traditional 'care'-based organisations continue to dominate the policy scene.
- Key developments that aim to bridge home and hospital/residential settings are slowly taking effect, but professional and budgetary boundaries continue to bedevil progress.
- Coalition government plans arguably set back self-direction where brokerage, adult support and coverage are made more limited by severe financial cuts that are beginning to impact on local authorities.

Questions

1. To what extent have social policies successfully grappled with the challenges faced by older disabled people?
2. Why do disability, poverty and old age continue to stubbornly co-exist despite policy efforts?
3. How might the lack of attention paid by the UK Disabled People's Movement to the needs of older disabled people affect the roll-out of the personalisation agenda?
4. Are assistive devices a panacea for older disabled people, given the cost challenges of traditional residential and community support models?

Further reading

There are few comprehensive pieces on older disabled people and the best materials are mostly found in reports or journal articles rather than books. However, **Harris and Roulstone (2011)** make good links between policy and practice realities. **Glendinning et al's (2008)** 'choices and change' article is a good overview. You ought to read the **Sutherland Report (RCLTC, 1999)** to get a firm grasp of the further funding of adult social care. You should also read **Priestley and Rabiee's (2002)** article on older people's organisations and disability issues to scope the issues around disability and ageing.

eight

Getting it right for all disabled people? The impact of disability policy on structured disadvantage

The field of disability policy is complex, and the many layers of services, benefits, initiatives and policy 'actors' makes an assessment of policy efficacy very challenging. Some policy areas can be more easily appraised where very specific interventions are at issue. For example, we can appraise the impact of work and welfare policies for a given target group or the degree to which direct payments are reaching their target audiences (Riddell et al, 2006). However, policy appraisal is much less clear when we attempt to assess the interplay of often disparate policies, or the broader economic and social position of disabled people in aggregate terms. Some policies fail to achieve benefits for their avowed beneficiaries or tend to be gendered in their assumptions (Walker and Walker, 1991).

Other policies may benefit disabled people in a serendipitous way (Skills for Care and IFF, 2007). Policies may conflict in purpose and impact (DWP, 2009a), while the complexities of the UK benefits system, to be discussed later in Chapter Nine, may at times present behavioural disincentives when they interact in unplanned ways to limit disabled people's economic and social progress (Roulstone and Barnes, 2005). We can analyse and assess policy effectiveness in a number of ways (see *Box 8.1*).

Box 8.1: Analysing disability policy

- Qualitative analyses of specific experiences of benefits (Corden et al, 2009).
- Macro-level national quantitative studies of the impacts of policy on a large population of disabled people (Pires et al, 2006).

> - Macro-level surveys of the wider economic and social position of disabled people, for example, the changing measures of poverty, worklessness and social class profiles (Labour Force Surveys, General Household Surveys).

This chapter focuses largely on the last of these options in looking at the wider national impact of a range of social policies on disabled people's lives. Indeed the types of policy appraisal detailed in the first and second bullet points above are dealt with elsewhere in this book. This chapter thus draws on survey findings on disabled people's economic and social circumstances more generally. Clearly some caution needs to be exercised in linking major policy developments with the social and economic progress of disabled people as the exact links between policy intention and outcomes are complex. However, as many policies claim to add to disabled people's life chances (PMSU, 2005) and social well-being (DH, 2005) more generally, it seems reasonable to judge major policy shifts, for example, poverty reduction strategies or employment readiness policy, in terms of these longer-term quantitative data measures. In strict sociological terms, the engrained barriers to paid work make the adoption of social class and socioeconomic group indicators a valid tool in appraising disabled people's social position. This is due to the largely employment-based official socioeconomic schemas (National Statistics, 2009a, 2009b). Here, social class and employment status represent an indispensable shorthand tool to compare the profiles of disabled and non-disabled populations. Woodin (2006), one of the few disability writers who connects disability and social class, draws on Bradley's classic formulation of social class as:

> ... a nexus of unequal lived relationships arising from the social organisation of production, distribution, exchange and consumption. (Bradley, 1996, p 46)

Although some authors reject such a productivist interpretation of social class, and attempt to operationalise social class using cultural, social capital, consumption patterns, these arguably fail as a workable comparative tool of social class analysis. If we include unemployment in such a social class schema we get a fuller sense of disabled people's social disadvantage (Woodin, 2006). The reassertion of the value of a social class schema seems ever more important at times of rapid social change and recessionary economic circumstances. Hilary Graham's (2009) exploration of socioeconomic position broadens the focus with attention being given to the three important factors of education, occupation and income. These aspects of socioeconomic position are seen by Graham to be important in influencing life chances and living standards. As Graham states, 'each can be used to provide a hierarchical classification of socioeconomic position: from no qualifications to degree-level qualifications, from unskilled manual jobs to professional jobs, and from low income to high income. Housing tenure and household assets (for example, car ownership) provide additional measures of socioeconomic position' (p 3). Graham concurs with Woodin that occupation is central to our understanding of the socioeconomic determinants of wider social opportunities. Graham sees social class gradients, based on occupational measures, attaching to health status, long-term conditions in populations, to 'cognitive' and psychological well-being/distress and to greater vulnerable to other health conditions (co-morbidity) (Graham, 2009).

We do, however, need to account for issues of gender here as an additional factor influencing disability, work and the overall provision of social welfare (Lonsdale, 1985, 1990). Not only do women face greater relative barriers to paid employment, in still being constructed as the primary 'carer' and nurturer, women also often forfeit employment opportunities and occupy the least valorised of social positions in the role of mother. As Twigg (2000) points out, the fact that assistance work is gendered means that it is viewed in contradictory ways. On the one hand, it is seen as low-level work; on the other, it is seen as being special, involving love and care for the person receiving assistance. In Woodin's survey of direct payments use, in very tangible terms middle-class disabled men were more likely to gain early and more substantial access to direct payments (Woodin, 2006).

Consequently, economic disadvantage has to be seen as the product of an interplay between class, gender and exclusionary cultures that continue to exclude some more than others from paid work and the least stigmatised benefits. Arguably, then, such key economic issues need to be more evident while policy discourses have moved further towards the more nebulous and almost liberal notion of life chances as opposed to substantive redistribution. Indeed, by failing to connect broader research on disabled people's economic position with the policy claims of government there is a risk of a policy 'disconnect' between such general surveys and more specific policy rhetoric and evaluations. This is made more acute by the increased use of such terms as 'social inclusion', 'life chances' and the lesser use of established comparable survey terms such as 'social class' and 'socioeconomic group' in official policy reviews. An example of this is the life chances report (PMSU, 2005) which, in focusing on the relatively new policy discourses of 'social inclusion' and 'life chances', aimed to offer a 'state of the art impression' of disabled people's social position in the early part of the 21st century, yet the report only gave one (limited) reference to social class.

In this vein, this chapter begins with a brief historical reflection on the broad economic position of disabled people in terms of their greater likelihood in experiencing poverty, poor housing and limited access to paid work. It then explores more recent measures of disabled people's social and economic opportunities set against the changing policy background of New Labour policies over the last 13 years.

Historical disadvantage of disabled people: early years of 'disability policy'

Disabled people had little explicitly badged 'disability policy' until the 1970s. The industrial injuries, war disablement and Disabled Persons' (Employment) Act 1944 (HM Government, 1944a) were the only substantively specific disability policies of note until the arrival of Mobility Allowance (MA), Attendance Allowance (AA) and Invalidity Benefit (IVB) in the early 1970s. Even the Chronically Sick and Disabled Persons Act of 1970 derived most of its statutory authority from the earlier National Assistance Act of 1948. Most poverty alleviation and income alternatives came via mainstream unemployment, sickness benefit or national assistance provision (Barnes, 1991; Walker and Walker, 1991). The acknowledgement early in the 1970s that incomes policy was 'not working' for many disabled people helped lead to policy reform and regular studies of the impact/ limitations of the latest policy development. Looking back through the telescope of history we now know the main causes of disabled people's economic disadvantage over time include worklessness (Walker, 1981; Martin et al, 1989; Burchardt, 2000) and the extra costs of impairment and overcoming social barriers (Martin and White, 1988; Matthews and Truscott, 1990; Berthoud, 1991; Woolley, 2004; Tibble, 2005). The complex link between impairment and disadvantage does, indeed, have different causal possibilities, with impairment leading to reduced social opportunities (the 'social drift' hypothesis) (Goldberg and Morrison, 2004) while social disadvantage itself can, of course, cause or exacerbate physical and mental ill health (Jahoda, 1982, 1988). The links between mental health and worklessness are well documented. The link between disability and disadvantage is also well established, as the following suggests:

> The Poor Law is at the present time only to a small extent concerned with the man who is able-bodied. The various sections of the non-able-bodied, the children, the sick, the mentally defective, and the aged and infirm make up today nine-tenths of the persons relieved by the Destitution Authorities.

(Royal Commission on the Poor Laws and the Relief of Distress (Minority Report), 1909, p 1)

Since the first official surveys of poverty, disabled, frail and sick people have all made up a large proportion of the stock of those at or below official poverty lines (National Statistics, 1971; Disability Alliance, 1975; Hyman, 1977; Stowell and Day, 1983; Buckle, 1984; Baldwin, 1985; Barnes, 1991). The suite of three surveys by Amelia Harris, completed in the late 1960s, made clear the engrained links between disablement and disadvantage (Harris et al, 1971). Survey 3 established that 30 per cent of the 'impaired group' of disabled adults studied were in receipt of supplementary benefit (a forerunner of Income Support [IS]) and an additional 7 per cent were judged to be entitled to these benefits but were not claiming them (Disability Alliance, 1975, p 15). Harris et al established that a third of the 'impaired group' population of the survey had at least one extra cost to meet which was disability related. This contrasted with the DHSS estimate of the time that only 10 per cent of this group had extra needs (DHSS, 1972). As the Disability Alliance report of 1975 pointed out, the survey by Harris et al established a whole array of comparative disadvantage among disabled people:

> ... [the] survey demonstrated that the disabled have incomes and other resources which are relatively low when compared with the non-disabled, even when standardised by age ... moreover, people in the more severe categories of disability tend to have lower incomes than those in the less severe categories of disability. Fewer of the disabled than of the non-disabled own their own homes. Fewer have substantial assets and large numbers of consumer durables in their homes. Fewer have rights to occupational pensions and other employers' welfare benefits. (Disability Alliance, 1975, p 18)

Despite the passing of the Chronically Sick and Disabled Persons Act in 1970, and its provision for greater community-based support and access and additional needs payments enshrined in IVBs and invalidity pensions, the link between economic disadvantage and disability was still a key finding of the Disability Alliance report in 1975. This link remained strong into the 1980s, with the Office of Population Censuses and Surveys (OPCS) reports on the position of disabled people in Great Britain establishing disabled people's relative poverty, inferior labour market position and inferior housing status compared to non-disabled people (Martin and White, 1988; Martin et al, 1988, 1989). The most shocking findings of these studies was that 54 per cent of disabled people lived in workless families and were thus reliant on benefits and/or savings for their income (Martin and White, 1988). Notably, the OPCS report on financial implications of being disabled was itself criticised for underestimating the real additional costs faced (Disability Alliance, 1988; Barnes, 1991).

While this engrained economic disadvantage prevailed, the state itself came under sustained attack from the political right during the 1980s. The newly elected Thatcher government of the time portrayed the state as a bloated regressive force holding back economic stealth and creativity. The ironic juxtaposition of disabled people's continuing economic disadvantage alongside the New Right rhetoric of 'rolling back the frontiers of the state' (Hall and Jacques, 1983; Gamble, 1988) cannot be overlooked. The position was reminiscent of the scene in *Alice in Wonderland* where the Mad Hatter's tea party was prematurely interrupted without any real explanation. Disabled people, to use this analogy, were not receiving anything akin to 'fair shares' in the distribution of the social goods, while the retraction of funding on welfare left disabled people even worse off. In concrete terms, the retraction of supplementary payments, a result of the Fowler reforms of IS in the mid-1980s, also signalled a reduction in disability income for disabled people outside of the paid labour market (PLM).

The increased emphasis on means testing and targeting at the heart of the Fowler reforms sat awkwardly with the developments of the 1970s which leant towards non-means-tested additional cost benefits and the supplements made available by the supplementary benefits system (Hills, 2003, p 10). A retrospective secondary analysis of government poverty statistics by the Institute for Fiscal Studies in 1990 (IFS, 1990) established that between 1979 and 1987 the numbers living at or under the poverty line had increased by 18 per cent. This figure is clearly going to be reflected in disabled people's experiences more specifically as their employment did not increase during this period as unemployment rose more generally.

Disability policy and the 1990s

The 1990s witnessed the revamping of MA and AA to introduce Disability Living Allowance (DLA) that had mobility and care components set at differential rates. This reflected the concerns identified in the OPCS studies that those with the least 'severe' impairments were receiving little if any support from the benefit system, while those with the 'most severe' impairments were not receiving enough support (Martin and White, 1988). The mid-1990s also witnessed additional funds being put into the Independent Living Fund (ILF), a sort of precursor to direct payments supporting those with the greatest support needs (*Hansard*, 1990).

Meanwhile, the introduction of the Disability Working Allowance (DWA) acknowledged the need to help more disabled people into the PLM as a source of greater economic security. The allowance, since mainstreamed into the tax credit system, was welcomed by those working more than 16 hours per week. For those regularly working less than 16 hours, or for those who wanted to increase their hours over time, the terms and conditions of the allowance's remit excluded them this extra benefit. What is very surprising is the almost total absence of evaluations of DWA in the public domain. What we do know, however, is that take-up increased relatively well between 1993 and 1998, but in absolute terms the numbers applying were extraordinarily low, growing from 903 in January 1993 to just 14,564 by January 1998 (when the allowance became a tax credit) (Rowlingson and Berthoud, 1996; HMRC, 2003). The successor to DWA, the Disabled Person's Tax Credit (DPTC), has proved to be more popular with recipients who crossed over and applied for DPTCs (HMRC, 2006). That said, Her Majesty's Revenue and Customs (HMRC) seem coy in providing any figures for increased take-up of these credits, compared to Working Families' Tax Credits (WFTCs) that are quantified in the same report as growing 5 per cent during the period 1999-2003. Furthermore, most DPTC recipients preferred these more generous benefits, although it is unclear whether the flagging of a person on a pay slip was a welcome development or not. In addition, the mainstreamed Working Tax Credit (WTC) also proved to be more attractive to disabled workers, with one study putting the figure at 103,000 disabled WTC recipients compared to the DPTC which only peaked at 37,500 in 2002 (HMRC, 2006).

Nevertheless, we should not get too carried away with this given that the numbers of disabled people of working age claiming income replacement benefits (both mainstream and incapacity-related) was growing at an alarming rate. This became a major concern for the incoming New Labour government throughout the 2000s as the growth in WTC take-up among disabled people was far outstripped by the growth in Incapacity Benefit (ICB) and Jobseeker's Allowance (disability supplement) headcount. While poverty and worklessness are clear bedfellows, it is important to also acknowledge that disabled people make up a disproportionate percentage of the working poor as they are historically more likely to be concentrated in lower pay/skill occupations (Berthoud, 2006). This in part reflects disabled people's poor relative educational attainments, but even when we hold constant wider variables, disabled people are seen to face greater horizontal and vertical labour market segregation, partially as a result of labour market discrimination and broader social class disadvantage that compounds negative views of disabled people (Burchardt, 2000; Labour Force Survey, 2003, 2009). Employed disabled people are disproportionately likely to be in manual occupations and they have lower average hourly earnings than their non-disabled peers, even after taking account of differences in age, education and occupation. According to Tania Burchardt, a leading authority on disabled workers and job seekers, the earnings gap appears to have grown substantially since 1985. Her analyses also revealed that greater 'severity' of impairment is generally associated with lower income despite the major changes in benefits and a shift to work-first policies. Burchardt, drawing on a range of data from the British Household Panel Survey (BHPS), the OPCS study of adults in private households, Family Resources Survey and Labour Force Survey tracking changes from the mid to late 1990s, noted that:

> ... the average income of this group has fallen relative to the general population since 1985. Overall, half of all disabled people have incomes below half the general population mean, after making an adjustment for extra costs. Disabled adults in families with children are even more likely to be in poverty: 60 per cent, by this measure. (Burchardt, 2000, p 52)

In terms of the social class position of disabled people there is little evidence of enhanced social mobility and, therefore, of improvement in the labour market. The *Health Survey for England* (DH, 2001a), for instance, established that disabled people in 2000/01 were still much more likely to be in social classes 4 or 5 and much less likely than their non-disabled comparators to occupy positions in social classes 1 and 2. The survey provides a useful guide to the degrees of success of New Labour's attempt to alter disabled people's economic and social contributions in their first term in office. These findings applied to both disabled men and women and they exposed a slightly greater preponderance of disabled women than men in social classes 4 and 5 (DH, 2001a). These data take account of age in their calculations. The Office for National Statistics also provides a new social class categorisation called the NS-SEC, the National Statistics socioeconomic classification. Although the class gradient was less steep with this formulation, with a less dramatic over-representation in the lower SEC, disabled people were still much more likely to be in these lower SEC categories. Disabled people were also 'significantly more likely' to be without formal educational credentials, to live in social housing, to be out of the labour market and when in work to receive less in remuneration (DH, 2001a).

Alongside broader, more abstract measures of socioeconomic disadvantage are the more specific forms of data that help us track the relative position of disabled people in an era of rapid policy change. For example, the housing position of disabled people, one which has always seen disabled people more reliant on often poorer quality social housing, had not improved dramatically during the 1990s. A study by Grewal et al (2002) for the DWP established that disabled people were much less likely (19 per cent difference) than their non-disabled counterparts to live in a private residence with a mortgage/loan. Interestingly, disabled people were more likely to own their own home (6 per cent difference). This may be age related, and requires further research. Taken together, owned outright and mortgaged property accounted for 57 per cent of disabled adult tenure in the UK, compared to 70 per cent of non-disabled people with such tenure (Grewal et al, 2002). Disabled people are significantly more likely to occupy social housing rented from a housing association or local authority (31 per cent disabled tenants versus 14 per cent non-disabled tenants). During the first term of the New Labour government between 1997 and 2003 there was a 44 per cent increase in the number of homeless households in priority need because a household member had a physical impairment, and a 77 per cent increase in the number of households where the priority need was someone with a mental illness (ODPM, 2005).

Disability policy impact and the 2000s

Given that disability-related policy has continued along the track of work-first principles, that the tax system features even more strongly and that incapacity-type benefits remain under the spotlight, it seems reasonable to look at poverty and worklessness as two key measures of policy effectiveness. The facts do not make good reading. Despite the many waves of activity to reduce worklessness, to make work pay and to reduce poverty for those unable to enter paid work, disability and poverty remain locked in a fatal embrace. Figures to emerge in a recent parliamentary answer, based on data from the 2008/09 Households Below Average Income (HBAI) survey, established that 3.9 million individuals who live in households with at least one disabled person in the household are living in income poverty (measured as 60 per cent below the median household income). In comparative terms, 23 per cent of individuals who live in a household with at least one disabled person are in official income poverty compared to 16 per cent for households with no disabled members, which represents a 7 per cent difference (*Hansard*, 2010b).

A key challenge alongside that of worklessness due to a mismatch of skills, opportunities, motivations and qualifications of often disabled men is the complex relationship between disabled women, caring roles and the benefits system. Evidence makes clear the challenge of locating paid work which pays enough to provide options for entering the formal PLM and leaving behind the more stigmatised role of childrearing. Notwithstanding the potentially pernicious assumptions that mothering and nurturing children is a form of dependency when paid for by the state via benefits (Levitas, 1998; Driver and Martell, 2002), the challenges of the poverty trap around women's work and benefits is a very real one (Daycare Trust, 2003; Johnson and Kossykh, 2008). The response by CPAG to the 2006 welfare reform Green Paper and the 2004 Spending Review pointed out that to date governments of all stripes have failed to square up to the difficulties of supporting disabled women in secure and well-remunerated work (CPAG, 2006b). The report emphasises the fact that disabled women not only support some of the most vulnerable children, but may also themselves be vulnerable in social and economic senses. The desire of the New Labour government to get an additional million disabled people into paid work (Centre for Economic Performance, 2006; DWP, 2007a) was seen to have clear implications for disabled parents. Of the estimated two million disabled, around half were disabled and largely female. The report noted:

> Parenting support is especially important for poor parents in vulnerable groups such as disabled parents, who face a particular risk of being in poverty. Over two million children live in families with one or more disabled adults. These children have an above average risk of living in low-income households. (CPAG, 2006b, p 56)

The CPAG report, drawing on the 2004/05 HBAI survey, also alerted readers to the rather alarming data that 24 per cent of Great Britain's poor children, amounting to over 800,000 children, live with one or more disabled adults, with a risk of income poverty for disabled children of 40 per cent. Disability once again seems to be a clear and present risk for both children and parents where it features in a household. The life chances report, completed in 2005 and commissioned by the Prime Minister's Strategy Unit (PMSU, 2005), revealed that entering paid work in the mid-2000s would not necessarily reduce poverty. Mothers of disabled children, for example, are historically less likely to take part in paid work. Research by the Daycare Trust, which drew on General Household Survey data, established that only 3 per cent of mothers with disabled children were in full-time work, compared with 22 per cent of mothers with non-disabled children, while 35 per cent of non-working lone parents were in full-time paid work (Daycare Trust, 2003). The degree to which policy strictures and targets connect with the dynamics of disabled parents and children's lives is a moot point. The exact calculations as to who can work, who should work, attitudes to childrearing/reward and rational alternatives to benefits have arguably only received cursory attention (Levitas, 1998; Roulstone and Barnes, 2005). Labour Force Survey data from 1999-2006, covering New Labour's second term in office, suggests the average gross hourly pay of disabled employees was £10.28 per hour, 10 per cent less than that of non-disabled employees (£11.30 per hour, based on the Labour Force Survey 1999-2006). The income gap stood at 10 per cent in the year 2009 towards the end of the New Labour period of office (Labour Force Survey, 2009, Quarter 1). Disabled people are also less likely to be able to compete on educational terms in the modern labour market, are still only half as likely as non-disabled people to be qualified to degree level and are twice as likely as non-disabled people to have no qualification at all (PMSU, 2005). Therefore, any crude numerical or throughput approach to getting disabled women into paid work had, according to commentators, to emphasise incentives, and could not simply rely on conditionality and sanctions. The latter would simply move disabled women and their families out of benefit-related poverty into work-related poverty. This is especially the case where severe Housing Benefit and Council Tax tapers make re-entering paid employment a particularly hazardous activity (Johnson and Kossykh, 2008).

The employment position of disabled people remains a major worry for policy makers and commentators, given that paid employment is recognised as a key route to greater economic stability and social status (DWP, 2007a). Of all economically active people, disabled people are closing the employment gap. Between 1998 and 2009 the employment gap reduced from 36 to 30 per cent (Labour Force Survey, 2009, Quarter 2). However, disabled people's employment rate remains lower than the rate for the lowest qualified portion of non-disabled jobseekers (Labour Force Survey, 2008). What these figures do not tell us about are those disabled people who may have dropped out of job seeking and economic activity more generally, for example, older workers placed on Pension Credit or younger workers with long-term conditions who have never claimed a benefit. Whichever way we look at it, the gap remains too great. This is somewhat ironic given the increasingly firm messages from New Labour and now the Coalition government about the need to end dependency. Indeed, the evidence over the last seven years suggests that about one million disabled people do want to work (Stanley and Regan, 2003; Shaw Trust, 2010). This rather challenges the construction of the problem of disabled worklessness as a form of rational choice.

Roulstone and Barnes (2005), in their analyses of disabled people and paid work, established that the government's targeted one million workless disabled people may not be synonymous with what the Institute for Public Policy Research (IPPR) have dubbed the missing million (Stanley and

Regan, 2003). Explicitly this suggests that many of those on incapacity (now Employment Support) allowances may not want to return to or commence paid work despite being closer to the labour market. While some of those furthest from the labour market who may want paid work may not get the chance as medical examination and 'objective' work capability tests are likely to deem these people 'worthy of support'. Meanwhile 23 per cent of disabled adults have no formal qualifications compared to 9 per cent in the general population (Labour Force Survey, 2009, Quarter 1). This is a clear challenge in policy terms for those furthest from economic stability in an era of work-first policies. What is becoming clear from both sides of the Atlantic is that anti-discriminatory policies outlawing inferior treatments in education and employment have at best made no difference to disabled people's employment status (Bambra and Pope, 2007) and, at worst, as the debates seem to be tentatively suggesting in the US, anti-discrimination legislation is leading to more employment-related discrimination (Stapleton and Burkhauser, 2003).

Other performance indicators for policy efficacy in the 2000s can be found in education, housing and crime data. In terms of reducing future educational disadvantage, there are some small but noteworthy improvements in disabled pupil performance. Between 2005 and 2008, the percentage of disabled pupils with a SEN statement attaining five plus A*–C grade GCSEs rose from 8.7 to 14.9 per cent. This is to be welcomed. Whether, in light of an increase in results more generally, the educational gap will remain, is hard to judge. The improvement does, however, point to increased aspirations for and by disabled people, which is very heartening (National Statistics, 2008).

The assumption that living lives free from paid work is somehow inherently pleasurable for disabled people also needs be challenged, with figures from the British Crime Survey (2008/09) pointing to a 10 per cent greater reported crime rate against younger disabled adults (16-34), with 42 per cent in the report year registering a crime against them compared to 32 per cent of non-disabled people (Home Office, 2008/09). Research by Sin et al (2009) at the Office for Public Management drew together the available evidence on disablist hate crime, noting that:

> The available evidence points to significant risk and prevalence of targeted violence and hostility against disabled people

> Disabled people are at higher risk of being victimised in comparison with non-disabled people. (Sin et al, 2009, p 10)

Conclusion

The longer-run efforts to disconnect disability from poverty and economic insecurity have proven of limited value, and perspectives on why this is the case may vary. Some would point to worklessness as at the core of the explanation of the links between poverty and disability. This is hard to contest as one major cause of engrained disadvantage. However, a reflexive approach would also need to link less eligible benefit rates to this poverty, something both the Harris (1971) and Martin et al (1988) studies confirmed some 20 years apart. The evidence that non-means-tested and non-contributory benefits have played a key role in stemming the most abject forms of poverty does not seem to be fully acknowledged. Recent shifts towards taking DLA into account in assessing charges for domiciliary care does not reflect the spirit of the legislation that established the allowances in the early 1970s. Recent attacks on DLA and ESA beneficiaries points to an increased conditionality and potential stigmatisation of these benefits. The widest differences in views attach to the reasons for worklessness and thus relative poverty whereby opinions are increasingly polarised into blaming discourses at one extreme and lost generation notions at the other. What is noteworthy is that the recent emphasis in the Coalition government's policy commitments to making work pay has to tackle barriers to work. The Coalition also needs to establish the threshold at which paid work begins to offer marginal utilities in compensating for benefits foregone in the housing and council tax systems. There is a real risk that people who were once deemed disabled by DWP-appointed assessors will be re-categorised for purely ideological reasons and will enter the Jobseeker's Allowance population. This could further engrain the link between poverty and disability, whether or not poverty stems from less eligible income replacement benefits or low paid work.

The question of the link between disability and poverty appears to be receiving renewed attention, yet a strongly ideological undercurrent detected by a number of commentators could simply make poverty a longer-term companion of many disabled people where employment, education and community barriers remain largely intact.

Summary

- Despite a range of anti-poverty measures, disability and poverty remain stubbornly close associates.
- Some policy interventions fail to consider their wider impact on disabled people and their families.
- Structural disadvantage arguably requires substantive equality rather than social inclusion processes alone in order to reduce long-term poverty.
- Worklessness remains a major source of relative poverty. Work-first approaches need to be carefully rolled out to tackle the lack of work opportunities in some areas.

Questions

1. What are the reasons for the largely ineffective anti-poverty measures as they relate to disabled households?
2. The poor are too well off and under-motivated, or structurally dis/advantaged. Which of these best sums up the position of disabled people in contemporary society?
3. What are likely to be the best ways to tackle social inequality among disabled people and their families?

Further reading

Tania Burchardt (2000, 2003) on disability and poverty/disadvantage provides robust and incisive reading, as do the CASEPapers constructed by LSE academics (see **Hills, 1998, 2003**). On worklessness **Beatty and Fothergill (2005)** and **Beatty et al (2009a, 2009b)** are key writers. **Levitas (1996, 1998), Dwyer (2004b)** and **Deacon (2002)** are useful on the poverty discourse, the weaknesses of New Labour's anti-poverty policy and the headlong shift into social inclusion discourses.

nine

Out of the labyrinth? The disability benefits system unpacked

The inclusion of a chapter on disability benefits in this book was prompted by the growing complexity of the UK benefits system and also the almost feverish attention afforded to disability welfare benefits by governments, the media and disability organisations in the late 20th and early 21st centuries (Piggott and Grover, 2009). The focus on 'sturdy beggars' in the early Poor Law has never fully gone away – this consideration has, in fact, remained in more contemporary concerns over a social underclass in 1980s welfare policy which, in time, has become equivalent to a 'moral panic' (Roulstone, 2000) over disabled people dependent on the welfare system. What is perhaps new about these debates is that disabled people, or to be precise those at some point deemed eligible for disability-related benefits, are now very much under the same spotlight as their non-disabled counterparts.

Today, alongside official guidance on benefit regulations are a myriad of articles, blogs, web pages and chat rooms all devoted to the detail, equity and 'injustices' of the disability benefits system. While direct payments and independent living has rightly exercised some disabled people to engage with policy discourses, a far greater number are actively engaged in a very real struggle over the future shape and eligibility of benefit entitlement. In a debate that does not engage with disabled people, decisions are being made as to whether they are 'disabled' or not. It is a debate that could seriously misrepresent the views of disabled people. The British press abounds with stories of disability benefit fraudsters. The Department for Work and Pensions has set up a fraud web page where neighbours or associates can inform on a benefit thief by filling in the 'Report a benefit thief' online form, which seems to act against the spirit of natural justice in assuming theft rather than alleged theft (DWP, 2011).

The equivalent of a pitched battle is taking place around the issue of who is or is not disabled. Legal actions have been taken by both the DWP and claimants around issues of process in assessing 'disability', most recently around the right to tape DWP medical assessments, which has become so heated that the DWP and Atos are trialling examination recording in one area (Jobcentre Plus, 2011). This form of contestation of welfare is relatively new, largely in response to often a quite arbitrary redrawing of the line at which eligibility for a given disability benefit is awarded. Views polarise strongly as to why the disability benefits system has come under such close scrutiny. The official position points to the undeniably dramatic growth in the headline figure spent on social security (as opposed to social care) and also the equally dramatic rise in the number of recipients. This growth is seen as counter-intuitive as, in the absence of war and increasing public health, claimancy ought to remain fairly steady (National Statistics, 2007b; Beatty and Fothergill, undated). At times, policy rhetoric has blamed the growth of claiming on people who have minor conditions or who are malingering and essentially jumping on the benefits bandwagon. However, a closer look reveals the picture is more complex. The most dramatic growth in disability benefit expenditure has been for the post-retirement age group. While the numbers of those of working age obtaining disability benefits has increased since the 1970s, the overall bill for this group has grown much less dramatically, even when mainstreamed disability tax credits is taken into account (UK Parliament, 2010a). The complex interplay of ageing, changing patterns of chronic ill heath and labour market opportunities seems more readily to lend assistance in providing clues here (Fothergill and Wilson, 2007).

A careful analysis needs to establish the finer details for the above growth and go beyond the policy rhetoric. For example, the 'moral panic' over fraud has never been substantiated. Even though the NAO posited a figure of 200,000 (out of 2.9 million) claims being fraudulent, a notable level of fraud, critics point to the methodology being based on extrapolations from a small sample, while 'strongly *suspected* fraud' accounted for over 80 per cent of these cases using the NAO's own rather vague definitions. A closer reading of the report suggests that only 1.5 per cent of the original sample of 1,200 had been confirmed as fraud cases. Indeed the comptroller general of the NAO was forced to admit that fraud and departmental errors were being conflated (NAO, 2009). Underclaiming is an even greater problem in monetary terms than either over or false claiming, but little policy concern is applied to the issue of underclaiming despite the social injustices involved (CAB, 2003). The growth in claimancy for working-age Incapacity Benefit (ICB) claimants can be better understood to link with a complex set of reasons that include poor job prospects in post-industrial contexts (Fothergill and Wilson, 2007), and very rational decisions to move onto or stay on ICBs as opposed to the less generous jobseekers benefits (Roulstone and Barnes, 2005).

Certainly the darkest images of a social underclass, promulgated from the 1980s onwards, have proven to be of very limited value in analysing the reasons for the growth in ICBs. It is worth pointing out that the move onto these benefits was assessed officially using medical assessors appointed by the DWP (Burchardt, 1999). Any post hoc rejection of the outcomes of such eligibility assessments has to cast doubt on the efficacy of the benefits system more generally. Indeed, while fraud and a seeking out of the better shelter of ICBs cannot be denied, policy writers have to disentangle the equally important question as to whether UK governments are simply shifting the 'disability category' to fit with its fiscal and spending plans and the real impact of the loss of large-scale manufacturing employment in the UK. This will likely become a more stark reality as unprecedented public spending cuts take effect throughout 2011 (DWP, 2010a; HM Treasury, 2010). At the time of writing a major backlash from disabled people's organisations is being mounted against possible cuts to the Disability Living Allowance (DLA).

To date, most disability benefits have been based on the Poor Law principle of less eligibility, except where personal sacrifice is the basis of the claim for disability benefits, for instance, where a person accrues an impairment in war or in industry. This leads to invidious distinctions being made historically around the cause of impairment. For example, if a person develops a chronic long-term condition due to operating machinery, this may be seen as more deserving than say an inflammatory condition which, despite being made worse by aspects of working life, is not easily attributable to that. This of course leads to a mismatch between levels of need and levels of desert in disability benefit systems.

Despite these inherent shortcomings, the UK disability benefits system has witnessed the further accretion of new benefits being grafted on to these older principles of eligibility and desert. The rise in disability benefit expenditure and numbers in receipt of benefits was first a major concern for the avowedly neoliberal Conservative government of the late 1970s, noting as it did: 'Public expenditure is at the heart of Britain's present economic difficulties' (HM Treasury, 1979). Specific concerns attached to the growth and need to curtail welfare spending as it was seen that such growth was encouraging rather than dispelling dependency. This concern led to a major policy review of disability benefits from the 1980s onwards, starting with the Fowler reforms which targeted mainly Income Support (IS), a mainstream income replacement benefit claimed by some disabled people (Barnes, 1991).

Of note, most forms of welfare spending increased during the Thatcher and Major government's tenure (Hills, 1998, p 2), with the largest growth being in the non-contributory universal benefits and means-tested benefits. This partly reflected an ageing population and the increase in unemployment and poverty-related claiming during the 1980s and early 1990s.

The continued growth throughout the 1980s and 1990s in ICBs and DLAs led to the biggest reviews of a range of disability-related welfare support since the welfare state was established (DWP, 2006). The Blair government's accession to power in 1997, under the reformulated image and philosophy of New Labour, made welfare benefits a key priority. As the then prime minister made clear:

> I vow we will have reduced the proportion [of national income that] we spend on the welfare bills of social failure. (Blair, 1996)

In the late 1990s, disability-related benefits came under scrutiny in a way previously unprecedented in UK policy terms. This reflected the continued growth in spending on social protection. HM Treasury figures suggest that in real terms expenditure on social protection grew from £108 billion in 1988 to £145 billion in 1998, and reached £208 billion in 2008. Therefore a doubling of spending was evident in the 20 years 1988-2008 (HM Treasury, 2009). However, closer scrutiny, one that takes economic growth in the British economy into account, suggests that the percentage spend as a proportion of GDP (gross domestic product) rose from 12.5 per cent of GDP in 1988 to 13.2 per cent in 2008, a 0.7 per cent increase (HM Treasury, 2009). What is noteworthy is that the real crisis, one often identified in neoliberal appraisals, was that despite this growth in spending, outcomes were poor. This contraction could certainly be explained by the limited success of getting disabled people off income replacement benefits, but is less helpful as an appraisal of, say, DLA and Attendance Allowance (AA) that clearly seem to be aiding disabled people's independence and quality of life (Corden et al, 2009). Nevertheless, by the late 1990s it was evident that a 'head of steam' had formed against any further growth in welfare spending. Perception, it seems, is very important in fuelling a moral panic around social expenditure. As the analysis below suggests, the actual growth in working-age benefits is less dramatic than that in post-retirement support. These subtleties of interpretation are often the first casualties in the war of words on reducing social dependency. Before we explore the reappraisal of disability benefits and the perceived fiscal crises of the state, it is necessary to undertake a brief historical reflection which reflects on the development of specific benefits and which also lays out the different principles that underpin the range of benefits available. Ahead of that it is also worth reflecting on Drake's (1999) typology of disability policy principles. His typology in ***Box 9.1*** below sums up the key principles behind a range of benefits.

Box 9.1: Drake's typology of disability benefits

- Containment
- Compensation
- Normalised support
- Rights

Historical context and the bases for benefit entitlements

Alongside Drake's useful typology, we might add the broader cross-cutting principles of 'active' versus 'passive' principles that have increasingly featured in the UK disability benefits system. For example, passive principles attach to DLAs where claimants have to emphasise what they *cannot* do, whereas recent shifts in ICB principles have shifted dramatically towards what disabled people *can* do (Roulstone and Barnes, 2005). This is significant as claimants could be subject to the regulations of each benefit and have to emphasise both active and inactive elements of their claim (Beatty et al, 2009a, 2009b), a continuing tension in the UK disability benefits system.

A more descriptive but equally useful typology is provided by Burchardt (1999), who provides the following scheme to aid interpretation of disability benefits:

- Compensatory benefits: for example, industrial injury and war disablement benefits where individuals are compensated for their industrial or combat sacrifices.
- Earnings replacement benefits: to provide an income for individuals unable to earn as a result of sickness or disability. This has taken the form of Invalidity Benefit (IVB), ICB and Employment and Support Allowance (ESA) respectively.
- Extra costs benefits related to benefits that aim to support the extra costs of disabled people (for example, transport, personal support), but which are not related to work contributions, as epitomised by the DLA and AA.
- Means-tested benefits: these are income top-up benefits, for example, IS, but also Housing or Council Tax Benefits. They are essentially mainstream benefits that disabled people may be eligible to apply for.

It is worth reflecting that the compensatory benefits above are for specified causes such as war and industrial injuries. If we take a broader view of disablement as the result of a hostile society, a much debated idea, then a radical policy agenda would be to review the possible expansion of the compensatory principle to a wider range of disabled people. Despite an evidence base on economic and social barriers, there is little likelihood that such an expansion of the compensatory principle will happen given the highly normative nature of constructions of desert in the compensatory benefits arena. Indeed the actual expansion is most likely to be that of conditionality in the area of earnings replacement benefits (DWP, 2010a).

The compensatory principle was rolled out early with the War Disability Pension following the First World War, and provided for those 'invalided' out of military service who could not avail themselves of the King's Roll (an early employment quota scheme aimed at work re-entry) as they were permanently disabled (Kowalsky, 2007). There was clear honour attached to combat for one's country and this connection has remained in place for much of the last 100 years (Barnes, 1991). The provision for industrial injuries was added in 1948 with the birth of the modern welfare state (Burchardt, 1999). Together, industrial and war injury compensation benefits have been set at generous levels, a far cry from the principle of less eligibility, with recognition that impairments are likely to be long-term and unchanging. Benefits have also been paid regardless of wider income sources and are not taxed. As Walker and Walker noted:

This was a crucial departure in the evolution of social security and represented the first recognition by society of the rights of disabled people to financial compensation irrespective of their earnings or other sources of income. (Walker and Walker, quoted in Dalley, 1991, p 22)

This latter point is controversial, as Beveridge had called for a unified disability scheme payable regardless of cause of impairment, a point overruled by the Labour government following the Second World War (Walker and Walker, quoted in Dalley, 1991). Disabled people who could not find work, or who were unable to work due to illness or impairment, had no formal recognition until the 1970s, and relied on mainstream, often stigmatised, means-tested benefits.

It is worth pointing out that disabled people have historically been disproportionately more likely to rely on general benefits (most notably retirement pension and social assistance) for a key part of their income (Walker and Walker, 1991). Disabled people were largely reliant on basic level sickness benefit (Barnes, 1991). In 1971, IVB was introduced to support those disabled people with a work and national insurance record. A non-contributory benefit entitled the 'non-contributory invalidity pension', later to become the Severe Disablement Allowance (SDA), was introduced to support disabled people who could not build up such a national insurance record (Burchardt, 1999). As with a range of benefits, feminist policy writers have criticised the insurance principle as sexist in overlooking the wider contributions of women in society (Lonsdale, 1985). Even the non-contributory element was not, at first, available to women outside of paid work, and it took a degree of struggle to gain parity between disabled men and women with the introduction of the SDA (*Hansard*, 1984).

ICB replaced IVB in 1994 with the passing of the Social Security (Incapacity for Work) Act (HM Government, 1994). The Act was not an attempt to grow IVB yet further and was introduced in part to stem the numbers who were accessing disability income replacement benefits. As Cooper and Vernon (1996) note, the Act was in part the result of concerns regarding benefit administration shortcomings over:

> ... the incorrect application of entitlement criteria or absence from work and fraud. One particular criticism was that the test for [incapacity] had only to relate to work that the claimant could reasonably be expected to undertake. This it was claimed suggested too much concern was being directed to non-medical criteria. (cited in Drake, 1999, p 57)

Despite this re-evaluation of the role and remit of ICB, claimant numbers continued to grow throughout the 1990s. Out-of-work disability income replacement benefits not surprisingly became a key concern of the incoming New Labour government in 1997:

> Labour was elected in 1997 with few specific proposals about social security reforms. But after over one parliament of reforms, we can clearly see explicit and consistent trends in welfare policy: there is a "work-first" focus; a new willingness to increase [some] social security benefits; a desire to redistribute and to reduce poverty, although in a manner which focuses on particular demographic groups; increasing centrality for benefits which relate to "need", which has involved expanded means-testing; and a downgrading of benefits that are contributory. (Brewer et al, 2002, p 1)

New Labour's emphasis on rights and responsibilities (Powell, 2002) underpinned the specific policy shifts to much firmer administration of out-of-work disability benefits with an attendant harsh rhetoric around the responsibilities of disabled people who they felt were capable of paid work:

> ... individual citizens ... need to meet their responsibility to take the necessary steps to re-enter the labour market when they have a level of capacity and capability that makes this possible ... the aim is to reduce the number of disability benefit claimants by 1 million over the next decade. (DWP, 2006, p 4)

New Labour managed to reduce the ICB headcount by 300,000 by 2009, much of which was achieved by reduced 'flow' on to the benefit and the shift of some claimants onto Jobseeker's Allowance or, for older claimants, Pension Credit (*Hansard*, 2009). The seeming inability of the New Labour government to dramatically reduce the 'stock' of ICBs remains a policy puzzle, while welfare spending has continued to rise overall. The identification of ICBs as a key focus can be seen to be motivated variously by genuine concerns for the wasted lives of those out of work, but can also be viewed as a shameless attack on those with impairments who have little electoral sympathy (Roulstone and Barnes, 2005).

The proportion of the welfare spend going on disability-related benefits is striking; however, some brief comparisons can be made with other mainstream benefits. This begs the question as to just where the wider problems lie. The year 2007/08 saw social security spending reach £158 billion, which amounted to 25.6 per cent of total government expenditure (11.4 per cent of GDP). Social security was the largest spending header, followed by health at 18.3 per cent of overall government spend. Of note, ICB formed £9.867 billion of the above spend, while DLA and AA took up £15 billion. These latter benefits, of course, support disabled people of all ages. It is also worth mentioning that Housing Benefit, a means-tested benefit supporting low-income families with housing needs, cost £15.732 billion in 2007/08, nearly 10 per cent of the country's GDP (HM Treasury, 2009).

There are at least two inferences that can be taken from the above. One is that disability support has become unaffordable, disproportionate, too easily accessible and overclaimed (Cawston et al, 2009). The other is that disability support has risen in response to engrained worklessness, an ageing population and the attempt by claimants to avoid the least attractive out-of-work benefits that are decidedly less eligible, but which compensate for lack of work in many areas (Piggott and Grover, 2009). This difference of opinion lies at the very heart of the conundrum regarding the attribution of causation to the 'disability welfare problem'. It is also worth pointing out that £16 billion of means-tested benefit goes unclaimed each year (Disability Alliance, 2010a).

Disability benefits spending in particular, and social security spending more generally, points to the challenges surrounding an evidence-based policy environment. Worryingly, the increased shift to conditionality, means testing and reduced take-up of ICBs is based on highly selective evidence as to the likely factors that continue to encourage claimancy. The speed and lack of clarity in introducing the successor to ICBs, the ESA, has wrought a range of criticisms of disabled people's organisations and governmental commentators alike. Despite the early discussion of ESA being for those clearly deserving of support, the reality has been perceived to be a rather harsher reformulation of earnings replacements benefits. The ESA is embedded in the more conditional (Dwyer, 2004b) welfare context of the late 1990s and 2000s, and proposed a lengthy assessment phase (13 weeks) and a work-focused interview for all applicants. This new assessment protocol places the onus on a disabled person to emphasise whether they can undertake paid work, and provides the test of Work Capability Assessment for sick and disabled individuals. The following is an excerpt from a 2006 parliamentary committee report on the proposed ESA benefit reforms:

We are disappointed that there are a range of issues requiring further clarification on the level at which the Employment and Support Allowance will be set. We recommend that the Department provide more detailed information in the response to this report. We urge the Department to work closely with disability organisations to ensure a proper assessment is made of the structure of the new benefit, how it will affect the income of ill or disabled people in comparison with the current system and work to alleviate inconsistencies within the system. DWP should ensure that the resulting benefit levels maintain the principle of no loss to existing claimants when a new benefit is introduced. (UK Parliament, 2006)

One major concern for the above commentators was the low level of basic ESA rate during the assessment period, which, in being set at less than the eligibility rates tagged to Jobseeker's Allowance, the main out-of-work benefit was seen as punitive of disabled people entering the benefit assessment. The ESA absorbed some of the criticisms levelled at it and now operates with three groupings which are treated as discrete claimant categories (DWP, 2008b):

- those with 'no limited capability' who will be channelled into work or Jobseeker's Allowance;
- those with 'some limited capability' who will form a work-related group and undergo regular assessment for work capability and work-focused interviews;
- those deemed too 'sick or disabled' to have work capability and who form the support group.

The middle group, those deemed to have limited but conceivable capability, receive a higher rate of ESA, but this is subject to their 'passing' a work activity test. There are some considerable concerns given that sanctions can be attached to this group, that workplace barriers cannot be denied and the fear that this group will face unreasonable pressure to achieve work based on abstract measures of work capability which ignore the behaviour and perceptions of employers towards those in this welfare category (Roberts et al, 2004). Here Stone's classic formulation of the shifting of the disability category to suit broader political expedients seems to apply neatly to this situation (Stone, 1984).

Disability Living Allowance: challenging the additional payments system

DLA is a non-means-tested, non-contributory benefit available for disabled people from the age of two to the maximum qualifying age of 64, although it can be continued beyond 64. It is made up of a mobility component (previously Mobility Allowance, MA) to help with costs in getting around and also a care component (formerly AA) to help pay for additional costs related to living in a disabling society (Burchardt, 1999). MA and AA had been introduced in 1975 and 1971 respectively with the aim of meeting the additional costs that disabled people were seen to face (Harris et al, 1971). Arguably, there was a clear early recognition that support for disabled people was unconditional on, say, their employment, good health or commitment to statutory constructions of independence. Even so, the absence of work, contributory insurance and the extra costs of being disabled were important background issues in the construction of the early forms of these benefits. Unlike national assistance, MA and AA in principle carried no stigma of social failure but were positive categorical treatments based on perceived needs.

DLA and the Social Security Act 1992 (HM Government, 1992) that underpinned it was itself recognition that many disabled people's needs were still not being met despite the advent of the above additional benefits. The (controversial) surveys of disability conducted in the mid-1980s established that disability, especially for those in the highest 'categories of disability', had significant unmet need (Martin and White, 1988). DLA was a response to this. It has proven invaluable to disabled people, and at the end of November 2009 there were 3,199,010 children and adults in receipt of the benefit (HM Treasury, 2009). It has more than one level of assessed need and more recently the care component of DLA has shifted to having three levels of assessed eligibility/need, while the mobility component has two levels.

The benefit has slowly if at times reluctantly expanded its remit. For example, the original operation of the mobility component of DLA operated more confidently and inclusively where a mobility impairment was at stake, but applicants with sensory and behavioural impairments struggled to gain support. Impairment charities continue to lobby for a more flexible interpretation of mobility needs and, indeed, a social model-informed approach to disability would point to commonalities in facing such barriers (Zarb, 1995). The UK Royal National Institute for the Blind (RNIB) was recently successful in getting the English Parliament to amend the Social Security Act 1992 (HM Government, 1992) to allow people with 'severe' visual impairments access to the higher rate of DLA, something that was previously disallowed unless a person was both deaf and blind (RNIB, 2009).

Alongside a review of ICB, a perhaps surprising parallel review of additional costs benefits was instigated in the late 1990s. The Benefit Integrity Project (BIP) aimed to identify and root out fraud in DLA claims. A moral panic attached to the growing numbers in receipt of DLA. Another possible reason for such a review was that research evidence (Beatty et al, 2009a, 2009b) was beginning to point to a growing overlap of ICB and DLA recipients (1.25 million adults by 2008). Although the UK benefits system had never outlawed this mixing of activity and inactivity benefits, suspicions were often raised in the welfare system where these were straddled and work/ICB was combined with DLA.

Although the inner logic of the DWP is very hard to comprehend compared to, say, the Department of Health, and little consultation takes place in the field of disability welfare (Roulstone and Barnes, 2005), there is evidence that straddling in/activity benefits, gaining a job and applying for work-based support can trigger a DLA review. In fact, the ability to combine (extra costs-related) benefits with ICBs or hopefully paid work can arguably be seen as a marker of a mature, flexible, nuanced disability benefits system. The reality, in policy and political terms in 2010, is closer to the suspicion that attached to the development of income replacement benefits for disabled people when they were first mooted. Income replacement benefits are seen as a threat to independence and self-reliance for all but the 'most disabled' of claimants. Notably, official research conducted for the DWP established that those claiming both ICBs (now ESA) and DLA were older claimants likely to be further away from the labour market. In this sense, any motivation based on beliefs that both ICB and DLA claimancy could be reduced by targeting this sub-group of DLA claimants is probably misplaced.

The official moral panic over DLA fraud more generally was not borne out in practice. In the first five months of the BIP's operation, just under

8,000 individuals of the 40,615 cases reviewed (themselves purposively sampled as being in need of 'review') had their benefit reduced (*Hansard*, 1998). The project sparked major controversy, with many disabled people's organisations making representations to the minister to review its operation. The perception was that some of the most needy and vulnerable disabled people were being targeted in what was seen as a cost-driven exercise. This drew a pre-emptive statement from the then DSS, denying that the BIP was part of the wider welfare reform programme:

> The Benefit Integrity Project (BiP) is entirely separate from welfare reform. It is about ensuring the correctness of payments of DLA under the current rules. It is a symptom of the need for reform rather than part of the reform process itself. DLA is a complex benefit and there is understandable confusion on the part of its recipients about whether or when to report changes in circumstances, particularly if a change has come about gradually or the level of need has been affected by other circumstances such as the acquisition of an aid. (Department of Social Security, 1998b)

Since the first attempts to strike out fraud in the welfare system, there has been evidence of muddle on the part of the chief officers taking fraud issues forward in government departments. The then head of fraud investigations at the DSS (a forerunner to the DWP), Peter Mathison, when giving evidence to the Public Accounts Committee on the difference between ove-claims and fraud, stated:

> I am not quite sure what you mean by robust. In terms of DLA [Disability Living Allowance], it is extremely difficult to identify quite whether it is fraud ... I do think it is about correctness and we are sure that there is a high level of incorrectness there. (UK Parliament, 1998)

The BIP was dropped in response to outcry from disabled people and critical parliamentary elements. Noticeably, many commentators viewed DLA as a protected benefit, one supporting disabled people with often significant extra costs, while ICB has received no such treatment. Despite this governmental climb down, a subsequent review programme entitled the 'Right Payments Programme' was recently rolled out. Significantly, little publicity was made around this latest review scheme, compared to further reviews of ICB. There is no evidence that the continued (and at times very stressful personal) review of DLA will abate, especially at a time of severe fiscal squeeze (DWP, 2010a; HM Treasury, 2010). DLA is clearly not now a sacrosanct territory and it is evident that the validity of historical assessment regimes is questionable given the large numbers of 'indefinite' claims that have now been overturned or even terminated.

One further development in the future of additional payments benefits is the review of AA. AA is not means tested, it is non contributory and, since 1992, has only been available for those who are deemed eligible for extra cost support having reached 65 years of age (DWP, 2009b). As with DLA, AA plays an important role in supporting disabled people. By November 2009, 1,621,030 disabled older people were in receipt of AA in the UK. The New Labour government's commissioning of the Wanless Review reflected the view that social security and social care systems were insufficiently engaged with each other, especially but not exclusively where they related to the most 'vulnerable' citizens who may be reliant on both systems. The social care review by Derek Wanless recommended the review of the relationship between AA and wider social care transfers via the social care system (Wanless, 2006). This has been met with varied responses. Those supportive of merging the social care and welfare budgets point to the popularity of seamless provision in wider adult social policy manifest in the form of individual budgets (IBs). Detractors point to the very different profiles of the AA claimant group, many of whom are more active and independent and a long way from social care professionals, while much social care provision is now means tested and heavily rationed. However, major concerns relate to the possibility of greater targeting of the merged provision that may well exclude many current AA claimants. It is interesting that for those with low to middle range support needs, AA has allowed access to benefits that until the 1990s afforded quasi-direct payments in not having to have professional prescription of just how money transfers were spent. There are some concerns that the merging of social welfare and social care could boost rather than diminish the role of social care professionals in the lives of AA claimants. Indeed, the growth of medical and social scrutiny in the AA system has the potential to place recipients between a rock and a hard place in having to deal with dominant disability professionals in their claims/reviews.

Conclusion

Clearly the additional payments system is hugely important for disabled people. Official evidence points to the positive role of DLA in fostering independence, improved quality of life, better physical and mental health. For those of working age DLA aids proximity to paid work (Corden et al, 2009). Strong anecdotal evidence points to the wider value of the benefit in keeping some disabled people out of income poverty. The additional payments benefits scheme is clearly in a state of flux, some would say disarray. It is certainly the case that DLA will be kept under continued review given the rise in claimant numbers. It is noteworthy that research on DLA and even AA have increasingly been linked to work-first agendas and looking at behavioural and disincentive effects of DLA claimancy. Given that we know too little about the actual benefits of DLA and AA to disabled people (Corden et al, 2009), it seems rather odd that such a shift in focus should attach to these benefits (Hancock et al, 2010; Thomas and Griffiths, 2010)

The role of critical policy analysts, therefore, is to cut through the policy rhetoric to arrive at a carefully nuanced understanding of the changing profile of claimants for DLA and AA. A recent study of age and care need projections of post-retirement British citizens by Malley et al (2005) established that the likely increased demand for AA and DLA (care component) will be as high as 4 per cent over the period 2005-25. This has huge implications for the UK government, while the DWP needs to open up its working and consult fully with disabled people if it is to regain any credibility in this area. Despite the moral panic over increased numbers of DLA, AA and ESA numbers of DLA/AA recipients are likely to rise where they reflect an ageing population, and for ESA the challenge of substituting economic activities for those lost during deindustrialisation will likely make the stock of people on this or related benefits very hard to move into paid employment. Disability benefits are likely to be more not less important as we move forward into a 21st century marked by uncertainty. As Hills remarked in 1998

> ... even the most optimistic assessments of the potential effect of such schemes suggest that a substantial proportion of benefit recipients pensioners, lone parents with pre-school children, and some of the long-term sick and disabled will continue to have their living standards determined by benefit levels, however successful other measures are. (Hills, 1998, p 40)

Summary

Welfare spending has increased markedly in real terms since the 1970s, however, most of the recent growth has been in spending on post-retirement benefits. Disability benefits have increased, most especially incapacity benefits (ICBs). It is erroneous to view claimants as inherently fraudulent as recipients were accessed, at some point, to be eligible for ICBs.

- Governments are seen to shift the disability category and who counts as disabled to fit wider policy and fiscal targets.
- Disabled people increasingly attract very negative attention as welfare recipients.
- ICB and DLA reform has made welfare claiming an increasingly precarious activity.
- Governments have been severely challenged in reforming the size of the disability welfare spend and are now resorting to harsh measures to reduce the flow and stock on ICBs and DLA.

Questions

1. Why have governments shifted the disability category to suit wider policy priorities?
2. Are attempts to toughen eligibility for ICB (now ESA) and DLA justified? Are they likely to work?
3. Why has welfare policy reform not involved disabled people in large-scale consultations in the way that adult social care has?
4. Is work the only legitimate means to social security? What are the barriers to greater working activity amont current ICB and DLA claimants of working age?

Further reading

The best work on disability welfare stems from **Piggott and Grover (2009)**, **Roulstone (2000, 2006)**, **Hyde (2000)** and **Burchardt (2004)**. Wider critical policy pieces on welfare reform are available in **Dwyer (2004b)**, **Levitas (1998)**, **Bagguley and Mann (1992)**, **Dean and Taylor-Gooby (1992)** and **Driver and Martell (2002)**.

Coalition dreams, new conditionality and disability policy

Introduction

When first conceived, this book was projected to end with an appraisal of the latest New Labour policies around disability. However, it soon became apparent that the New Labour era was to end before the book was to be completed. The accession to power of the Conservative-Liberal Democrat Coalition in June 2010 thus requires a snapshot appraisal of the key policy changes proposed and a prediction of the impact these policies could have on disabled people. Before embarking on an exploration of Coalition policy it is worth, in the spirit of the wider book, reflecting on the ideological positioning of these policies. The Coalition brings together a clear commitment to neoliberal values alongside a continuation of communitarianism captured in the notion of the 'Big Society'. Here, the increased role of civil society, community, neighbourhood and localised voluntary activity are seen to complement a reduced role and reach of the state. The public sector has come in for sustained criticism for being wasteful and supposedly sapping the economic vigour of UK society. The proposal to cut up to 40 per cent from some departments sat alongside an initial 'cordon sanitaire' of protection for health and overseas development (HM Treasury, 2010a). The erstwhile Coalition Chief Secretary to the Treasury, David Laws, laid out the government's view on public spending:

But the worst choice of all would be to fail to put in place a credible plan to reduce Britain's bloated budget deficit. We cannot afford to continue to increase public debt at the rate of £3 billion each week. Our huge public debts threaten financial stability and if left unchecked would de-rail the economic recovery. Public borrowing is only taxation deferred, and it would be deeply irresponsible to continue to accumulate vast debts which would have to be paid off by our children and our grandchildren for decades to come. (Laws, 2010)

Mr Laws relinquished his position shortly after making this comment due to alleged financial impropriety.

On the very same day the Chancellor George Osborne provided a similar apocalyptic message:

The years of public sector plenty are over, but the more decisively we act the quicker and stronger we can come through these tough times.... (Osborne, 2010a)

There was indeed cause for concern, with welfare spending increasing in real terms by 40% in the financial years 2000-2010 (HM Treasury, 2010b). The OECD's Economic Outlook review in 2010 placed Britain in the highest structural deficit placing (OECD, 2010). The Treasury's budget document makes clear the major reasons for this mismatch was the growth of bad debt, inappropriate behaviour in the financial sector to fuel a fool's paradise of debt-fuelled spending by both individuals and the British state (HM Treasury, 2010b). Of note the coalition government aside from introducing a bank tax levy, has focused much of its attention on groups who would not have gained from this financial bonanza. Those on out-of-work benefits have come in for the most sustained criticism this side the 1940s welfare settlement. This mismatch of cause and remedy in British policy response has led to the largest revolt from erstwhile traditional welfare, disability and carers organisations. The public sector, despite having many of the lowest paid workers has also taken much of the blame for our fiscal crisis.

The incoming Coalition government also announced that a range of quasi-autonomous non-governmental organisations (quangos) would be reviewed alongside major IT projects and governments' use of external consultants (Osborne, 2010b). The 'bonfire of the quangos', as it was dubbed, witnessed the end of the Independent Living Fund (ILF), the Disability and Employment Advisory Committee (DEAC) and the Audit Commission. The latter was an odd decision given the Audit Commission's central role in safeguarding public finances. Quangos had been under sustained attack from the political right, who described quangos as a key part of a wasteful and unaccountable (UK Parliament, 2010b).

Clearly some elements of state activity are more valued than others. At the time of writing the Liberal Democrat policy elements of the Coalition seem not to be in the foreground, with heavy concessions being given in terms of increased tuition fees and even a cross-party backlash against the key Liberal Democrat quest to instigate electoral reform (Stevenson,

2010). The messages coming from the Coalition are complex and, at times, contradictory. Welfare reform is a prime example. Here there is the harsher tone taken by the Coalition, one that is being picked up by most of the UK media. As George Osborne put it:

> I want to support the person who leaves their house at six or seven in the morning, goes out and does perhaps a low-paid job in order to provide for their family and is incredibly frustrated when they see on the other side of the street the blinds pulled down and someone sitting there and living on out-of-work benefits. (Osborne, 2010c)

This presentation of the binary dilemma of those who will work, often against all odds, and those who will not whatever the conditions, helps create an image of a wasteful state and a parasitic sub-populace. At times, however, the political rhetoric is much more sympathetic and alludes to worklessness as the result of social circumstances and previously being written off. In the words of the then Secretary of State for Work and Pensions, Iain Duncan Smith:

> A system that was originally designed to help support the poorest in society is now trapping them in the very condition it was supposed to alleviate. Instead of helping, a deeply unfair benefits system too often writes people off. The proportion of people parked on inactive benefits has almost tripled in the past 30 years to 41% of the inactive working age population. (Duncan Smith, 2010)

An advocate of the Coalition's concerns would point to their early assessment of the issues in a divided society and their genuine concern to attack the root causes of the problems they have inherited. For example, a key document outlining *The state of the nation* (HM Government, 2010a) points to the growth of 'out-of-work' benefits and the greater income inequality that has arisen in the preceding 10 years. The report notes that 1.4 million people have been out of work for 9 of the last 10 years of New Labour's time in office. The report also notes that despite the previous administration's anti-poverty agenda and tax credits systems, income inequality is at its highest levels since 1961 (HM Government, 2010a). This latter point seems to blame previous administrations for poverty, inequality and worklessness. Taken together, the very different discourses of the debilitating state versus blaming the individual take some unravelling. Indeed they beg questions as to just what the true beliefs of government are on these issues. However, these dual sentiments are not new and were an abiding feature of New Labour rhetoric (Roulstone and Barnes, 2005; Grover and Piggott, 2007) around workless disabled people.

In terms of longer-run policy shifts, Coalition policy appears to advocate a consolidation of neoliberal aims for a free economy, an enlivened private sector and a reaffirmation of the value of 'organic communities'. Lister and Bennett provide an early appraisal of the Coalition government's welfare and work policy programme, noting that it did not escape '... out of the policy paradigm established by Labour' (Lister and Bennett, 2010, p 102). The Coalition Prime Minister David Cameron summed up his vision of the 'Big Society' as based on: 'Things that fire you up in the morning, that drive you, that you truly believe will make a real difference to the country you love' (Cameron, 2010). A more worked-up statement is made clear in the Coalition's *Our programme for government*:

> We share a conviction that the days of big government are over; that centralisation and top-down control have proved a failure. We believe that the time has come to disperse power more widely in Britain today; to recognise that we will only make progress if we help people to come together to make life better. In short, it is our ambition to distribute power and opportunity to people rather than hoarding authority within government. (HM Government, 2010b)

Interestingly, the planned cuts in policing might suggest that authoritarianism is less a feature of this new conservatism. This may be true in strict law and order terms, yet there is evidence of increasingly harsh welfare discourses. Arguably, authoritarianism is taking on a new form, while populism, in rhetorical terms around welfare dependency and rolling back the state, has reached new heights. In concrete terms, these discourses are being realised in severe benefit withdrawal sanctions in, for instance, the failure to look for work. This is nothing new, but the stated policy intention to make it work at all costs is new. The increase in personal tax allowance for basic rate tax payers is for example seen to benefit 800, 000 of the lowest paid in Britain (HM Treasury, 2010b). The extent to which these reforms however take account of the contradictions of welfare policy, and 'make work pay', are open to question. Certainly the first sighting of disability welfare policy seems unduly harsh and based on highly selective appraisals of the problem at hand. Indeed the extent to which evidence underpins the proposed policy reforms is highly questionable. For example, the notion that worklessness is too easy, that the public sector drains the lifeblood of the economy and that unleashed community energies exist to underpin new social policies all lack substance in evidential terms. In terms of disability policy, the effects of imagined communities at the heart of first wave community care reforms seem not to have survived in the policy memory. To argue for greater community volunteering seems, for some, to reflect a degree of desperation on the part of the incoming Coalition government.

The Coalition and disability-related policy

The blueprint for disability policy is framed within the Coalition's *Our programme for government*. In a somewhat regressive fashion, disability and social care are tagged together (see ***Box 10.1***) in a way that pays no dues to independent living ideas that want to transcend the link between care and disability (Barnes and Mercer, 2006). The following are the highlighted priorities laid out in *Our programme*:

Box 10.1: The Coalition programme for social care and disability

- We will break down barriers between health and social care funding to incentivise preventative action.
- We will extend the greater roll-out of personal budgets to give people and their carers more control and purchasing power.
- We will use direct payments to carers and better community-based provision to improve access to respite care.
- We will reform Access to Work, so disabled people can apply for jobs with funding already secured for any adaptations and equipment they will need. (HM Government, 2010b, p 30)

The Coalition's disability reforms in detail

Disabled people have largely been protected from *major* welfare retractions during periods of fiscal crisis. But this stance has recently changed, and rather dramatically. A key target for policy reform is those disabled people claiming Employment and Support Allowance (ESA), and Incapacity Benefit (ICB)(ICB claimants not immediately deemed work-able will be migrated to the ESA). More differentiated approaches have already been introduced in the newly established and piloted ESA system to establish 1) those disabled people too sick/disabled to work, 2) those who should move rapidly into work or mainstream Jobseeker's Allowance and 3) a review group who will face continual Work Capability Assessments. It is assumed many will be moved off ESA where work capability is in evidence.

Those ESA recipients deemed closest to the labour market and allocated to the work-related activity group will have their claim limited to one year (DWP, 2010b). The key benefits that make work possible for those on a low income are also being reappraised and a new universal credit is being introduced to streamline out-of-work benefits and tax credits. The following, which will become effective in 2013 aims to:

- Bring together different forms of income-related support and provide a simple, integrated, benefit for people in or out of work.
- It will consist of a basic personal amount (similar to the current Jobseeker's Allowance) with additional amounts for disability, caring responsibilities, housing costs and children.
- As earnings rise, we expect Universal Credit will be withdrawn at a constant rate of around 65 pence for each pound of net earnings. Higher earnings disregards will also reinforce work incentives for selected groups.
- When introduced, Universal Credit will initially apply to new claims. It will be phased in for existing benefit and Tax Credit recipients. There will be no cash losers at the point of change, ensuring that no one will see their benefits reduced when Universal Credit is introduced.

However, there are contradictory issues developing in policy terms even before the roll out begins, for example, the tightening of eligibility for new Housing Benefit claimants (HM Treasury, 2010b) will impact disproportionately on disabled people contemplating entry into lower paid work. Universal credit (UC) aims to incentivise greater access to work and hours build-up. The exact impact of the universal credit on the five million claimants is very hard to gauge in the absence of detailed proposals. The benefit withdrawal rate is all-important here, with initial details suggesting a benefits withdrawal of 65/100 as opposed to the current 75/100. However, as Pearce has noted (IPPR, 2010), job creation and support is not receiving the same degree of attention as welfare reform. The objective of diminishing the public sector workforce, one where disabled people are largely concentrated (Hirst et al, 2004), may inadvertently limit the number shifting from the out-of-work claimant count for UC (UC is claimable both in and out of paid work). The claim by the Department for Work and Pensions that their single-handed management of the UC system will lead to more efficient administration of support might be seen as optimistic given the historic failure of DWP to avoid under-payments especially for those with most severe impairments (DWP, 2011c).

The government is also planning to scrap the current complex array of Work programmes (such as the New Deal, Work Step, Work Preparation) for disabled people. It intends to introduce a single Work Programme for all 'out-of-work' benefit claimants. The Work Programme according to the DWP' early assertions: 'will also ensure good value for money for the taxpayer by basing payments largely on results, and paying providers from the benefits saved from getting people into work. It is very much a partnership between Government and providers from across the public, private and third sectors – including social enterprises' (DWP, 2011d). Concerns attach to these assertions. Previous schemes including Pathways to Work and Workstep claimed to offer just such personalised forms of support, while the former proved limited and the latter though more effective was discontinued (see Roulstone and Barnes, 2005). The decision to pay by results is also not new, the notion that benefit savings will underpin future Work Programme funding makes a major gamble that sustained work placements occur. To date payments by results approaches have led contractors to aim for high throughput as opposed to quality sustained support approaches (Roulstone and Barnes, 2005). Conditionality and proposed harsh and incremental sanctions are central to the new programme which will be firmly based on supply-side measures (Deacon and Patrick, 2010). Although the detail is limited, it appears some disabled people closer to the labour market will be supported via this single gateway of support. For disabled people with more obvious support needs, a Work Choice programme (formerly the specialist disability employment programe) is being introduced to provide intensive support. The details provided on intensive support suggest CV writing, brokerage and closer working with employers will form the main support activities.

In truth, these forms of support have been available under previous schemes (Purvis et al, 2006; Roulstone and Barnes, 2005), while the more hands-on approach to employers seems at odds with the proposed review of disability discrimination legislation that may be viewed as reducing the power of anti-discrimination legislation in the disability field. Many bidders for Workchoice are the same traditional disability organisations that devlivered the previous specialist programs (DWP, 2011d) (Workstep, Work Preparation Job Introduction Scheme). No figures are available for the savings of an additional entry of large numbers of disabled people into paid work. Although benefits savings will be evident where someone enters work, where extra hours are worked and where withdrawal rates are made to benefit the claimant, this will obviously cost more.

The key assertion that benefits are more attractive than paid work because of disincentives in the benefits system is borne out by some evidence (OECD, 2004). Nevertheless, this OECD report (2004) failed to find one key programme or approach across OECD (Organisation for Economic Co-operation and Development) countries that substantially improved disabled people's path into paid work. The government has, however, increased the tax allowances for low-income earners in 2011, which may benefit some disabled people. Also helpful may be the reforming of Access to Work, a key workplace support fund to allow funding before a job is secured so that a disabled person can enter employment with support in place. The recent Sayce review, one funded by the DWP asserted that Access to Work, one of the government's best 'kept secrets' should be doubled from its current base and particularly aim to support those that had not been major beneficiaries (for example those with mental health problems and learning difficulties) in the past gain support (Sayce, 2011, p 1). This recommendation reflects the commitment of the Labout government before losing the election in 2010 (Shaw, 2010). Whether the DWP follow this advice is a moot point. The exact role of an employer's financial contribution, a current feature of the scheme, is unclear at this point, however. Local labour market conditions are closely linked to rates of 'out-of-work' disability benefit recipients. Research (Beatty and Fothergill, 2005) points to the absence of job opportunities, benefit traps and also cycles of worklessness all being important. Most ESA claimants are at more generalised higher risk of unemployment due to having lower educational and skill profiles. In this sense, the Coalition government may be fighting with the 'wrong shadow'. Harsher welfare regimes in the absence of greater employment opportunities may simply lead to movement onto less generous benefits which, in turn, become another important policy consideration where genuine extra costs are no longer met. Evidence from the mainstream Jobseeker's Allowance population of churning, repeat entry and exit to the jobs market suggests that sustained employment for some disabled people leaving ESA may be limited (Beatty and Fothergill, 2005).

Perhaps the most surprising development has been the government's commitment to reassessing all current Disability Living Allowance (DLA) claims by 2013. Or at least this is one interpretation (HM Treasury, 2010c). HM Treasury's budget highlights the need to make savings by reforming the 'gateway' to DLA by 2013/14. The latter might suggest just new claimants will face the new 'objective' test for the benefit (HM Treasury, 2010b). The position is unclear at the time of writing. What is noteworthy is the assertion that an objective medical tests is required; what one wonders underpinned the previous DLA assessments? Certainly the recent Harrington report of ICB work-related medical assessments might suggest that current medical assessments of disability have been unduly harsh rather than too easy (The same contractor completes ICB/ESA and DLA medicals) (Harrington, 2010). DLA mobility and care components provide key forms of support for extra costs related to getting about and getting support. DLA does not attract the stigma or professional gate keeping of applying for adult social care as it is firmly part of the social welfare system. The exact reasons for reviewing DLA claimants is less clear than for, say, ESA, as DLA is generally claimed by those with more obvious and enduring impairments – differential levels of award are made depending on levels of 'disability'. This is clearly an attempt to review the threshold for support and the development is clearly premised on the view that access to DLA has been too generous. There is no evidence available to support this assertion, however, and this is borne out by the high levels of successful appeals for refused claims (CPAG, 2001; Disability Law Service, 2009). The government has also said it would prioritise the review of working-age DLA recipients who are not in paid work. The coalition also committed in its 2010 Budget and Spending Reviews to cut DLA (mobility component) from current and future recipients living in residential accommodation. This would see the withdrawal of benefits for over 50,000 claimants and would save 75 million sterling (HM Treasury, 2010d; UK Parliament, 2010c). The exact reasons for this withdrawal are unclear; however, governmental comments align the withdrawal with loss of DLA while in hospital. These are quite different contexts. Although social care may be funded in residential care, living options in getting out and being part of the wider community arguably necessitates the continued payment of the benefit. This seems a particularly harsh and regressive policy move. Personal budgets can of course cover additional transport costs. However, this is no current evidence that a transfer of monies to underpin such additional payments is taking place between the DWP and DoH.

For those with the highest levels of social support needs, the news that around £2 billion is being made available from previous health budget commitments to support adult social care by 2014/15 is to be welcomed. These funds are not guaranteed with the current fiscal uncertainty and with the U-Turn on health restructuring effected by powerful medical professionals/bodies. No similar powerful professional or lobbying power exists which arguably could lead to social welfare and social care each been disproportionately hard hit by the proposed cuts of 32 billion per annum by 2014/15 (HM Treasury, 2010a & b). The recent report on the future funding of adult social care, the Dilnot Review (DoH and Care Commission, 2011) established that root and branch changes to funding are required and laid out the following key recommendations:

1. That personal contributions are capped at 35,000 sterling
2. That means-test thresholds should begin at 100, 000 sterling
3. A national agreed eligibility criterion
4. Those young disabled people entering adult residential services should not have their support means tested.

The Dilnot Review has estimated the costs of implementation of its ideas would initially be 1.7 billion. There is now fevered debate as to whether the review recommendations will be heeded by the Treasury/DH or whether they will be 'kicked into the long grass'. The Disabled Facilities Grant, a means-tested fund supporting accessible homes, is being increased from £169 million in 2010/11 to £185 million in 2014/15 (HM Treasury, 2010, p 49). These commitments are appreciated by some disability organisations, but the timetable, in taking the commitments to 2014/15, has prompted concerns that actual uplifts in 2011/12 will not be anything approaching this sum. This news comes in the wake of major reviews (that is, the Wanless Review and the Sutherland Report) on funding in this area (RCLTC, 1999; Wanless, 2006).

An ageing population, personalisation and user-led organisations (ULOs) are, of course, premised on further budgetary investment. Arguably, however, these extra monies, if they materialise, will do little to ameliorate already severely strained budgets for adult social support. Many ULOs and Centres for Inclusive/Integrated Living (CILs) are under threat (NCIL, 2008), and many local authorities are now restricting their funding to the top category of eligibility. It seems reasonable to assume that given wider local authority budget cuts, and the reliance for up to half the new monies coming from health budgets, that adult social care funding is likely to be extremely limited in the years 2011/12. The figure of circa 500,000 fewer jobs in the public sector is unlikely to leave social care funding unscathed. New developments sit alongside withdrawn services. A prime example is the Independent Living Fund (ILF) which provided funding for the most complex needs. It will no longer be taking new applicants as the scheme is gradually being withdrawn.

The Coalition also aims to end the Child Trust Fund for disabled children and will likely redirect funding to direct payments for children and carers to provide greater respite care and hospice provision, with an extra £10 million per annum from 2011. While welcome, these are essentially funded relief to prevent physical deterioration; the funding makes no connection to positive empowering life choices. Concern does attach to the changes to children's tax credit being rolled up into the Universal Credit (UC) which sees more 'severely' disabled children receive more and 'less severely' disabled chidren receive less (DWP, 2011). The government's statements on education are, however, the most worrying aspect of their proposed reforms. With little evidence to back up their assertions, the Coalition government has stated they 'will improve diagnostic assessment for schoolchildren, prevent the unnecessary closure of special schools and remove the bias towards inclusion' (HM Government, 2010b, p 29). What is meant by removing the bias 'towards inclusion' is entirely unclear. How inclusion, a key plank of child policy for 13 years, can now be viewed as a bad thing raises major questions about the underlying philosophical changes occurring in some parts of the Coalition.

Overall, the Emergency Budget of May 2010 and the Comprehensive Spending Review outcomes in November present some positive developments for disabled people. Yet the pledges of increased spending by 2014/15 seem to offer 'jam tomorrow' for many disabled adults. The ability to fund these uplifts appear to be heavily dependent on reduced benefit payments given the wider fiscal squeeze on spending up to 2015. This is a major gamble with public finances (HM Treasury, 2010). The challenge to encourage more disabled people into paid work while respecting their human rights to good treatment and not being forced to take poverty level benefits is a very real one. Critics have tended to view the rhetoric of ending the 'tragic waste' of disabled worklessness as simply a smokescreen to save money and to redefine the disability category regardless of the altered economic position of those moved out of the more generous disability benefits. The proposed cuts in health and social care may well result in a reversal of hard-won debates around personalised and enabling packages in the form of direct payments and personal budgets.

Possible impact of the proposed reforms

A critical longer-term perspective on disability policy might question some of the arguably populist strands of Coalition thinking and provide an alternative policy agenda. The evidence firmly points to the need to link work programmes to greater economic opportunities. The discussion of unfilled vacancies for which disabled people might apply ignores the geographical mismatch of opportunity and geographical location of disabled people. The Coalition's suggestion of encouraging greater mobility to match the person and opportunity ignores the cost of relocation, something likely to be made worse by the capping of Housing Benefit in high cost areas. Informal care networks could also suffer when forced relocation increases the necessity to access funded formal care. It is hoped that the revised Work and Work Choice programmes will provide the sustained and tailored support that proved successful in, say, the intensive Workstep programme for disabled people (Ofsted, 2010). The mooting of a more 'realistic' operation of disability discrimination legislation can be read as an attempt to water down its legislative 'burden'. The available evidence suggests a *more* demanding operation of the legislation is required to support the reciprocal relationship between the disabled jobseeker and the welcoming employer.

Of all the proposed reforms, adult social care may prove to be the most contested policy area. The raised expectations of personalisation, alongside an ageing population, demands significant investments into the second decade of the 21st century to support user-led innovations. The review of all DLA and ESA claimants will be a very expensive process, and on current evidence, reviews will lead to many successful appeals. For many, DLA makes the difference between significant poverty and managing some additional disability-related costs. The loss of DLA may simply see more people applying for tax and pension credits. The loss of the DLA higher rate mobility component may cause disproportionate hardship where the Motability scheme is being used to fund a car. Mid-award withdrawal of DLA would threaten the functioning of arguably the most successful disability mobility scheme globally, one that sees 6 per cent of new car sales in the UK funded via DLA and Motability (Motability Operations, 2011). The economic multipliers of disabled people often tend to get lost in evaluations based on the 'burden' of disability costs. A more effective and affordable approach is to undertake a six-yearly review for all higher rate claimants based on independent medical evidence aligned to Motability cycles. The abrupt volte-face on educational inclusion goes against a burgeoning evidence base on the cultural and economic value of mainstreamed education. Evidence-based policy has been the mantra of the last 15 years; the sidelining of the considerable evidence on what works in disability policy may simply store up problems for the future.

Conclusion

The very real need to reform the foundations of public finances have afforded the space for far-reaching reforms to the general size and specific function of the public sector and social policies in the UK. However, the lack of Treasury impact assessments and modelling of these policy changes means a major gamble is being made in rebalancing public finances. The proposed simpliflication of the benefits system is, of course, welcome, yet the reform of ESA runs the risk of returning us to firm policy categories on disability which consign some to lifelong 'support' (or worklessness) and others to the vaguaries of the labour market, with few demand-side measures in evidence. The attempt to make work pay by less severe benefits withdrawal is also welcome, but the greater restriction of Housing Benefits may well negate the value of these changes, especially in high rent areas. The effects of the reform of DLA is less easy to predict, but given the severe restrictions on public funding, the inevitable reduction of the DLA claimant count seems a fair prediction to make. This is concerning for those getting the highest rates of DLA who have rightly been deemed to have the greatest needs and extra care and mobility costs. The reforms, more generally the emphasis on conditionality and greater targeting, risk leaving more disabled people in enduring poverty and social isolation.

A final word

Disabled people's wider social and economic well-being is an increasingly important issue in the 21st century, and disability policy is a rich but challenging area for analysis. The overlay of more traditional paternalist policies alongside very new developments in self-direction and personalisation make for a very complex policy terrain. The established theories and concepts of policy shape, development and philosophy do not neatly fit the unravelling of disability policy and the way it is experienced. While the state has shifted from a provider to an enabling format, the impact and influence of policy are much more fragmented than could ever have been imagined from the postwar welfare settlement. This could be viewed as a healthy outcome of welfare pluralism and greater choice making by disabled people. The changes could also be viewed as a further ideological cleaving between and within the welfare and social care systems. While many disabled people benefit from good protection and from some self-direction, many are being pushed out of the disability category. The same government that once deemed them disabled is now redefining them as able to enter paid work or as ineligible for disability benefits.

Personalised models of welfare increasingly sit alongside greater rationing of services and the widespread introduction of means testing for some support. The binary between those 'deserving' support and those who 'need' to enter the work-based welfare system is becoming ever more starkly defined, even though many disabled people do not fit neatly into a policy category. Highly differentiated definitions and eligibility criteria apply to a range of social goods that the same person may have to navigate. The muddle of activity versus inactivity-based benefits remains very real. The recent discussion of a streamlining of the disability welfare system while promising is short on detail, and only a radical review of the system will erase these major accretions of inconsistent approaches to disability. And the hard-won gains of personalisation and self-direction may be viewed as under threat given the harsh budgetary plans of the Coalition government. For those disabled people needing more intensive support in residential contexts, the future looks even more uncertain. We can only hope that disabled people and their advocates gain further voice in shaping future policy.

Summary

- Coalition thinking seems rooted in neoliberalism and the communitarianism encapsulated in the notion of a 'Big Society'.
- Conditionality continues to pervade new policy design – severe sanctions are promised for those who fail to conform to these conditions.
- Disabled people look set to be placed in firm categories in the future symbolised in the 'support', 'work' and 'review' groups – this is arguably a return to paternalist thinking and at times has commonalities with Poor Law thinking on 'sturdy beggars' and feigned disablement.
- While a much harsher discourse attaches to new welfare, for those deemed eligible for packages of support greater self-direction is being fostered. This risks writing off this disabled sub-group.
- A significant gamble is being made in continuing to commit to the expansion of self-directed options alongside the planned cost savings in DLA and ESA benefits. A failure to achieve the latter could severely restrict progress in the former.

Questions

1. What does the Coalition government see as the major challenges in disability policy?
2. What are their key weapons in the battle against dependency?
3. How likely are the Coalition to be effective in increasing disabled people's self-direction and economic inclusion?

Further reading

You might like to read some good general readings on the reforms, for example, **Lister and Bennett (2010)** and **Deacon and Patrick (2010)** available at: www.social-policy. org.uk/lincoln/Deacon.pdf

On the specific disability reforms you may wish to look at the government's detailed proposals in *Our programme for government* (**HM Government, 2010b**). See also **Iain Duncan Smith**'s speech, 'Welfare for the 21st century', at www.dwp.gov.uk/ newsroom/ministers-speeches/2010/27-05-10.shtml

You also may like to read *The state of the nation report: Poverty, worklessness and welfare reform in the UK* (**HM Government, 2010a**) which provides greater background reading on the Coalition reforms: www.cabinetoffice.gov.uk/publications/ state-of-nation-report.aspx **www.marmotreview.org/AssetLibrary/resources/ new%20external%20reports/cabinet%20office%20-%20state%20of%20 the%20nation.pdf**

References

Abbott, D. (2003) *Direct payments and young people*, York: Joseph Rowntree Foundation.

Ackers, L. and Dwyer, P. (2002) *Senior citizenship? Retirement, migration and welfare in the European Union*, Bristol: The Policy Press.

Action for Blind People (2010) 'Benefits for children 2010/11' (www.actionforblindpeople.org.uk/assets/Uploads/downloads/Benefits-for-children-factsheet-2010-11.pdf).

Adams, F. (1980) *Apart or a part?*, Milton Keynes: Open University Press.

Ahmed, M. (2008) 'Social workers vague on personal budgets', *Community Care*, 22 October (www.communitycare.co.uk/Articles/2008/10/22/109755/social-workers-lack-knowledge-of-personalisation-survey-finds.htm).

Ainscow, M. and Miles, S. (2008) 'Making education for all inclusive: where next?', *Propects*, vol 38, no 1, pp 15-34.

Alcock, P., Beatty, C., Fothergill, S., Macmillan, R. and Yeandle, S. (2003) *Work to welfare: How men become detached from the labour market*, Cambridge: Cambridge University Press.

Arthur, S., Corden, A., Green, A., Lewis, J., Loumidis, J., Sainsbury, R., Stafford, B., Thornton, P. and Walker, R. (1999) *New Deal for disabled people: Early implementation*, DWP Research Report No 106, London: Department for Work and Pensions.

Atkinson, A.B. et al (1981) 'Poverty in York: a re-analysis of Rowntree's 1950 Survey', *Bulletin of Economic Research*, vol 33, no 2, pp 59-71.

Atkinson, D., Jackson, M. and Walmsley, J. (1997) *Forgotten lives: Exploring the history of learning disability*, Kidderminster: BILD Publications.

Audit Commission (1994) *Finding a place: A review of mental health services for adults*, London: Audit Commission.

Audit Commission (2002) *Special educational needs: A mainstream issue*, London: Audit Commission.

Audit Commission (2003) *A review of services for disabled children and their families*, London: Audit Commission.

Audit Commission (2006) *Choosing well: Analysing the costs and benefits of choice in local public services*, London: Audit Commission.

Bagguley, P. and Mann, K. (1992) 'Idle thieving bastards? Scholarly representations of the underclass', *Work, Employment and Society*, vol 6, no 1, pp 113-26.

Bailey, S.J. and Davidson, C. (1999) 'The purchaser–provider split: theory and UK evidence', *Environment & Planning*, vol 17, no 2, pp 161-76.

Baldwin, S.M. (1985) *The costs of caring: Families with disabled children*, London: Routledge & Kegan Paul.

Baldwin, S.M. and Lunt, N. (1996) *Charging ahead: Local authority charging policies for community care*, Bristol: The Policy Press for the Joseph Rowntree Foundation.

Bambra, C. and Pope, D.P. (2007) 'What are the effects of anti-discriminatory legislation on socio-economic inequalities in the employment consequences of ill health and disability?', *Journal of Epidemiology and Community Health*, vol 61, pp 421-6.

Barker, R.L. (1998) *Milestones in the development of social work and social welfare*, Washington, DC: National Association of Social Work Press.

Barlow, J. and Venables, T. (2004) 'Will technological innovation create the true lifetime home?', *Housing Studies*, vol 19, no 5, pp 795-810.

Barnes, C. (1991) *Disabled people in Britain and discrimination: A case for anti-discrimination legislation*, London: Hurst & Company.

Barnes, C. (1994) *Disabled people in Britain and discrimination: A case for anti-discrimination legislation* (2nd edn), London: Hurst & Company.

Barnes, C. and Mercer, G. (2006) *Independent futures: Creating user-led disability services in a disabling society*, Bristol: The Policy Press.

Barnes, C. and Mercer, G. (2010) *Exploring disability* (2nd edn), Cambridge: Polity Press.

Barnes, C., Mercer, G. and Shakespeare, T. (1999) *Exploring disability: A sociological introduction*, Cambridge: Polity Press.

Barton, L. and Oliver, M. (eds) (1997) *Disability studies: Past, present and future*, Leeds: The Disability Press.

Bauer, M., Fitzgerald, L., Haesler, E. and Manfrin, M. (2009) 'Hospital discharge planning for frail older people and their family. Are we delivering best practice? A review of the evidence', *Journal of Clinical Nursing*, vol 18, no 18, pp 2539-46.

Baxter, K., Wilberforce, M. and Glendinning, C. (2011) 'Personal budgets and the workforce implications for social care providers: expectations and early experiences', *Social Policy and Society*, vol 10, no 1, pp 55-65.

Bayley, M. (1973) *Mental handicap and community care*, London: Routledge & Kegan Paul.

Beatty, C. and Fothergill, S. (undated) *Incapacity benefits in the UK: An issue of health or jobs?*, Sheffield: Centre for Regional Economic and Social Research, Sheffield Hallam University (www.social-policy.org.uk/lincoln/Beatty.pdf).

Beatty, C. and Fothergill, S. (2005) 'The diversion from "unemployment" to "sickness" across British regions and districts', *Regional Studies*, vol 39, pp 837-54.

Beatty, C., Fothergill, S. and Platts-Fowler, D. (2009a) *DLA claimants – A new assessment: The characteristics and aspirations of the Incapacity Benefit claimants who receive Disability Living Allowance*, DWP Research Report No 585, London: Department for Work and Pensions.

Beatty, C., Crisp, R., Foden, M., Lawless, P. and Wilson, I. (2009b) *Understanding and tackling worklessness: Lessons and policy implications. Evidence from the New Deal for communities programme*, London: Department for Communities and Local Government.

Beckett, A. (2006) *Citizenship and vulnerability: Disability and issues of social and political engagement*, Basingstoke: Palgrave Macmillan.

Benson, T.B. and Williams, E. (1979) 'The Younger Disabled Unit at Fazakerley Hospital', *British Medical Journal*, vol 11, no 2, pp 369-71.

Beresford, B. and Oldman, C. (2002) *Housing matters*, Bristol: The Policy Press.

Beresford, B., Rabiee, P. and Sloper, P. (2007) *Outcomes for parents with disabled children*, Research Works, 2007-03, York: Social Policy Research Unit.

Beresford, P. and Jones, R. (2008) 'Fair shares!', *Guardian Society*, 23 January.

Berthoud, R. (1991) 'Meeting the costs of disability', in G. Dalley (ed) *Disability and social policy*, London: Policy Studies Institute, pp 64-100.

Berthoud, R. (2006) *The employment rates of disabled people*, London: Department for Work and Pensions.

Beveridge, S. (1999) *Special educational needs in schools*, London: Routledge.

Beveridge, W. (1942) *Social insurance and allied services*, Cmd 6404, London: HMSO.

Bewley, C. and Glendinning, C. (1992) *Involving disabled people in community care planning: The first steps. An analysis of community care plans for England and Wales*, Manchester: Department of Social Policy and Social Work, University of Manchester.

Birmingham Post (2008) 'Atos Origin staff awarded erroneous Incapacity Benefit claims', 9 April (www.meassociation.org.uk/?p=349).

Black, P. (2000) *Why aren't person centred approaches and planning happening for as many people and as well as we would like?*, York: Joseph Rowntree Foundation.

Blair, A. (1996) Speech to Labour Party Conference, Blackpool Winter Gardens, 1 October.

Blair, A. (2002) 'Mutual respect the key to welfare reform', Downing Street Press Release, 10 June.

Blakemore, K. (2003) *Social policy: An introduction* (2nd edn), London: McGraw Hill.

BMA (British Medical Association) (undated) *Guidance for medical services doctors undertaking work for the Department of Work and Pensions* (www. bma.org.uk/employmentandcontracts/fees/medicalservicesdoctors.jsp).

Bornat, J., Johnson, J., Pereira, C., Floris, T., Pilgrim, D. and Williams, F. (1997) *Community care* (2nd edn), Basingstoke: Palgrave.

Borsay, A. (1986) 'Personal trouble or public issue? Towards a model of policy for people with physical and mental disabilities', in L. Barton and M. Oliver (eds) (1997) *Disability studies: Past, present and future*, Leeds: The Disability Press.

Borsay, A. (2005) *Disability and social policy in Britain since 1750: A history of exclusion*, Basingstoke: Macmillan.

Boxall, K., Dowson, S. and Beresford, P. (2009) 'Selling individual budgets, choice and control: local and global influences on UK social care policy for people with learning difficulties', *Policy & Politics*, vol 27, no 4, pp 499-515.

Boyle, G. (2008) 'Autonomy in long-term care: a need, a right or a luxury?', *Disability & Society*, vol 23, no 4, pp 299-310.

Boyson, R. (1978) *Centre forward – A radical conservative programme*, London: Temple Smith.

Bradley, H. (1996) *Fractured identities: Changing patterns of inequality*, Oxford: Blackwell.

Brechin, A., Liddiard, P. and Swain, J. (eds) (1981) *Handicap in a social world*, Sevenoaks: Hodder & Stoughton.

Brewer, M., Clarke, T. and Wakefield, M. (2002) *Social security under New Labour: What did the third way mean for welfare reform?*, London: Institute for Fiscal Studies.

Brisenden, S. (1986) 'Independent living and the medical model of disability', *Disability, Handicap and Society*, vol 1, no 2, pp 173-8.

British Geriatrics Society (2008) *Intermediate care guidance for commissioners and providers of health and social care* (www.bgs.org.uk/Publications/Compendium/compend_4-2.htm).

Brown, J.C. (1984) *The disability income system*, London: Policy Studies Institute.

Brown, P. and Sparks, R. (eds) (1989) *Beyond Thatcherism*, Milton Keynes: Open University Press.

Buckle, J. (1984) *Mental handicap costs more*, London: Disablement Income Group.

Burchardt, T. (1999) *The evolution of disability benefits in the UK: Reweighting the basket*, CASEPaper 26, London: London School of Economics and Political Science.

Burchardt, T. (2000) *Enduring economic exclusion: Disabled people, income and work*, York: Joseph Rowntree Foundation.

Burchardt, T. (2003) 'Disability, capability and social exclusion', in J. Millar (ed) *Understanding social security*, Bristol: The Policy Press, pp 145-66.

Burchardt, T. (2005) *The education and employment of disabled young people: Frustrated ambition*, Bristol: The Policy Press.

Burden, T. and Hamm, T. (2000) 'Responding to socially included groups', in J. Perry-Smith (ed) *Policy responses to social inclusion*, Buckingham: Open University Press.

Burns, N. (2004) 'Negotiating difference: disabled people's experiences of house builders', *Housing Studies*, vol 19, no 5, pp 765-81.

Burton, M. and Kagan, C. (2006) 'Decoding *Valuing People*', *Disability & Society*, vol 21, no 4, pp 299-313.

Butler, P. (2010) 'The next child protection crisis will tell if reforms have worked', *The Guardian*, 15 June.

Butler, P. (2011) 'Women and the coalition: mothers' and child benefits', *The Guardian*, 20 May.

CAB (Citizens' Advice Bureaux) (2003) *Serious benefits: The success of CAB benefit take up campaigns*, London: CAB.

Cameron, D. (2010) Speech on the 'Big Society', Liverpool, 19 July (www. number10.gov.uk/news/speeches-and-transcripts/2010/07/big-society-speech-53572).

Campbell, J. and Oliver, M. (1996) *Disability politics: Understanding our past, changing our future*, London: Routledge.

Care & Repair (2007) *Future of Disabled Facilities Grant – Consultation responses summary*, London: Care & Repair.

Cawston, T., Haldenby, A. and Nolan, P. (2009) *The end of entitlement*, London: Reform.

Centre for Economic Performance (2006) *Incapacity Benefit reform: Tackling the rise in labour market inactivity*, London: Centre for Economic Performance (http://cep.lse.ac.uk/pubs/download/pa005.pdf).

Chadwick, R. and Russell, G. (1989) 'Hospital discharge of frail elderly people: social and ethical considerations in the discharge decision-making process', *Ageing & Society*, vol 9, pp 277-95.

Charlesworth, J., Clarke, J. and Cochrane, A. (1995) 'Managing local mixed economies of care', *Environment & Planning*, vol 27, no 9, pp 1419-35.

Charlton, J.I. (2000) *Nothing about us without us: Disability oppression and empowerment*, Berkeley, CA: University of California Press.

Clements, L. (2008) 'Individual budgets and irrational exuberance', 11 CCLR (Community Care Law Reports) 413-430 (pre-publication draft available at www.lukeclements.co.uk/downloads/UpdatePDF01-Oct08. pdf).

CLG (Department for Communities and Local Government) (2007) *Disabled Facilities Grant programme: The government's proposals to improve programme delivery*, Consultation, London: CLG.

CLG (2008) *Lifetime homes, lifetime neighbourhoods: A national strategy for housing in an ageing society*, London: CLG.

CLG and Welsh Assembly (2009) *Disabled Facilities Grant: Updated guidance*, London: CLG.

Cohen, R., Coxall, J., Craig, G. and Sadiq-Sangster, A. (1990) *Hardship Britain*, London: Child Poverty Action Group.

Coid, J. (1994) Editorial: 'Failure in community care: psychiatry's dilemma', *British Medical Journal*, no 308, p 805.

Contact a Family (2010) *Counting the cost: The financial reality for families of disabled children*, London: Contact a Family.

Cooper, V. and Vernon, S. (1996) *Disability and the law*, London: Jessica Kingsley.

Corden, A. and Thornton, P. (2002) *Employment programmes for disabled people: Lessons from research evaluations*, DWP In-house Report No 90, London: Department for Work and Pensions.

Corden, A., Sainsbury, R., Irvine, A. and Clarke, S. (2009) *The impact of Disability Living Allowance and Attendance Allowance: Findings from exploratory qualitative research*, DWP Research Report No 649, London: Department for Work and Pensions.

CPAG (Child Poverty Action Group) (2001) 'Decisions and appeals – what is going on?', *Welfare Rights Bulletin*, 164 (www.cpag.org.uk/cro/wrb/wrb164/appeals.htm).

CPAG (2006a) '"Make child benefit count" say campaigners celebrating 60 years of support for children', 6 August (www.cpag.org.uk/press/060806. htm).

CPAG (2006b) *A route out of poverty: Disabled people, work and welfare reform*, London: CPAG.

Craig, G. (2004) 'Citizenship, exclusion and older people', *Journal of Social Policy*, vol 33, no 1, pp 95-114.

Craig, P. and Greenslade, M. (1998) *First findings from the disability follow-up to the Family Resources Survey*, London: Department of Social Security Social Research Branch.

Crawford, R., Emmerson, C., Phillips, D. and Tetlow, G. (2011) *Public spending cuts: Pain shared?*, London: Institute for Fiscal Studies.

Cree, V.E. (ed) (2010) *Social work: A reader*, London: Routledge.

Croft, S. and Beresford, P. (1992) 'The politics of participation', *Critical Social Policy*, vol 12, no 35, pp 20–44.

CSCI (Commission for Social Care Inspection) (2008) *The state of social care report*, London: CSCI.

CSCI and HCC (Health Care Commission) (2009) *The state of social care in England, 2007-8*, London: CSCI.

CSIP (Care Services Improvement Partnership) (2006) *Out and about: Wheelchair services for disabled children*, London: CSIP and Department of Health.

Dalley, G. (1991) *Disability and social policy*, London: Policy Studies Institute.

Darwin, C.R. (1859) *On the origin of species by means of natural selection*, London: John Murray.

Davey, V., Fernández, J.L., Knapp, M., Vick, N., Jolly, D., Swift, P., Tobin, R., Kendall, J., Ferrie, J., Pearson, C., Mercer, G. and Priestley, M. (2006) *Direct payments in the UK: A national survey of direct payments policy and practice*, London: Personal Social Services Research Unit, London School of Economics and Political Science.

Davis, K. (1998) 'The Disabled People's Movement: putting the power in empowerment', Paper for a seminar at the Sociology Department, University of Sheffield (1996, updated 1998) (www.leeds.ac.uk/disability-studies/archiveuk/DavisK/davis-empowerment.pdf).

Daycare Trust (2003) *Informal care: Bridging the childcare gap for families*, London: Daycare Trust.

DCSF (Department for Children, Schools and Families) (2006) *Greater expectations: Learners with disabilities*, London: DCSF.

DCSF (2008a) *Sure Start children's centres: Building brighter futures*, London: DCSF.

DCSF (2008b) *Better communication: Improving services for children and young people with speech, language and communication needs* (Bercow Report), London: DCSF.

DCSF (2008c) *The Children's Plan: Building brighter futures*, London: DCSF.

DCSF (2008d) *Transforming short breaks for families with disabled children*, London: DCSF.

DCSF (2009) *Early Years Quality Improvement Support Programme (EYQISP)*, London: DCSF.

Deacon, A. (2002) *Perspectives on welfare*, Buckingham: Open University Press.

Deacon, A. and Patrick, R. (2010) 'A new welfare settlement? The Coalition government and welfare to work', Paper presented to symposium on 'Prospects for the Coalition: The Conservative Party and social policy', Annual Conference of the Social Policy Association, University of Lincoln, Tuesday 6 July (www.social-policy.org.uk/lincoln/Deacon.pdf).

Dean, H. and Taylor-Gooby, P. (1992) *Dependency culture: The explosion of a myth*, Hemel Hempstead: Harvester Wheatsheaf.

Dewson, S., Hill, D., Meager, N. and Willison, R. (2002) *Evaluation of Access to Work: Core evaluation*, DWP Research Report No 619, London: Department for Work and Pensions.

DfE (Department for Education) (2011) *Short Breaks Pathfinder Evaluation* (www.education.gov.uk/publications/standard/publicationdetail/page1/DFE-RR062).

DfES (Department for Education and Skills) (1997) *Excellence for all: Meeting special educational needs*, Green Paper, London: The Stationery Office.

DfES (2003) *Every Child Matters*, London: DfES.

DfES and DH (Department of Health) (2002) *The Early Support Programme: Professional guidance*, London: The Stationery Office.

DH (Department of Health) (1989) *Caring for people: Community care in the next decade and beyond*, White Paper, London: HMSO.

DH (1998) *Modernising social services*, White Paper, London: The Stationery Office.

DH (2001a) *Health Survey for England*, London: The Stationery Office.

DH (2001c) *Valuing People: A new strategy for the 21st century*, London: The Stationery Office.

DH (2001d) *Intermediate care*, LAC (2001)1, London: The Stationery Office.

DH (2002) *Fair Access to Care Services: Guidance on eligibility criteria for adult social care*, LAC13, London: The Stationery Office.

DH (2003a) *Community Care (Delayed Discharges etc) Act (Qualifying Services) (England) Regulations*, London: The Stationery Office.

DH (2003b) *Fair Access to Care Services: Guidance on eligibility criteria for adult social care*, London: The Stationery Office.

DH (2003c) *Keeping children safe: The government's response to the Victoria Climbié Inquiry report and Joint Chief Inspectors' report Safeguarding children*, London: The Stationery Office.

DH (2003d) *Guidance for service users*, Mental Health Task Force, London: The Stationery Office.

DH (2004) *National Service Framework for children*, London: The Stationery Office.

DH (2005) *Independence, wellbeing and choice*, Green Paper, London: The Stationery Office.

DH (2006) *Our health, our care, our say: A new direction for community services*, White Paper, London: The Stationery Office.

DH (2007) *Putting people first: A shared vision and commitment to the transformation of adult social care*, London: The Stationery Office.

DH (2008a) *Transforming social care*, LAC DH 2001/8, London: DH.

DH (2008b) *Independent living: A cross-government strategy about independent living for disabled people*, London: Office for Disability Issues.

DH (2008c) *High quality care for all: NHS next stage review. Final report*, Cm 7432 (Darzi Report), London: The Stationery Office.

DH (2008d) *The case for change*, London: The Stationery Office.

DH (2009a) *Personalisation of social care services*, London: The Stationery Office.

DH (2009b) *Shaping the future of care together*, London: The Stationery Office.

DH (2009c) *Health Survey for England*, London: The Stationery Office.

DH (2010a) *Putting people first: A whole system approach to eligibility for social care*, London: The Stationery Office.

DH (2010b) *Prevention package for older people: Resources*, London: DH (www.dh.gov.uk/en/Publicationsandstatistics/Publications/dh_103146).

DHSS (Department of Health and Social Security) (1969) *Report of the Committee of Inquiry into allegations of ill-treatment of patients and other irregularities at the Ely Hospital, Cardiff*, London: HMSO.

DHSS (1971) *Better services for the mentally handicapped*, London: HMSO.

DHSS (1972) *Families receiving supplementary benefit*, May, London: HMSO.

DHSS (1977) *The way forward*, White Paper, London: DHSS.

Dickinson-Lilley (2010) *Behaviour and discipline in schools – House of Commons Education Committee: Examination of Witnesses*, Questions 176-207, 27 October, London: The Stationery Office.

Dilnot, A. (2011) Fairer Care Funding: Report of the Commission on Funding of Care and Support (Dilnot Review). London: Care Commission & DoH (www.wp.dh.gov.uk/carecommission/files/2011/07/Fairer-Care-Funding-Report.pdf).

Directgov (2010) *Access to Work – Practical help at work*. www.direct.gov.uk/en/DisabledPeople/Employmentsupport/WorkSchemesAndProgrammes/DG_4000347

Disability Alliance (1975) *Poverty and disability: The case for a comprehensive income scheme for disabled people*, London: Disability Alliance.

Disability Alliance (1988) *The financial position of disabled people living in private households: A Disability Alliance briefing on the second OPCS report*, London: Disability Alliance.

Disability Alliance (2010a) Disability Alliance factsheet, 'A guide to tax credits', London: Disability Alliance.

Disability Alliance (2010b) 'Disability Alliance joins campaign to challenge the government over £16bn unclaimed benefits', 3 February (www.disabilityalliance.org/damanifesto3.htm).

Disability Law Service (2009) DLA Appeals Factsheet. Available at: http://www.dls.org.uk/advice/factsheet/welfare_benefits/DLA_appeals/DLA%20Appeals%20Factsheet.pdf

Disability Rights Task Force (1999) *From exclusion to inclusion: A report of the Disability Rights Task Force on civil rights for disabled people*, DRC legacy document (www.leeds.ac.uk/disability-studies/archiveuk/disability%20 rights%20task%20force/From%20exclusion%20to%20inclusion.pdf).

Dobson, B. and Middleton, S. (1998) *Paying to care: The cost of childhood disability*, York: York Publishing Services.

DoE (Department of Employment) (1990) *Employment and training for people with disabilities: Consultative document*, London: DoE.

DRC (Disability Rights Commission) (2007) *Disability rights agenda*, London: DRC.

Drake, R. (1999) *Understanding disability policies*, Basingstoke: Macmillan.

Driver, S. and Martell, L. (2002) 'New Labour, work and the family', *Social Policy & Administration*, vol 36, no 1, pp 46-61.

DSS (Department of Social Security) (1990) *The way ahead: Benefits for disabled people*, Cm 917, London: HMSO.

DSS (1998a) *New ambitions for our country: A new contract for welfare*, London: The Stationery Office.

DSS (1998b) *Memorandum submitted by the Department of Social Security to the Select Committee on Social Security*, Minutes of Evidence, 12 May, London: DSS.

Duffy, S. (2010) 'The citizenship theory of social justice: exploring the meaning of personalisation for social workers', *Journal of Social Work Practice*, vol 24, no 3, pp 253-67.

Duncan Smith, I. (2010) 'Reforms will tackle poverty and get Britain working again', DWP Press Release, 27 May (www.dwp.gov.uk/newsroom/press-releases/2010/may-2010/dwp070-10-270510.shtml).

Dunning, J. (2010) 'Personalisation may force day centre closures in Liverpool', *Community Care*, 30 June.

DWP (Department for Work and Pensions) (2006) *A new deal for welfare: Empowering people to work* (www.dwp.gov.uk/aboutus/welfarereform/docs/A_new_deal_for_welfare-Empowering_people_to_work-Full_Document.pdf). www.dwp.gov.uk/policy/welfare-reform/legislation-and-key-documents/a-new-deal-for-welfare-empowering/

DWP (2007a) *Ready for work: Full employment in a generation*, Cm 7290, London: DWP.

DWP (2007b) *Helping people achieve their full potential: Improving specialist disability employment services*, Consultation, London: DWP.

DWP (2008a) *Pathways to Work* (www.dwp.gov.uk/policy/welfare-reform/pathways-to-work/).

DWP (2008b) Employment and Support Allowance Regulations 2008 (http://dwp.gov.uk/policy/welfare-reform/legislation-and-key-documents/employment-and-support-allowance/).

DWP (2009a) *Supporting people into work: The next stage of Housing Benefit reform*, Public Consultation Document, London: DWP.

DWP (2009b) *Attendance Allowance and Disability Living Allowance: Retrospective equality impact assessment report*, London: DWP.

DWP (2010a) *21st century welfare*, Cm 7913, London: DWP.

DWP (2010b) *Employment and Support Allowance* (www.dwp.gov.uk/policy/welfare-reform/employment-and-support/).

DWP (2011a) 'Report a benefit thief' online form (https://secure.dwp.gov.uk/benefitfraud/).

DWP (2011b) *Disability Living Allowance Reform: Impact Assessment*, London: DWP

DWP (2011c) *Department for Work and Pensions Main Estimate 2011-2012* (www.hm-treasury.gov.uk/d/dwp_main_supply_estimates_april11.pdf).

DWP (2011d) *Work Choice: Information and Bidding Document* (www.dwp.gov.uk/supplying-dwp/what-we-buy/welfare-to-work-services/specialist-disability-employment/).

DWP (2011e) *Universal Credit Briefing Note 1* (www.dwp.gov.uk/docs/ucpbn-1-additions.pdf).

Dwyer, P. (2000) *Welfare rights and responsibilities: Contesting social citizenship*, Bristol: The Policy Press.

Dwyer, P. (2004a) *Understanding social citizenship*, Bristol: The Policy Press.

Dwyer, P. (2004b) 'Creeping conditionality in the UK: from welfare rights to continued entitlements', *The Canadian Journal of Sociology*, vol 29, no 2, pp 265-87.

Dwyer, P. (2010) *Understanding social citizenship: Themes and perspectives for policy and practice* (2nd edn), Bristol: The Policy Press.

Easterlow, D. and Smith, J. (2003) 'Health and employment: towards a New Deal', *Policy & Politics*, vol 31, no 4, pp 511-33.

EDCM (Every Disabled Child Matters) (2010) Priorities for the 2010 Spending Review (www.ncb.org.uk/edcm/2010_government_spending_review_edcm_key_recommendations.pdf).

EHRC (Equality and Human Rights Commission) (2009) *Inquiry into disability-related harassment*, London: EHRC (www.equalityhumanrights.com/legal-and-policy/inquiries-and-assessments/inquiry-into-disability-related-harassment/).

Emerson, E. et al (2009) *The association between child disability and poverty dynamics in British families: Non-technical summary (Research summary)*, ESRC End of Award Report, RES-000-22-2874, Swindon: Economic and Social Research Council.

Etzioni, A. (1995) *The spirit of community: Rights, responsibilities and the communitarian agenda*, London: Fontana Press.

Etzioni, A. (1997) *The new golden rule: Community and morality in a democratic society*, London: Profile Books Ltd.

Etzioni, A. (1998a) 'A matter of balance, rights and responsibilities', in A. Etzioni (ed) *The essential communitarian reader*, Oxford: Rowman and Butterfield Publishers Inc, pp ix–xxiv.

Etzioni, A. (ed) (1998b) *The essential communitarian reader*, Oxford: Rowman and Butterfield Publishers Inc.

Etzioni, A. (2000) *The third way to a good society*, London: Demos.

Family Fund (2010) *Ensuring fairness across the UK for disabled children's families*, London: Family Fund.

Ferguson, I. (2008) *Reclaiming social work: Challenging neo-liberalism and promoting social justice*, London: Sage Publications.

Fergusson, R. (2002) 'Rethinking youth transitions: policy transfer and new exclusions in New Labour's New Deal', *Policy Studies*, vol 23, no 3, pp 173–190.

Finch, J. (1990) 'Gender, employment and the responsibilities of kin', *Work, Employment and Society*, vol 4, no 3, pp 349–61.

Finkelstein, V. (1980) *Attitudes and disabled people*, New York: World Rehabilitation Fund Monograph.

FLHN (Foundation for Lifetime Homes and Neighbourhoods) (2010) *Consultation response on lifetime homes*, London: FLHN.

Fothergill, S. and Wilson, I. (2007) 'A million off *Incapacity Benefit*: how achievable is Labour's target?', *Cambridge Journal of Economics*, vol 31, pp 1007–24.

Foucault, M. (2001) *Madness and civilisation*, London: Routledge.

Fraser, D. (1984) *The evolution of the British welfare state: A history of social policy since the Industrial Revolution* (2nd edn), Basingstoke: Macmillan.

Fulcher, G. (1989) *Disabling policies? A comparative approach to education policy and disability*, London: Falmer Press.

Galton, F. (1883) *Inquiries into human faculty and its development*, New York: AMS Press.

Galton, F. (1904) 'Eugenics: its definition, scope and aims', *The American Journal of Sociology*, vol 10, no 1, pp 1–25.

Gamble, A. (1988) *The free economy and the strong state*, Basingstoke: Palgrave.

George, V. and Wilding, P. (1985) *Ideology and social welfare* (revised edn), London: RKP.

Giddens, A. (1998) *The Third Way*, Cambridge: Polity Press.

Glasby, J. and Littlechild, R. (2002) *Social work and direct payments*, Bristol: The Policy Press.

Gleeson, B. (1999) *Geographies of disability*, London: Routledge.

Glendinning, C. (1991) '*Losing ground*: social policy and disabled people in Britain 1980-90', *Disability, Handicap and Society*, vol 6, no 1, pp 3-19.

Glendinning, C., Halliwell, S., Jacobs, S., Rummery, K. and Tyrer, J. (2000) 'Bridging the gap: using direct payments to purchase integrated care', *Health and Social Care in the Community*, vol 8, no 3, pp 192-200.

Glendinning, C., Challis, D., Fernandez, J., Jacobs, S., Jones, K., Knapp, M., Manthorpe, J., Moran, N., Netten, A., Stevens, M. and Wilberforce, M. (1998) *Evaluation of the Individual Budgets Pilot Programme: Final report*, York: Social Policy Research Unit, University of York.

Glendinning, C. et al (2011) *Choice and change: extending choice and control over the lifecourse: A qualitative longitudinal panel study*, York: DoH and Social Policy Research Unit.

Glennerster, H. (2007) *British social policy 1945 to the present* (3rd edn), Oxford: Blackwell.

Glennerster, H. and Evans, M. (1994) 'Beveridge and his assumptive worlds: the incompatibilities of a flawed design', in J. Hills, J. Ditch and H. Glennerster (eds) *Beveridge and social security: An international retrospective*, Oxford: Clarendon Press, pp 56-72.

Goffman, E. (1961) *Asylums: Essays on the social situation of mental patients and other inmates*, New York: Doubleday.

Goldberg, E.M. and Morrison, S.L. (2004) 'Schizophrenia and social class', in C. Buck et al *The challenge of epidemiology: Issues and selected readings*, Washington: Pan American Health Organisation, pp 368-83.

Gooding, C. (1995) *Disabling laws, enabling acts*, London: Pluto.

Goodley, D. (2011) *Disability studies: An interdisciplinary approach*, London: Sage Publications.

Gordon, D. and Pantazis, C. (1997) *Breadline Britain in the 1990s*, Aldershot: Ashgate.

Graham, H. (ed) (2009) *Understanding health inequalities*, Maidenhead: Open University Press.

Grant, G., Goward, P., Richardson, M. and Ramcharan, P. (eds) (2005) *Learning disability: A life cycle approach to valuing people*, Maidenhead: Open University Press.

Grewal, I., Joy, S., Lewis, J., Swales, K. and Woodfield, K. (2002) *Disabled for life? Attitudes towards, and experiences of, disability in Britain*, DWP Research Report No 148, London: Corporate Document Services.

Griffiths, R. (1988) *Community care: Agenda for action* (Griffiths Report), London: Department of Health and Social Security.

Grover, C. and Piggott, L. (2005) 'Disabled people, the reserve army of labour and welfare reform', *Disability & Society*, vol 20, no 7, pp 705-17.

Grover, C. and Piggott, L. (2007) 'Social security, employment and Incapacity Benefits: critical reflections on *A new deal for welfare*', *Disability & Society*, vol 22, no 7, pp 733-46.

Hall, S. and Jacques, M. (1983) *The politics of Thatcherism*, London: Lawrence & Wishart.

Hancock, R., Morciano, M. and Pudney, S. (2010) *Attendance Allowance and Disability Living Allowance claimants in the older population: Is there a difference in their economic circumstances?*, ISER Working Paper, Colchester: Institute for Social and Economic Research.

Hansard (1969) HC Debate, 27 January, vol 776, col 936-7.

Hansard (1984) HC Debate, 26 March, vol 57, col 61W.

Hansard (1990) HC Oral Answers, 21 May, vol 173, col 3.

Hansard (1998) HC Written Answers, 11 March, col 243.

Hansard (2009) HC Debate, 29 March, col 87 WS.

Hansard (2010a) HC Written Answers, 26 June, col 96W.

Hansard (2010b) HC Debate, 4 October, col 1342W.

Harrington, M. (2010) An Independent Review of the Work Capability Assessment. Report for the Department for Work and Pensions, London: The Stationery Office.

Harris, A., Cox, E. and Smith, C.R.W. (1971) *Handicapped and impaired in Great Britain*, Part 1, Office of Population Censuses and Surveys, Social Survey Division, London: HMSO.

Harris, J. (1994) 'Beveridge's social and political thought', in J. Hills, J. Ditch and H. Glennerster (eds) *Beveridge and social security: An international retrospective*, Oxford: Clarendon Press, pp 26-42.

Harris, J. and Roulstone, A. (2011) *Disability policy and professional practice*, London: Sage Publications.

Harrison, J. and Wooley, M. (2004) *Debt and disability: The impact of debt on families with disabled children*, York: Contact a Family and Family Fund.

Hasler, F., Campbell, J. and Zarb, G. (1999) *Direct routes to independence: A guide to local authorities' implementation and management of direct payments*, London: Policy Studies Institute.

Hendrick, H. (2003) *Child welfare: Historical dimensions, contemporary debates*, Bristol: The Policy Press.

Hewitt, M. (2002) 'New Labour and the redefinition of social security', in M. Powell (ed) *Evaluating New Labour's welfare reforms*, Bristol: The Policy Press, pp 189-209.

Heywood, F. (2004) 'Understanding needs: a starting point for quality', *Housing Studies*, vol 19, no 5, pp 709-26.

Hills, J. (1998) *Thatcherism, New Labour and the welfare state*, CASEPaper 13, London: London School of Economics and Political Science.

Hills, J. (2003) *Inclusion or insurance? National insurance and the future of the contributory principle*, CASEPaper 63, London: London School of Economics and Political Science.

Hills, J. and Stewart, K. (eds) (2005) *A more equal society? New Labour, poverty, inequality and exclusion*, Bristol: The Policy Press.

Hills, J., Ditch, J. and Glennerster, H. (eds) (1994) *Beveridge and social security: An international retrospective*, Oxford: Clarendon Press.

Hirsch, D. (2006) *Paying for long-term care: Moving forward*, York: Joseph Rowntree Foundation (www.jrf.org.uk/sites/files/jrf/0186.pdf).

Hirst, M., Thornton, R., Dearey, M. and Maynard-Campbell, S. (2004) *The employment of disabled people in the public sector*, London: Disability Rights Commission.

HM Government (1913) Statute: *The Mental Deficiency Act*, London: HMSO.

HM Government (1944a) Statute: *Disabled Persons' (Employment) Act*, London: HMSO.

HM Government (1944b) Statute: *Education Act*, London: HMSO.

HM Government (1946a) Statute: *National Insurance (Industrial Injuries) Act*, London: HMSO.

HM Government (1946b) Statute: *National Insurance Act*, London: HMSO.

HM Government (1948a) Statute: *National Health Service Act*, London: HMSO.

HM Government (1948b) Statute: *National Assistance Act*, London: HMSO.

HM Government (1968) Statute: *Health Services and Public Health Act*, London: HMSO.

HM Government (1970a) Statute: *Local Authority Act*, London: HMSO.

HM Government (1970b) Statute: *Chronically Sick and Disabled Persons Act*, London: HMSO.

HM Government (1981) Statute: *Education Act*, London: HMSO.

HM Government (1985) *Welfare reform*, Green Paper, London: HMSO.

HM Government (1990) Statute: *National Health Service and Community Care Act*, London: HMSO.

HM Government (1992) Statute: *Social Security Act*, London: HMSO.

HM Government (1993) Statute: *Disability Grants Act*, London: HMSO.

HM Government (1994) Statute: *Social Security (Incapacity for Work) Act*, London: HMSO.

HM Government (1995a) Statute: *Carers (Recognition) Act*, London: HMSO.

HM Government (1995b) Statute: *Disability Discrimination Act*, London: HMSO.

HM Government (1996a) Statute: *Disabled Persons (Services, Consultation and Representation) Act*, London: The Stationery Office.

HM Government (1996b) Statute: *Community Care (Direct Payments) Act*, London: The Stationery Office.

HM Government (1999a) Statute: *Welfare Reform and Pensions Act*, London: The Stationery Office.

HM Government (1999b) Statute: *Health Act*, London: The Stationery Office.

HM Government (2000a) Statute: *Special Educational Needs and Disability Act*, London: The Stationery Office.

HM Government (2000b) Statute: *Carers and Disabled Children Act*, London: The Stationery Office.

HM Government (2004) Statute: *Children Act*, London: The Stationery Office.

HM Government, (2006) Bill: *Education and Inspections Bill*, London: The Stationery Office

HM Government (2008) Statute: *Children and Young Persons Act*, London: The Stationery Office.

HM Government (2009) *Shaping the future of care together*, Green Paper, Cm 7673, Norwich: The Stationery Office.

HM Government (2010a) *The state of the nation report: Poverty, worklessness and welfare dependency in the UK*, London: The Stationery Office.

HM Government (2010b) *The Coalition: Our programme for government*, London: Cabinet Office.

HMRC (Her Majesty's Revenue and Customs) (2003) *Disabled Person's Tax Credit statistics*, Summary statistics, United Kingdom, January (www.hmrc.gov.uk/dptctables/dptc_jan03.pdf).

HMRC (2005) *Disability Discrimination Act: New access requirements: Tax guidance*, London: HMRC.

HMRC (2006) *Personal Tax Credits* (www.hmrc.gov.uk/stats/personal-tax-credits/cwtc-geog-stats.htm).

HM Treasury (1979) *The government's spending plans 1980-81*, Cmnd 7746, London: HMSO.

HM Treasury (1998) *Pre-budget report 2001: Steering a stable course for lasting prosperity*, Cm 4076, London: The Stationery Office.

HM Treasury (2009) *Public expenditure statistical analyses*, London: The Stationery Office.

HM Treasury (2010a) *Spending Review framework*, Cm 7872, London: The Stationery Office.

HM Treasury (2010b) *Budget: 2010*, London: The Stationery Office.

HM Treasury (2010c) *Spending Review: Distributional Impact Analysis*: Data Series, London: The Stationery Office.

HM Treasury (2010d) *Budget Policy 2010 Costings*, London: The Stationery Office.

HM Treasury and DCSF (Department for Children, Schools and Families) (2007) *Aiming high for disabled children: Better support for families*, London: DCSF.

Hodgson, S. and Blackman-Woods, R. (2008) 'Free school meals: debate', *Hansard*, 30 June 2010, col 223WH, London: The Stationery Office.

Home Office (2008/09) *British Crime Survey*, London: The Stationery Office.

House of Commons Employment Committee (1994) *The operation of the Disabled Persons' (Employment) Act 1944*, Minutes of Evidence, Tuesday 8 March, 281-i, London: The Stationery Office.

House of Commons Select Committee on Work and Pensions (2006) *Incapacity Benefits and Pathways to Work: Third report of session 2005-06, Volume I*, London: The Stationery Office.

Howard, M. (2005) 'Disability: rights, work and security', *Benefits*, vol 13, no 3, pp 93-7.

Hoyes, L., Means, R. and Le Grand, J. (1992) *Made to measure? Performance measurement and community care*, Bristol: School for Advanced Urban Studies, University of Bristol.

Humphries, S. and Gordon, P. (1992) *Out of sight: The experience of disability 1900-1950*, Plymouth: Northcote House.

Hunt, P. (1966) *Stigma: The experience of disability*, London: Chapman.

Hurstfield, J., Meager, N., Aston, J., Davies, J., Mann, K., Mitchell, H., O'Regan, S. and Sinclair, A. (2004) *Monitoring the Disability Discrimination Act (DDA) 1995: Phase 3*, London: Department for Work and Pensions and Disability Rights Commission.

Hyde, M. (2000) 'From welfare to work? Social policy for disabled people of working age in the United Kingdom in the 1990s', *Disability & Society*, vol 15, issue 2, March, pp 327-41.

Hyman, M. (1977) *The extra cost of disabled living*, London: National Fund for Research into Crippling Diseases.

IFS (Institute for Fiscal Studies) (1990) *Poverty in official statistics*, London: IFS.

Imrie, R. (2003) 'Housing quality and the provision of accessible homes', *Housing Studies*, vol 18, no 3, pp 387-408.

Imrie, R. (2004) 'Disability, embodiment and the meaning of home', *Housing Studies*, vol 19, no 5, pp 745-63.

Imrie, R. (2006) 'Independent lives and the relevance of lifetime homes', *Disability and Society*, vol 21, no 4 pp 359-76.

IPPR (Institute for Public Policy Research) (2010) *Working, working less and worklessness*, London: IPPR.

Jahoda, M. (1982) *Employment and unemployment: A social-psychological analysis*, Cambridge: Cambridge University Press.

Jahoda, M. (1988) 'Economic recession and mental health: some conceptual issues', *Journal of Social Issues*, vol 44, pp 13-23.

Jenkins, R. (1994) 'The Health of the Nation: recent government policy and legislation', *Psychiatric Bulletin*, vol 18, pp 324-7.

Jobcentre Plus (2011) Audio recording of Medical Assessments Pilot (www.disabilityalliance.org/audio.doc).

Johnson, A. (2005) Ministerial speech at the University of London Senate House on welfare reform, June.

Johnson, P. and Kossykh, Y. (2008) *Early years, life chances and equality*, London: Equality and Human Rights Commission.

Jones, K. (2000) *The making of social policy in Britain*, London: Athlone.

Jones, K. et al (1983) *Issues in social policy* (2nd edn), London: Routledge & Kegan Paul.

Kempson, E. (1996) *Life on a low income*, York: York Publishing Services.

Kestenbaum, A. (1993) *Making community care a reality*, London: LSE Pamphlet Collection.

Kettle, M. (1979) *Disabled people and their employment*, London: RADAR.

Kowalsky, M. (2007) 'This honourable obligation: the King's National Roll Scheme for disabled ex-servicemen 1915-1944', *European Review of History*, vol 14, no 4, December, pp 567-84.

Labour Force Survey (2003) *Labour Force Survey*, London: Office for National Statistics.

Labour Force Survey (2007) *Labour Force statistics: Quarters 1 and 2*, London: Office for National Statistics.

Labour Force Survey (2008) *Labour Force Survey*, London: Office for National Statistics.

Labour Force Survey (2009) *Labour Force statistics: Quarters 1 and 2*, London: Office for National Statistics.

Ladyman, S. (2004) 'Health and social care advisory service: new directions in direct payments for people who use mental health services', Speech, Department of Health, London, 18 May.

Langan, M. and Clarke, J. (1994) 'Managing in the mixed economy of care', in J. Clarke et al (eds) *Managing social policy*, Buckingham: Open University Press, pp 73-92.

Larson, M.L. (1977) *The rise of professionalism: A sociological analysis*, Berkeley, CA: University of California Press.

Laws, D. (2010) Chief Secretary to the Treasury, Statement, BBC News, 24 May (http://news.bbc.co.uk/1/hi/8699522.stm).

Lawson, A. (2008) *Disability and equality law in Britain: The role of reasonable adjustments*, Oxford: Hart Publishing.

Lawton, D. (1992) *Education and politics in the 1990s: Conflict or consensus?*, London: Routledge.

LCF (Leonard Cheshire Foundation) (2010) *Disability and the downturn*, London: LCF.

Leadbeater, C., Bartlett, J. and Gallagher, N. (2008) *Making it personal*, London: Demos.

Leece, D. and Leece, J. (2006) 'Direct payments: creating a two-tiered system in social care', *British Journal of Social Work*, vol 36, pp 1379-93.

Le Grand, J. (1991) 'Quasi-markets and social policy', *Economic Journal*, vol 101, no 408, pp 1256-67.

Levitas, R. (ed) (1986) *The ideology of the New Right*, Cambridge: Polity Press.

Levitas, R. (1996) 'The concept of social exclusion and the new Durkheimian hegemony', *Critical Social Policy*, vol 16, no 1, pp 5-20.

Levitas, R. (1998) *The inclusive society: Social exclusion and New Labour*, Basingstoke: Macmillan.

Levitas, R. (2005) *The inclusive society? Social exclusion and New Labour* (2nd edn), Basingstoke: Palgrave Macmillan.

Lister, R. (1990) *The exclusive society: Citizenship and the poor*, London: Child Poverty Action Group.

Lister, R. (1997) 'From fractured Britain to one nation? The policy options for welfare reform', *Renewal*, vol 5, no 3/4, pp 11-23.

Lister, R. (2009) 'Labour must do more on child poverty', *The Guardian*, 12 June.

Lister, R. and Bennett, F. (2010) 'The new "champion of progressive ideals"? Cameron's Conservative Party: poverty, family policy and welfare reform', *Renewal*, vol 18, no 1, pp 84-109.

Local Government Association (2009) *Adults' Social Services Expenditure Survey 2008-2009*, London: LGA.

Loney, M. (ed) (1987) *The state or the market? Politics and welfare in contemporary Britain*, London: Sage Publications.

Lonsdale, S. (1985) *Work and inequality*, London: Longman.

Lonsdale, S. (1990) *Women and disability: The experience of physical disability among women*, London: Macmillan.

Lukes, S. (1974) *Power: A radical view*, London: Macmillan Press.

Lund, B. (2002) *Understanding state welfare: Social justice or social exclusion?*, London: Sage Publications.

Macdonald, K. (1995) *The sociology of the professions*, London: Sage Publications.

McLaughlin, J., Goodley, D. and Clavering, E. (2008) *Families raising disabled children*, Basingstoke: Palgrave Macmillan.

Magadi, M. (2010) 'Risk factors for severe child poverty in the UK', *Journal of Social Policy*, vol 39, no 2, pp 297-316.

Malley, J., Wittenberg, R., Comas-Herrera, A., Pickard, L. and King, D. (2005) *Long-term care expenditure for older people, Projections to 2022 for Great Britain*, Report to the Institute for Public Policy Research, PSSRU Discussion Paper 2252, Canterbury: Personal Social Services Research Unit.

Mann, K. and Roseneil, S. (1994) 'Some mothers do "ave' em": backlash and the gender politics of the underclass debate', *Journal of Gender Studies*, vol 3, no 3, pp 317-31.

Marcuse, H. (1964) *One dimensional man: Studies in the ideology of advanced industrial society*, Boston, MA: Beacon Press.

Marshall, T.H. ([1949] 1992) 'Citizenship and social class', in T.H. Marshall and T. Bottomore, *Citizenship and social class*, London: Pluto Press, pp 3-51.

Martin, F.C. and Sturdy, D. (2010) *Half-way home? Updated guidance from the Department of Health on intermediate care in England*, British Geriatrics Society (www.bgsnet.org.uk/index.php?option=com_content&view=article&id=12:mar10intermediatecare1&catid=1:april2010&Itemid=11).

Martin, J. and White, A. (1988) *The financial circumstances of disabled adults living in private households*, OPCS Report 2, London: HMSO.

Martin, J., White, A. and Meltzer, H. (1989) *Disabled adults: Services, transport and employment*, OPCS Report 4, London: HMSO.

Martin, K., Meltzer, H. and Elliott, D. (1988) *The prevalence of disability among adults*, OPCS Surveys of Disability in Great Britain, London: HMSO.

Matthews, A. and Truscott, P. (1990) *Disability, household income and expenditure: A follow-up survey of disabled adults in the Family Expenditure Survey*, DSS Research Report No 2, London: HMSO.

Mead, L. (1987) 'The obligation to work and the availability of jobs: a dialogue', *Focus*, vol 10, no 2, pp 11-19.

Means, R. (2007) 'Safe as houses? Ageing in place and vulnerable older people in the UK', *Social Policy & Administration*, vol 41, no 1, pp 65-85.

Melis, R., Rikkert, M., Parker, S. and van Eijken, M. (2004) 'What is intermediate care?', *British Medical Journal*, vol 329, p 360.

Mencap (2008) 'Disabled Facilities Grant not enough says Mencap', Response to the government consultation on the Disabled Facilities Grant (www.mencap.org.uk/news.asp?id=6791).

Merriman, S. (2009) *TransMap: From theory into practice. The underlying principles in supporting disabled young people in transition to adulthood*, London: Council for Disabled Children (www.transitionsupportprogramme.org.uk/pdf/TransMap_Final.pdf).

Millar, J. (ed) (2003) *Understanding social security: Issues for policy and practice*, Bristol: The Policy Press.

Miller, E. and Gwynne, G. (1972) *A life apart: A pilot study of residential institutions for the physically handicapped and the young chronic sick*, London: Tavistock.

Minister of Health (1961) Address to the National Association of Mental Health Annual Conference, 9 March ('Watertower Speech') Church House, Westminster.

Ministry of Health (1962) *National Health Service: A hospital plan for England and Wales*, Cmnd 1604, London: HMSO.

Ministry of Health (1963) *Health and welfare: The development of community care. Plans for the health and welfare services of local authorities in England and Wales*, London: HMSO.

'Minority Report of the Royal Commission on the Poor Laws and the Relief of Distress, 1905-9' (1909) *British Medical Journal*, vol 2, no 1415.

Mooney, A., Owen, C. and Statham, J. (2008) *Disabled children: Numbers, characteristics and local service provision*, Report to the Department for Children, Schools and Families (http://eprints.ioe.ac.uk/61/1/Numbers_and_characteristics_of_disabled_children.pdf).

Moreton, T. (1992) 'Sheltered employment: gateway or "roadblock"?', *Personnel Review*, vol 21, issue 6, pp 37-54.

Morris, J. (1993) *Independent lives: Community care and disabled people*, Basingstoke: Macmillan.

Morris, P. (1969) *Put away: A sociological study of the institutions for the mentally retarded*, London: Routledge & Kegan Paul.

Murray, C. (1984) *Losing ground*, New York: HarperCollins.

Murray, C. (1986) 'No, welfare isn't really the problem', *Public Interest*, no 84, pp 3-11.

Murray, C. (1996a) 'The emerging British underclass', in R. Lister (ed) *Charles Murray and the underclass: The developing debate*, London: Health and Welfare Unit, Institute of Economic Affairs, pp 23-53.

Murray, C. (1996b) 'Underclass: the crisis deepens', in R. Lister (ed) *Charles Murray and the underclass: The developing debate*, London: Health and Welfare Unit, Institute of Economic Affairs, pp 99-135.

NAO (National Audit Office) (2006) *Sure Start children's centres*, Report by the Comptroller and Auditor General, HC 104 session 2006-2007, 19 December, London: NAO.

NAO (2009) *Department for Work and Pensions: Resource account 2009-10*, London: NAO (www.nao.org.uk/publications/1011/dwp_account_2009-10.aspx).

NAO (2010) *Support to incapacity claimants through Pathways to Work*, Report to the Comptroller and Auditor General, HC 21, May.

National Pensioners Commission (2005) *A new pension settlement for the twenty-first century*, Second Report of the Pensions Commission (www.webarchive.org.uk/wayback/archive/20070801230000/http://www.pensionscommission.org.uk/publications/2005/annrep/main-report.pdf).

National Statistics (1971) *General Household Survey 1971*, London: Office for National Statistics.

National Statistics (2001a) *National Statistics Bulletin 10/01*, London: Office for National Statistics.

National Statistics (2001b) *Health Survey for England*, London: Office for National Statistics.

National Statistics (2005) *Statistical first release: Fixed and permanent exclusions*, London: Office for National Statistics.

National Statistics (2007a) *Statistical first release: Fixed and permanent exclusions*, London: Office for National Statistics.

National Statistics (2007b) *General Household Survey*, London: Office for National Statistics.

National Statistics (2008) *National pupil database*, London: Office for National Statistics.

National Statistics (2009a) *Statistical first release: Fixed and permanent exclusions*, London: Office for National Statistics.

National Statistics (2009b) *Labour market statistics: Statistical bulletin*, London: Office for National Statistics.

NCIL (National Centre for Independent Living) (2008) *Review of adult social care*, London: NCIL.

NDCS (National Deaf Children's Society) (2010) 'Gains in GCSEs under threat from cuts to help for deaf children', 20 December (www.ndcs.org.uk/about_us/campaign_with_us/england/campaign_news/2010ks4.html).

Netten, A., Malley, J., Forder, J. and Flynn, T. (2009) *Outcomes of Social Care for Adults (OSCA). First consultation exercise feedback*, PSSRU Discussion Paper 2634, Canterbury: Personal Social Services Research Unit.

NHS Information Centre (2010) *Social care and mental health indicators from the National Indicator set: Provisional further analysis, England 2009-10* (www.ic.nhs.uk/pubs/socmhi09-10).

Nichols, T. and Beynon, H. (1977) *Living with capitalism*, London: Routledge & Kegan Paul.

Nickell, S. (2003) 'Poverty and worklessness in Britain', Royal Economic Society (RES) Presidential Address at the RES Conference, University of Warwick, 8 April.

Nuffield Foundation (2009) *Education for all: The future of education and training for 14-19 year olds*, London: Routledge.

O'Brien, P. (2003) 'Disabled Facilities Grants: are they meeting the assessed needs of children in Northern Ireland?', *British Journal of Occupational Therapy*, vol 66, no 6, pp 277-80.

ODI (Office for Disability Issues) (2009) *Independent living: A cross-government strategy about independent living for disabled people*, London: ODI.

ODI (2010) *Key facts and figures*, August, London: ODI.

ODPM (Office of the Deputy Prime Minister) (2000) *Building Regulations: Part M*, London: The Stationery Office.

ODPM (2005) *Third Report of the 2004/5 Session. Homelessness*, House of Commons Housing, Planning, Local Government and the Regions Committee, London: The Stationery Office (www.publications.parliament.uk/pa/cm200405/cmselect/cmodpm/61/61i.pdf).

OECD (Organisation for Economic Co-operation and Development) (2004) *Transforming disability welfare policies: Towards work and equal opportunities*, Aldershot: Ashgate.

OECD (2006) *Jobs strategy*, Paris: OECD.

OECD (2010) *Economic Outlook 87*, Paris: Organisation for Economic Co-operation and Development.

Ofsted (Office for Standards in Education) (2004) *Special educational needs and disability: Towards inclusive schools*, London: Ofsted.

Ofsted (2010) *Improving progression to sustainable unsupported employment*, 4 February, London: Ofsted (www.ofsted.gov.uk/Ofsted-home/Publications-and-research/Browse-all-by/Documents-by-type/Thematic-reports/Improving-progression-to-sustainable-unsupported-employment).

Oliver, M. (1990) *Politics of disablement*, Basingstoke: Macmillan.

Oliver, M. and Barnes, C. (1998) *Disabled people and social policy: From exclusion to inclusion*, London: Longman.

O'Neal, A. and Lewis, J. (2001) *Cost-effectiveness and independent living*, York: Joseph Rowntree Foundation.

Osborne, G. (2010a) Chancellor of the Exchequer, Statement, BBC News, 24 May (http://news.bbc.co.uk/1/hi/8699522.stm).

Osborne, G. (2010b) Chancellor of the Exchequer Budget Speech, 22 June 2010 (http://news.bbc.co.uk/democracylive/hi/house_of_commons/newsid_8751000/8751754.stm).

Osborne, G. (2010c) Pre-budget Discussion of Welfare Reform, BBC Andrew Marr Show, June 19 (http://news.bbc.co.uk/1/hi/programmes/andrew_marr_show/8750301.stm).

Oswin, M. (1975) 'Handicapped children and the "hospital scandal reports"', *Child Care, Health and Development*, vol 1, no 1, pp 70-7.

Page, R. (2007) *Revisiting the welfare state*, Maidenhead: McGraw Hill/Open University Press.

Pantazis, C. and Gordon, D. (eds) (2000) *Tackling inequalities: Where we are now and what can be done?*, Bristol: The Policy Press.

Parker, H. (ed) (2000) *Low cost but acceptable incomes for older people*, Family Budget Unit and Age Concern, Bristol: The Policy Press.

PCS (Public and Commercial Services Union) (2010) 'Atos healthcare ballot' (www.pcs.org.uk/en/commercial_sector/Atos-Origin-Healthcare/bulletins/atos- healthcare-ballot-.cfm).

Pearson, C. (2004) 'The implementation of direct payments: issues for user-led organisations in Scotland', in C. Barnes and G. Mercer (eds) *Disability policy and practice: Applying the social model*, Leeds: The Disability Press.

Peck, J. and Theodore, N. (2000) 'Beyond "employability"', *Cambridge Journal of Economics*, vol 24, pp 729-49.

Pelling, H. (1971) *A history of British trade unions*, Harmondsworth: Penguin.

Perry-Smith, J. (ed) (2000) *Policy responses to social inclusion*, Buckingham: Open University Press.

Piggott, L. and Grover, C. (2009) 'Retrenching Incapacity Benefit: Employment Support Allowance and paid work', *Social Policy and Society*, vol 8, pp 159-70.

Pires, C., Kazimirski, A., Shaw, A., Sainsbury, R. and Meah, A. (2006) *New Deal for disabled people evaluation: Survey of eligible population, Wave Three*, DWP Research Report No 324, London: Department for Work and Pensions.

Pitt, V. (2010) 'One in five councils illegally charge for reablement services', *Community Care*, 20 September.

PMSU (Prime Minister's Strategy Unit) (2005) *Improving the life chances of disabled people*, A joint report with the Department for Work and Pensions, Department of Health, Department for Education and Skills and the Office of the Deputy Prime Minister, London: PMSU.

Powell, M. (ed) (2002) *Evaluating New Labour's welfare reforms*, Bristol: The Policy Press.

Powell, M. (2007) *Understanding the mixed economy of welfare*, Bristol: The Policy Press.

Powell, T.H. (1996) *What's New in Day Care?* MA Dissertation University of York.

Preston, G. (2006) *A route out of poverty? Disabled people, work and welfare reform*, London: Child Poverty Action Group.

Prideaux, S. (2001) 'New Labour, old functionalism: the underlying of welfare reform in the US and the UK', *Social Policy & Administration*, vol 35, no 1, pp 85-115.

Prideaux, S. (2005) *Not so New Labour: A sociological critique of New Labour's policies and practices*, Bristol: The Policy Press.

Prideaux, S. (2006) *Good practice for providing reasonable access to the physical built environment for disabled people*, Leeds: The Disability Press.

Prideaux, S. and Roulstone, A. (2009) 'Good practice for providing disabled people with reasonable access to the built environment: a comparative study of legislative provision', *International Journal of Law in the Built Environment*, vol 1, no 1, pp 59-81.

Prideaux, S., Roulstone, A., Harris, J. and Barnes, C. (2009) 'Disabled people and self directed support schemes: re-conceptualising work and welfare in the 21st century', *Disability & Society Special Edition*, vol 24, no 5, pp 557-69.

Priestley, M. (1998) 'Listening to disabled children', *British Journal of Social Work*, vol 28, no 6, pp 969-73.

Priestley, M. (2002) 'Whose voices? Representing the claims of older disabled people under New Labour', *Policy & Politics*, vol 30, no 3, pp 361-72.

Priestley, M. and Rabiee, P. (2002) 'Same difference? Older people's organisations and disability issues', *Disability & Society*, vol 17, no 6, pp 597-611.

Purvis, A., Lowery, J. and Dobbs, L. (2006) *Workstep Evaluation Case Studies*, Research Report No 348, London: Department for Work and Pensions.

Quigley, M. (1995) 'The roots of the IQ debate: eugenics and social control', *Public Eye*, 13 October (www.hartford-hwp.com/archives/45/034.html).

Rabiee, P., Moran, N. and Glendinning, C. (2009) 'Individual budgets: lessons from early users' experiences', *British Journal of Social Work*, vol 39, no 5, pp 918-35.

RCLTC (Royal Commission on Long-term Care) (1999) *With respect to old age: Long-term care: Rights and responsibilities* (Sutherland Report), London: The Stationery Office.

Reiser, R. (2006) 'Confronting the oppression of the past', in M. Cole (ed) *Education equity and human rights: Issues of gender, 'race', sexuality, disability and social class* (2nd edn), London: Routledge.

Riddell, S., Priestley, M., Pearson, C., Mercer, G., Barnes, C., Jolly, D. and Williams, V. (2006) *Disabled people and direct payments: A UK comparative study*, ESRC final report (www.leeds.ac.uk/disability-studies/projects/UKdirectpayments/UKDPfinal.pdf).

Rioux, M. (1994) 'Towards a concept of equality of well-being: overcoming the social and legal construction of inequality', *Canadian Journal of Law and Jurisprudence*, vol VII, pp 127-47.

Rioux, M. (2002) 'Disability, citizenship and rights in a changing world', in C. Barnes, M. Oliver and L. Barton (eds) *Disability studies today*, Cambridge: Polity Press, pp 210-27.

RNIB (Royal National Institute for Blind People) (2009) *Taken for a ride*, London: RNIB.

Roberts, S., Heaver, C., Hill, C., Rennison, J., Stafford, B., Howat, N., Kelly, G., Krishnan, S., Tapp, P. and Thomas, A. (2004) *Disability in the workplace: Employers' and service providers' responses to the Disability Discrimination Act in 2003 and preparation for the 2004 changes*, London: Department for Work and Pensions.

Roulstone, A. (1998) *Enabling technology: Disabled people, work and new technology*, Milton Keynes: Open University Press.

Roulstone, A. (2000) 'Disability, dependency and the New Deal for disabled people', *Disability & Society,* vol 15, no 3, pp 427-43.

Roulstone, A. (2002) 'Disabling pasts, enabling futures? How does the changing nature of capitalism impact on the disabled worker and jobseeker?', *Disability & Society*, vol 17, no 6, October, pp 627-42.

Roulstone, A. (2003) 'The legal road to rights, obiter dicta and the limits of the Disability Discrimination Act 1995', *Disability & Society*, vol 18, no 2, pp 117-31.

Roulstone, A. and Barnes, C. (2005) *Working futures: Disabled people, policy and social inclusion*, Bristol: The Policy Press.

Roulstone, A. and Hudson, V. (2007) 'Carer participation in England, Wales and Northern Ireland', *Journal of Inter-Professional Care*, vol 23, issue 3, pp 303-13.

Roulstone, A. and Morgan, H. (2009) 'Neo-liberal individualism or self-directed support: are we all speaking the same language on modernising adult social care?', *Social Policy and Society*, vol 8, no 3, pp 333-45.

Roulstone, A. and Prideaux, S. (2009) 'Constructing reasonableness: environmental access policy for disabled wheelchair users in four EU countries', *ALTER: European Journal of Disability Research*, vol 4, no 3, pp 360-77.

Roulstone, A. and Warren, J. (2006) 'Applying a barriers approach to monitoring disabled people's employment: implications for the Disability Discrimination Act 2005', *Disability & Society*, vol 21, no 2, pp 115-31.

Roulstone, A. and Yates, S. (2009) 'Formation professionnelle et jeunes handicapés en Grande-Bretagne', in A. Philip and D. Velche, *La nouvelle revue de l'adaptation et de la scolarisation*, Référence No 48, 4ème trimestre, Paris: CTHERNI.

Roulstone, A. et al (2006) *Working together: Carer participation in England, Wales and Northern Ireland*, Bristol: The Policy Press.

Rowlingson, K. and Berthoud, R. (1996) *Disability, benefits and employment*, DSS Research Report No 54, London: Department for Social Security.

Royal College of Physicians (1986) 'Physical disability in 1986 and beyond', *Journal of the Royal College of Physicians*, vol 20, pp 160-94.

Royal Commission on the Poor Laws and Relief of Distress (1909) *Minority Report by H.R. Wakefield, F. Chandler, G. Lansbury and B. Webb*, London: HMSO.

Rummery, K. (2002) *Disability, citizenship and community care: A case for welfare rights?*, Aldershot: Ashgate.

Rummery, K. (2006) 'Partnerships and collaborative governance in welfare: the citizenship challenge', *Social Policy and Society*, vol 5, no 2, pp 293-303.

Rushefsky, M.E. (2002) *Public policy in the United States: At the dawn of the 21st century*, New York: Sharpe Publishing.

Russell, M. (1998) *Beyond ramps: Disability at the end of the social contract*, New York: Common Courage Press.

Russell, M. (2002) 'What disability civil rights cannot do: employment and political economy', *Disability & Society*, vol 17, no 2, pp 117-35.

Rustemier, S. and Vaughan, M. (2005) *Segregation trends in LEAs in England 2002-2004*, Bristol: Centre for Studies in Inclusive Education.

Ryan, J. and Thomas, F. (1980) *The politics of mental handicap*, Harmondsworth: Penguin.

Sadiq-Sangster, A. (1991) *Living on Income Support: An Asian experience*, London: Family Services Unit.

Samuel, M. (2009) 'Direct payments, personal budgets and individual budgets', Briefing document for *Community Care* (www.communitycare. co.uk/Articles/2011/08/19/102669/direct-payments-personal-budgets-and-individual-budgets.htm).

Sayce, L. (2011) *Getting in, staying in and getting on: Disability employment support fit for the future*, Cm 8081, London: DWP.

Schneider, J., Simons, K. and Everatt, G. (2001) 'Impact of the National Minimum Wage on disabled people', *Disability & Society*, vol 16, no 5, pp 729-47.

SCIE (Social Care Institute for Excellence) (2006) *Community-based day activities and supports for people with learning disabilities, Messages from 'Having a good day': Good transition planning*, Guide 16, London: SCIE.

SCIE (2009) *Co-production: An emerging evidence base for adult social care transformation*, Research Briefing 31, London: SCIE.

Scottish Parliament (2008) *Care at home services: Briefing note* (http://www2. scottish.parliament.uk/s3/committees/lgc/inquiries/HomeCareServices/CareCommission.pdf).

Scull, A. (1984) *Decarceration: Community treatment and the deviant: A radical view* (2nd edn), Oxford/New Brunswick, NJ: Polity Press/Rutgers University Press.

Secretary of State for Work and Pensions (2006) *A new deal for welfare: Empowering people to work*, Cm 6730, London: The Stationery Office.

Seebohm, F. (1968) *Report of the Committee on local authority and allied personal social services* (Seebohm Report), London: HMSO.

Shah, S. (2005) *Career success of disabled high-flyers*, London: Jessica Kingsley Publishers.

Shakespeare, T. (2006) *Disability rights and wrongs*, London: Routledge.

Sharma, N. and Morrison, J. (2007) *Don't push me around! Disabled children's experiences of wheelchair services in the UK*, London: Barnardo's and Whizzkids.

Shaw, J. (2010) Minister sets targets to help people with mental health conditions and learning disabilities. Available at : http://www.dwp.gov.uk/previous-administration-news/press-releases/2010/march-2010/dwp039-10-040310.shtml

Shaw Trust (2010) *Disability and employment statistics*, London: Shaw Trust.

Sin, H.C., Mguni, N., Cook, C., Comber, N. and Hedges, A. (2009) *Targeted violence, harassment and abuse against people with learning disabilities in Great Britain*, London: Office for Public Management.

Sixsmith, A. and Sixsmith, J. (2008) 'Ageing in place in the United Kingdom', *Ageing International*, vol 32, no 3, pp 219-35.

Skills for Care and IFF (2007) *Employment aspects and workforce implications of direct payments*, London, Skills for Care and IFF.

Smiles, S. (1859) *Self help: With illustrations of character, conduct and perseverance*, London: Murray.

Sopp, L. and Wood, L. (2001) *Consumer and industry views of lifetime homes*, York: Joseph Rowntree Foundation.

Spencer, H. (1864) *Principles of psychology*, London: Longman, Brown and Green.

Stafford, B. (2003) 'In search of a welfare-to-work solution: the New Deal for disabled people', *Benefits*, vol 11, no 3, pp 181-6.

Stafford, B. (2005) 'New Deal for disabled people: what's new about New Deal?', in A. Roulstone and C. Barnes (eds) *Working futures: Disabled people, policy and social inclusion*, Bristol: The Policy Press, pp 17-28.

Stafford, B., Kellard, K., Hill, K., Hai Phung, V., Greenberg, D., Davis, A., Magadi, M., Pound, E. and Legge, K. (2007) *New Deal for disabled people*, DWP Report, London: Department for Work and Pensions (www.crsp.ac.uk/projects/nddp.html).

Staincliffe, S. (2003) 'Wheelchair services and providers: discriminating against disabled people', *International Journal of Therapy and Rehabilitation*, vol 10, no 4, pp 151-9.

Stanley, K. and Regan, S. (2003) *The missing million: Supporting disabled people into work*, London: Institute for Public Policy Research.

Stapleton, D.C. and Burkhauser, R.V. (2003) *The decline in employment in people with disabilities: A policy puzzle*, Kalamazoo, MI: Upjohn.

Stevenson, A. (2010) 'Electoral reform rebels hold fire – for now', 7 September (www.politics.co.uk/news/2010/9/7/electoral-reform-rebels-hold-fire-for-now).

Stone, D. (1984) *The disabled state*, Philadelphia, PA: Temple University Press.

Stowell, R. and Day, F. (1983) *Tell me what you want and I'll get it for you: A study of shopping when disabled*, London: Disablement Income Group.

Swain, J., French, S., Barnes, C. and Thomas, C. (eds) (2004) *Disabling barriers, enabling environments* (2nd edn), London: Sage Publications.

Tawney, R.H. (1931) *Equality*, New York: Harcourt, Brace & Company.

Thane, P. (1982) *The foundations of the welfare state*, London: Longman.

Thomas, A. and Griffiths, R. (2010) *Disability Living Allowance and work: Exploratory research and evidence review*, DWP Research Report, London: Department for Work and Pensions.

Thornton, P. and Lunt, N. (1995) *Employment for disabled people: Social obligation or individual responsibility?*, Occasional Paper, York: Social Policy Research Unit.

Thornton, P., Corden, A. and Byrne, C. (2002) *Evaluation of the impact of Access to Work*, London: Jobcentre Plus.

Tibble, M. (2005) *Review of existing research on the extra costs of disability*, Working Paper 21, London: Department for Work and Pensions.

Tinker, A. (1983) 'Housing elderly people: some themes of current research', *Public Health*, vol 97, no 5, pp 290-5.

Tomlinson Report (1942) *Report of the Inter-departmental Committee on the rehabilitation and resettlement of disabled persons, Appendix G to the Beveridge Report*, Cmd 6405, London: HMSO.

Tomlinson, S. (1982) *A sociology of special education*, London: Routledge & Kegan Paul.

Topliss, E. (1982) *Social responses to handicap*, Harlow: Longman.

Townsend, P. (1979) *Poverty in the United Kingdom: A survey of household resources and standards of living*, Harmondsworth: Penguin Books.

Townsend, P. and Walker, A. (1981) *Disability in Britain: A manifesto of rights*, Oxford: Martin Robertson.

Townsley, R., Abbott, D. and Watson, D. (2003) *Making a difference? Exploring the impact of multi-agency working on disabled children with complex health care needs, their families and the professionals who support them*, Bristol: The Policy Press.

Twigg, J. (2000) *Bathing: The body and community care*, London: Routledge.

UK Parliament (1998) *Public Accounts Committee: Examination of witnesses*, Questions 80-99, 18 February (www.publications.parliament.uk/pa/cm199798/cmselect/cmpubacc/570/8021806.htm).

UK Parliament (2006) *Select Committee on Work and Pensions: Third report, 2006* (www.publications.parliament.uk/pa/cm200506/cmselect/cmworpen/616/61607.htm).

UK Parliament (2010a) *Briefing Paper: DWP benefit spending: Age-based client group 1991/2 to 2010/11 (plans), real terms, 2010/11 prices* (www.parliament.uk/briefingpapers/commons/lib/research/briefings/snsg-02656.pdf).

UK Parliament (2010b) *Parliamentary business: Quangos* (www.parliament.uk/business/publications/research/key-issues-for-the-new-parliament/decentralisation-of-power/quangos/).

UK Parliament (2010c) *Parliamentary business: Comprehensive Spending Review debate*, 1 November, col 1467.

UN (United Nations) (2006) *Convention on the Rights of Persons with Disabilities* (www.un.org/disabilities/convention/conventionfull.shtml).

Ungerson, C. (1987) *Policy is personal: Sex, gender and informal care*, London: Tavistock.

Ungerson, C. and Yeandle, S. (eds) (2007) *Cash for care in developed welfare states*, Basingstoke: Palgrave Macmillan.

UPIAS (Union of Physically Impaired Against Segregation) (1976) *Fundamental principles of disability*, London: UPIAS.

Wainwright, R. and O'Brien, D. (2010) *An overview of the UK domiciliary care sector*, UKHCA Summary Paper, Sutton: UKHCA Ltd (www.ukhca.co.uk/pdfs/domiciliarycaresectoroverview.pdf).

Walker, A. (1981) *Unqualified and underemployed: Handicapped young people and the labour market*, Basingstoke: Macmillan.

Walker, A. and Walker, L. (1991) 'Disability and financial need', in G. Dalley (ed) *Disability and social policy*, London: Policy Studies Institute.

Walker, R. and Wiseman, M. (2003) 'Making welfare work: UK activation policies under New Labour', *International Social Security Review*, vol 56, no 1, pp 3-29.

Wanless, D. (2006) *Securing good care for older people: Taking a long-term view* (Wanless Review), London: The King's Fund.

Warnock, M. (1978) *Special educational needs report of the Committee of Enquiry into the education of handicapped children and young people* (Warnock Report), London: HMSO.

Watson, N. (2002) '"Well, I know this is going to sound very strange to you, but I don't see myself as a disabled person": identity and disability', *Disability & Society*, vol 17, no 5, pp 509-27.

Westcott, H.L. (1991) *Institutional abuse of children: From research to policy: A review*, London: NSPCC.

Williams, B., Copestake, P., Eversley, J. and Stafford, B. (2008) *Experiences and expectations of disabled people*, London, Office for Disability Issues.

Williams, F. (1989) *Social policy: A critical introduction. Issues in race, gender and class*, Cambridge: Polity Press.

Woodin, S.L. (2006) 'Social relationships and disabled people: the impact of direct payments', Unpublished PhD, University of Leeds (www.leeds. ac.uk/disability-studies/archiveuk/woodin/FinalThesis.pdf).

Woolley, M. (2004) *Income and expenditure of families with a severely disabled child*, York: Family Fund.

Zadek, S. and Scott-Parker, S. (2003) *Unlocking potential: The new disability business case*, London: Employers Forum on Disability.

Zarb, G. (ed) (1995) *Removing disabling barriers*, London: Policy Studies Institute.

Index